POETIC INQUIRY

Poetic Inquiry: Craft, Method and Practice examines the use of poetry as a form of qualitative research, representation, and method used by researchers, practitioners, and students from across the social sciences and humanities. It serves as a practical manual for using poetry in qualitative research through the presentation of varied examples of Poetic Inquiry. It provides how-to exercises for developing and using poetry as a qualitative research method.

The book begins by mapping out what doing and critiquing Poetic Inquiry entails via a discussion of the power of poetry, poets', and researchers' goals for the use of poetry, and the kinds of projects that are best suited for Poetic Inquiry. It also provides descriptions of the process and craft of creating Poetic Inquiry, and suggestions for how to evaluate and engage with Poetic Inquiry. The book further contends with questions of method, process, and craft from poets' and researchers' perspectives. It shows the implications for the aesthetic and epistemic concerns in poetry, and furthers transdisciplinary dialogues between the humanities and social sciences.

Faulkner shows the importance of considering the form and function of Poetic Inquiry in qualitative research through discussions of poetry as research method, poetry as qualitative analysis and representation, and Poetic Inquiry as a powerful research tool.

Sandra L. Faulkner is Professor of Communication at Bowling Green State University. Her interests include qualitative methodology, Poetic Inquiry, and the relationships among culture, identities, and sexualities in close relationships. She received the 2014 Knower Outstanding Article Award from the National Communication Association and the 2016 Norman K. Denzin Qualitative Research Award.

DEVELOPING QUALITATIVE INQUIRY

Series Editor: Janice Morse
University of Utah

Books in the *Developing Qualitative Inquiry* series, written by leaders in qualitative inquiry, address important topics in qualitative methods. Targeted to a broad multi-disciplinary readership, the books are intended for mid-level to advanced researchers and advanced students. The series forwards the field of qualitative inquiry by describing new methods or developing particular aspects of established methods.

Volumes in this series include:

Poetic Inquiry
Craft, Method and Practice
Sandra L. Faulkner

Qualitative Analysis Using Atlas.ti
The Five-Level QDA® Method
Nicholas H. Woolf and Christina Silver

Qualitative Analysis Using MAXQDA
The Five-Level QDA® Method
Nicholas H. Woolf and Christina Silver

Qualitative Analysis Using NVivo
The Five-Level QDA® Method
Nicholas H. Woolf and Christina Silver

For a full list of titles in this series, please visit www.routledge.com/Developing-Qualitative-Inquiry/book-series/DQI

POETIC INQUIRY

Craft, Method and Practice
Second Edition

Sandra L. Faulkner

Routledge
Taylor & Francis Group

NEW YORK AND LONDON

Second edition published 2020
by Routledge
52 Vanderbilt Avenue, New York, NY 10017

and by Routledge
2 Park Square, Milton Park, Abingdon, Oxon, OX14 4RN

Routledge is an imprint of the Taylor & Francis Group, an informa business

First edition published by Left Coast Press, Inc 2009

Library of Congress Cataloging-in-Publication Data
A catalog record for this title has been requested

ISBN: 978-1-138-48694-2 (hbk)
ISBN: 978-1-138-48695-9 (pbk)
ISBN: 978-1-351-04423-3 (ebk)

Typeset in Bembo
by Newgen Publishing UK

CONTENTS

ILLUSTRATIONS

Figures

Tables

PREFACE

"Poetic inquiry" is the use of poetry crafted from research endeavors, either before project analysis, as a project analysis, and/or poetry that is part of or that constitutes an entire research project. The key feature of poetic inquiry is the use of poetry as/in/for inquiry.

Faulkner, 2017, p. 210

Poetry has become a valuable research tool and method for researchers in fields such as anthropology, communication, education, mathematics, sociology, and social work, contributing to an interdisciplinary dialogue between the social sciences and the humanities. The poet and social scientist share a common approach; both ground their work in meticulous observation of the empirical world, have the ability to be self-reflexive about their work and experience, and the capacity to foreground how subjective understanding influences their work. A critical issue, then, is the creation and evaluation of poetic forms used as research, analysis, and representation. If researchers are going to use poetry of all types in their work, we need a critical discussion about how we understand poetry, the process of using poetry as research, and how it informs our work and scholarly endeavors. Researchers interested in poetry must be aware of poetic traditions and techniques and study the craft as they study research writing.

First, this project extends my own and others' work on issues of poetic and arts-based research craft/method through an examination of explicit, and often implicit, writing and beliefs about what constitutes effective poetry and qualitative and arts-based research. The focus on poetic craft and research method through an examination of Poetic Inquiry and writing about poetic craft contributes to dialogue about the power of poetry. This project contends with questions of method, process, and craft from poets' and researchers' perspectives to show the implications for the aesthetic and epistemic concerns in poetry and for further interdisciplinary dialogues between the humanities and social sciences. This examination acts as a heuristic in the development, refinement, and teaching of what doing and critiquing Poetic Inquiry entails. In addition, the dialogue between poets and researchers promises to demonstrate the relevance and importance of poetry in other venues outside of the small poetry sub-culture as poetry is used for such things as preserving the "lived experience" of research participants and for poetry therapy. I answer questions about how we can use poetry to represent research and the research process:

What does it mean to use poetry in research?

How can you transform interviews and observations into poetry?

How do you write poetry as research?

How can poetry be used in and as qualitative analysis?

How can we evaluate the use of poetry in/as/for research?

Second, this book acts as a teaching guide that will enhance discussion of poetry writing as a method and encourage students to consider the importance of form and function in the process, craft, and use of poetry as/in/for research. In addition, the text will serve as an extended example of how one can use poetry to represent research and the research process. Students who wish to learn more about how to transform interviews, research observations, and archival work into poetry can use this book as it describes the process and craft of that writing. Students who want to use poetry as part of the analysis process will find the exercises and examples included to be helpful. How do you decide what poetic form to use? Do you need to read other poets? What about other researchers writing poetry? What issues are there when using poetry as/in/for research? These questions will be addressed, and the text will provide point-by-point topics based on example Poetic Inquiry texts with suggested guidelines for representing research through poetry.

ACKNOWLEDGMENTS

The following articles were adapted for inclusion in Chapters 1–4:

Faulkner, S. L. (2005). Method: 6 poems. *Qualitative Inquiry*, 11(6), 941–949.

Faulkner, S. L. (2006). Reconstruction: LGBTQ and Jewish. *International and Intercultural Communication Annual*, 29, 95–120.

Faulkner, S. L. (2007). Concern with craft: Using *ars poetica* as criteria for reading research poetry. *Qualitative Inquiry*, 13(2), 218–234.

Faulkner, S. L. (2009). Research/poetry: Exploring poet's conceptualizations of craft, practice, and good and effective poetry. *Educational Insights*, 13(3). Available at: www.ccfi.educ.ubc.ca/publication/insights/v13n03/articles/faulkner/index.html

Faulkner, S. L. (2012). Frogging it: A poetic analysis of relationship dissolution. *Qualitative Research in Education*, 1(2), 202–227. doi:10.4471/qre.2012.10

Faulkner, S. L., & Ruby, P. D. (2015). Feminist identity in romantic relationships: A relational dialectics analysis of email discourse as collaborative found poetry. *Women's Studies in Communication*, 38(2), 206–226. doi:10.1080/07491409.2015.1025460

Faulkner, S. L. (2016). TEN: The promise of arts-based, ethnographic, and narrative research in critical family communication research and praxis. *Journal of Family Communication*, 16(1), 9–15. doi:10.1080/15267431.2015.1111218

Faulkner, S. L. (2016). The art of criteria: *Ars Criteria* as demonstration of vigor in poetic inquiry. *Qualitative Inquiry*, 22(8), 662–665. doi:10.1177/1077800416634739

Faulkner, S. L. (2016). Postkarten aus Deutschland: A chapbook of ethnographic poetry. *Liminalities*, 12(1). Available at: http://liminalities.net/12-1/postkarten.html

Faulkner, S. L. (2017). MotherWork collage (a queer scrapbook). *QED: A Journal in GLBTQ Worldmaking*, 4(1), 166–179.

Faulkner, S. L. (2017). Poetry is politics: A poetry manifesto. *International Review of Qualitative Research*, 10(1), 89–96. doi:10.1525/irqr.2017.10.1.89

Faulkner, S. L. (2018). Crank up the feminism: Poetic inquiry as feminist methodology. *Humanities*, 7(3), 85. doi:10.3390/h7030085

In Chapter 1, excerpts of *Pendleton Poems* (p. 25; pp. 29–30) and *From Love and Death in California* (p. 122) from Hartnett, S. J. (2003). *Incarceration Nation: Investigative Prison Poems of Hope and Terror.* Walnut Creek, CA: AltaMira. Reprinted by permission of Rowan and Littlefield.

In Chapter 2, excerpts of the poems *Que, Que* and *Que, Que: Tanka* from Furman, R., Lietz, C., & Langer, C. L. (2006). The research poem in international social work: Innovations in qualitative methodology. *International Journal of Qualitative Methods*, 5(2). Available at: www.ualberta.ca/~iiqm/backissues/5_3/PDF/furman.pdf. Copyright © 2006 by R. Furman. Used with the permission of the first author.

In Chapter 2, excerpt of Ron Pelias' poem *How to Watch Your Father Die* (p. 74), from Pelias, R. J. (2004). *A Methodology of the Heart: Evoking Academic & Daily Life.* Walnut Creek, CA: Altamira. Reprinted by permission of Rowan and Littlefield.

In Chapter 2, excerpt of Ron Pelias' poem *Acid Attack* from Pelias, R. J. (2007). Jarheads, girly men, and the pleasures of violence. *Qualitative Inquiry*, 13(7), 945–959. Copyright © 2007 by Sage. Reprinted by Permission of Sage Publications.

In Chapter 2, excerpt of Corrine Glesne's poetic transcription from Glesne, C. (1997). That rare feeling: re-presenting research through poetic transcription. *Qualitative Inquiry*, 3, 202–222. Copyright © 1997 by Sage. Reprinted by Permission of Sage Publications.

In Chapter 2, excerpt of Frank X. Walker's poem *Role Call* from Walker, F. X (2008). *When Winter Come: The Ascension of York.* Lexington: University Press of Kentucky. Copyright © 2008 by Frank X. Walker. Used with the permission of the author.

In Chapter 2, excerpt of Gabe Welsh's poem, *Pennsylvania*, from *Dirt and All Its Dense Labor*, by Gabriel Welsh, 2006, WordTech Editions, used with the permission of the author.

In Chapter 2, excerpt of Laham's (Laham, Teman, & Richard, 2019) poem *risk.*, *Qualitative Inquiry*, 25(2) 200–214. doi:10.1177/10778, Copyright © 2019 by Sage. Reprinted by Permission of Sage Publications.

In Chapter 2, excerpt of Michelle Reale's poem, *from Suleiman* in Reale, M. (2015). "We never thought it would be like this": Refugees' experiences in Sicily. *The Qualitative Report*, 20(1), 107–114. Available at: https://nsuworks.nova.edu/tqr/vol20/iss1/8, used with permission of the author.

In Chapter 3, *You Are Worth Many Sparrows*, from *Threat of Pleasure*, Word Press, 2008, by Philip Memmer, reprinted with the permission of the author.

In Chapter 3, Kay Boyle, excerpt from *Poets* from *This is Not a Letter and Other Poems*. Copyright © 1985 by Kay Boyle. Reprinted with the permission of The Permissions Company, Inc., on behalf of Green Integer, www.greeninteger.com

In Chapter 3, excerpt of R. Seiferle's poem *Poetic Voice* from Wiegers, M. (ed.) (2003). *This Art: Poems about Poetry*. Port Townsend, WA: Copper Canyon Press. Reprinted with the permission of Rebecca Seiferle.

In Chapter 1, Sandra Faulkner's poems *Crank Up the Feminism, I'm Not What Lisa Expected, Letter to the IRB from South Jersey, Instructions for Surviving Infant, Make Two, Feminist Theory Class Cento, Haiku as Running Log, Reconstructionist, When She Passes by Her Professor's Door, Hello Kitty Spits on His Creepy Poetry, Hello Kitty Goes to College,* Dissertation Abstracts International *Feminist Standpoint Theory: An Examination by a Post Modern Two-Dimensional Cat with No Mouth and 22,000 Products Bearing Her Image,* and *After the Faculty Meeting* used with the permission of the author.

In Chapter 2, Sandra Faulkner's poems *Method, The Jewish Table 31 Ways, In Your Interview Dream, When Hello Kitty Registers for the Working Cats Conference, Security Confiscates Her Catnip, Orthodoxy, 1. Die Trauer (The Sadness), 2. Die Angst (The Fear), 3. Der Stolz (The Pride), 4. Der Ärger (The Annoyance), 5. Die (Un) Ordnung (The (Dis)Order),* and *On Inauguration Day* used with the permission of the author.

In Chapter 2, Sheila Squillante's poem, *The Hive Responds* used with the permission of the author.

In Chapter 3, Sandra Faulkner's poems *Letter to Faulkner from the Fluff and Fold, Dr. H. Kitty Considers Her Dissertation as* Ars Poetica, and *Hoagland Writes to Faulkner about Thingitude* used with the permission of the author.

In Chapter 4, Sandra Faulkner's poems *The Jewish Question, A.L.I.C.E. Training, I was to be an Orthodox Rabbi, Letter to Sol after the SSSS Presentation, The Suicide Window, Outside the Suicide Window,* and *Suicide Window, Detroit* used with the permission of the author.

Thank you to Hannah Shakespeare, Acquisitions Editor, for taking a chance on another edition. Thank you to Janice Morse, Series Editor, who gave the first edition a home. And a special shout out to my feminist posse, Patricia Leavy and Jessica Smartt Guillion, who provided me with "energy gel" to keep going during the painful last mile of finishing this book. You two are living proof that building each other up is living the feminist life.

As always, thank you to my partner, Josh, and my kid, Mimi, for understanding that poetry is life to me. Your support for me and my work is life.

THE BOOK

+ How does she construct this statement?

+ what do you think of these questions?

Welcome to the revised edition of *Poetry as Method* wherein I examine the use of poetry as a form of research, representation, and method used by researchers, practitioners, and students from across the social sciences and humanities. Through discussions of poetry as research method, poetry as qualitative analysis and representation, and Poetic Inquiry as a powerful research tool, I make an argument for the importance of considering the form and function of Poetic Inquiry in qualitative research. This project extends my own and others' work on issues of poetic and arts-based research methodology through an examination of explicit, and often implicit, writing and beliefs about what constitutes effective poetry and arts-based research. This project contends with questions of method, process, and craft from poets' and researchers' perspectives to show the implications for the aesthetic and epistemic concerns in poetry and to further transdisciplinary dialogues between the humanities and social sciences. I argue for Poetic Inquiry as a feminist, liberatory methodology that will enhance our teaching, research, and practice. This revision also serves as a practical manual for using poetry in qualitative research through the use of varied examples of Poetic Inquiry and providing how-to exercises for developing and using poetry as qualitative research method. I map out what doing and critiquing Poetic Inquiry entails by beginning with a discussion of the power of poetry, moving to poets' and researchers' goals for the use of poetry in their work and the kinds of projects that are best suited for Poetic Inquiry, then describing the process and craft of that writing, and suggesting ways that we may evaluate and engage with Poetic Inquiry.

Chapter 1 introduces the idea of poetry as research, method, and methodology by defining poetry and Poetic Inquiry and making the argument for the power of poetry by addressing the following questions:

- What is poetry as research?
- What does it mean to say that poetic practice is a research method?
- What do we label poetry used in and as research?
- What is poetry as research methodology?
- How is poetry praxis and response?

I begin with an autoethnographic account of my move to Poetic Inquiry in my research as a social scientist to position myself in the conversation and demonstrate reflexivity. Next, I define poetry and Poetic Inquiry, synthesize and discuss the scope of Poetic Inquiry, before moving to the goals and kinds of projects that are best suited for Poetic Inquiry. This includes framing Poetic Inquiry within feminist, queer, narrative, and identity theories to show how we can use poetry as research method, to represent research and the research process, and as praxis. I show that poetry as/in/for research offers scholars, teachers, and practitioners a means of doing, showing, and teaching embodiment and reflexivity, a way to refuse the mind-body dialectic, a form of ethnography and qualitative research, and a catalyst for social agitation and change.

In Chapter 2, I describe the process, method, and craft of Poetic Inquiry through exemplars and discussion of how we can use poetry to represent research and the research process to address the following questions:

- What goals do Poetic Inquirers hope to achieve in their work?
- How can you transform interviews, archival research, and observations into poetry?
- How do you write poetry as research?
- How can poetry be used in qualitative analysis or even as qualitative analysis?
- How can you use poetry as political activism?

I show the doing of Poetic Inquiry through examples of different poetic forms including the lyric, narrative, long forms and poetry series, collaborative, and collage work. I open the chapter with researchers' goals for using poetry in their work to put the use of poetry in qualitative research practice in context.

In Chapter 3, I wrestle with the questions of whether one should use criteria to evaluate Poetic Inquiry, and if so, what criteria would be appropriate for such an evaluation and why? I argue for the importance of considering criteria for Poetic Inquiry, and perhaps more importantly, I argue for a *willingness* to engage in dialogue about the creation and use of criteria as a concentrated focus on craft issues promises to help us fulfill our poetic goals. I present phenomenological interviews with 14 poets about craft issues, their practice of writing and teaching poetry, and ideas of good and effective poetry to pose these questions:

- What is "good" poetry used as/in qualitative research?
- What should Poetic Inquiry accomplish?

- How should we evaluate Poetic Inquiry?
- What does it mean to call poetry good or bad?
- Is there room for "good enough" poetry?

I offer ways to help us evaluate the merits of research poetry- the use of *ars poetica* (i.e., the art of poetry) and *ars criteria* poems as well as the application of poetic criteria—artistic concentration, embodied experience, discovery/surprise, conditionality, narrative truth, and transformation. Specifically, I present a discussion of the function and utility of *ars poetica* for poetic craft, a means of articulating one's own *ars poetica* and *ars criteria* poems, the implications of using poetic criteria, and the possibilities of good enough poetry.

Chapter 4 acts as a heuristic offering suggestions, questions, and challenges for Poetic Inquirers to consider in their work by focusing on poetic inspiration through the use of writing exercises intended to train the poetry muscle. I wrote this chapter to make the process of Poetic Inquiry less mysterious while concomitantly acknowledging that individual and groups of researcher-poets will find and develop their own creative processes. I address the following questions through specific and detailed writing exercises:

- In what ways can you transform research, interviews, reflections, and observations into poetry?
- How do you move from research problem to poetry?
- What are the best exercises for the type of work you want to do and your research goals?
- How can you best collaborate with other poets and poet-researchers?

I end with some reflections on how regular poetic practice may help in your poetry making through habit, mindfulness, and finding joy in the necessity of revision, and I offer selected books on craft and critique for further reference and reading.

1

THE POWER OF POETRY

Poetry allows us to hear the tread of another through their experiences and it compels us to explore a different way of capturing social science research.

Gradle, 2017, p. 234

Poetry is another way of singing. Language is wearing its other story.

Rita Dove, 2018

Poetic Inquiry Is ...

At its best, Poetic Inquiry bootstraps comprehension of a research topic, energizes inquiry, and challenges how we come to knowledge and what we think we know, undercutting disciplinary, discursive norms.

James, 2017, p. 23

Welcome to the revised edition of *Poetry as Method* wherein I examine the use of poetry as a form of research, representation, and method used by researchers, practitioners, and students from across the social sciences and humanities. Through discussions of poetry as research method, poetry as qualitative analysis and representation, and Poetic Inquiry as a powerful research tool, I make an argument for the importance of considering the form and function of Poetic Inquiry in qualitative research. This project extends my own and others' work on issues of poetic and arts-based research methodology through an examination of explicit, and often implicit, writing and beliefs about what constitutes effective poetry and arts-based research. This project contends with questions of method, process, and craft from poets' and researchers' perspectives to show the implications for the aesthetic and epistemic concerns in poetry and to further transdisciplinary dialogues between the humanities and social sciences. I argue for Poetic Inquiry as a feminist, liberatory methodology that will enhance our teaching, research, and practice. This revision also serves as a practical manual for using poetry in qualitative research through the use of varied examples of Poetic Inquiry and providing how-to exercises for developing and using poetry as qualitative research method. I map out what doing and critiquing Poetic Inquiry entails by beginning with a discussion of the power of poetry, moving to poets' and researchers' goals for the use of poetry in their work and the kinds of projects that are best suited for Poetic Inquiry, then describing the process and craft of that writing, and suggesting ways that we may evaluate and engage with Poetic Inquiry.

This chapter introduces the idea of poetry as research, method, and methodology by defining poetry and Poetic Inquiry and making the argument for the power of poetry by addressing the following questions:

- What is poetry as research?
- What does it mean to say that poetic practice is a research method?
- What do we label poetry used in and as research?
- What is poetry as research methodology?
- How is poetry praxis and response?

I begin with an autoethnographic account of my move to Poetic Inquiry in my research as a social scientist to position myself in the conversation and demonstrate reflexivity. Next, I define poetry and Poetic Inquiry, synthesize and discuss the scope of Poetic Inquiry, before moving to the goals and kinds of projects that are best suited for Poetic Inquiry. This includes framing Poetic Inquiry within feminist, queer, narrative, and identity theories to show how we can use poetry as research method, to represent research and the research process, and as praxis. I show that poetry as/in/for research offers scholars, teachers, and practitioners a means of doing, showing, and teaching embodiment and reflexivity, a way to refuse the mind-body dialectic, a form of ethnography and qualitative research, and a catalyst for social agitation and change.

Moving to Poetic Inquiry

Crank Up the Feminism

We declare feminist law
like shrews in heat
dial up the belligerent bass
from the front seat.

We do our hair in rosy rage
smear righteous red on our cheeks
as we pull on our combat best dress
the anti-patriarchy patrol in suffragette white.

The usual boys have no idea
what to do as we shank
the good girl in the mirror:
You're all lesbians now, America!

Our art bleeds down our legs
pools like rubies on piles of rubble
that can't be swept under rugs:
our rage refuses to ride shotgun.

We skip the protest and go
right for the throat, steal bologna
sandwiches from the Boy Scout's
tent yawping, *You want to see rogue?*

We snap the elastic in your pants,
show up five minutes late
with wet hair and chipped nails,
hit send without proofreading:

you can type your own template
as we crush the control panel
throttle up the appropriate volume
smashing the baby over your knees.
Faulkner, 2018a

I begin with a poem I wrote in response to Alex Ruth Bertulis-Fernandes' art piece called *Dial Down the Feminism*, which consists of a photo of a control panel with a dial and two volume settings—complicit in my own dehumanization and raging feminist—with the dial turned to raging feminist (Grasso, 2018). Alex's art professor told her to dial down the feminism in her work, and Alex responded with feminist art. As I wrote my ekphrastic poetic response to Bertulis-Fernandes' work, I thought of all of the ways I've been told in my life and career that "my feminism has ruined me," that my work is too critical, that I should be the "Good White Girl," that I have destroyed others' altruistic visions of motherhood, and that I shouldn't put that "poetry stuff" on my vitae (Faulkner, 2016a). I am a poet, a feminist ethnographer, partner, and teacher who studies close relationships and uses Poetic Inquiry as a way to show the messy work of living a feminist life (Ahmed, 2017), being a feminist scholar and teacher, being a feminist partner and mother, and doing feminist relationship research. You can use poetry in your research, teaching, and praxis as a (YOU FILL IN THE BLANK) scholar. I show you my evolution from a traditional qualitative researcher to an Arts-Based Research Practitioner who uses poetry in teaching and as a feminist research method.

"Poetic Inquiry is the use of poetry crafted from research endeavors, either before a project analysis, as a project analysis, and/or poetry that is part of or that constitutes an entire research project" (Faulkner, 2017a, p. 210). I argue that Poetic Inquiry can be a qualitative and feminist research methodology because of what poetry can do and be.

> I write poetry because I am a bad (BAD!) social scientist. I study personal relationships; I am most interested in what relationships feel like and sound like and smell like more than how they function as some kind of analytic variable to be deconstructed. I believe in poetic truth(s) more than social science Truth punctuated with a capital T … What I understand is that one can write poetry as social science. What I believe in is the value of poetry as relationship research.
>
> *Faulkner, 2017b, p. 148*

I began using poetry in my work as a scholar who studies close relationships when I needed to talk about identity and communication in a more nuanced fashion and wanted to describe the physicality and emotionality of doing research (Faulkner, 2005). I have written poetry since childhood and often write poems when I am trying to make sense of difficult life experiences such as cancer and motherhood (e.g., Faulkner, 2014a, 2017c). Shortly after finishing my PhD when I was engaged in a project on LGBTQ Jewish identity (Faulkner and Hecht, 2011), I merged my poetry practice with my social science training by presenting the narrative research as poetry (Faulkner, 2006). "Writing poetry helped me recover from my training in graduate school and the numbing realities of academic writing. It helped me reclaim creativity and its rhythms" (Faulkner, 2014a, p. xiii). I felt that the twists and turns in the research study, showing my reflexivity as a feminist scholar, and the bodily experience of doing and being a feminist ethnographer were best presented as poetry. I wrote the method's section of the work (Faulkner, 2005) as a series of six poems to show the research story (L. Richardson, 1997a), my subjective emotional processes, difficulties of identities in fieldwork, and the challenges of conducting interviews while being reflexive and conscientious. In the poems, I was able to highlight how identities as researcher and participant were negotiated in situ. For example, the following poem about a participant's reaction to me as a researcher is a story a traditional method section couldn't tell:

I'm Not What Lisa Expected

no blonde bunned hair
like the researcher in her mind,

like my second grade teacher, glasses,
but blue and stylish and young.

I'm 31 and old enough to teach,
ask others about their identities,

though I have scant lines on face and vita,
wear shirts without collars.

I talk as a friend—except those questions
about being gay and Jewish—

as I shift, catch words with my recorder,
camo cargo pants belie my worry with uniform.

Another participant claims I walk lesbian-
like, confident stride and spiky cut hair,

into her usual diner on 7th Avenue where
we eat rice pudding like family. She knew

who I was without my description—
5 feet 5 inches, red hair, short and sapphire spectacles—

How do I tell them that I live and flirt
and fight with a man now, that my

ex-girlfriend calls me semi-straight
and semi-gay and too interested in labels?

Faulkner, 2005

A method section as poetry highlighted a different story—a not so neatly packaged story of how we negotiate our identities in the field. I longed to send the poem, *Letter to the IRB from South Jersey*, as a response to my Institutional Review Board instead of the typical template to ask for continued approval to talk with LGBTQ Jews about their identities and life. This epistolary poem let me use an intimate tone and talk about becoming friends with research participants, how I managed my identities as a researcher and a human being, and the influences that life and values have on what I noticed and commented on in a research setting:

Letter to the IRB from South Jersey

Dear Institutional Review Board:
I know it has been a year, but I am still in the field.
The renewal form for study 11147 (Gay Jewish Identity)
is mostly complete. As usual, you provide too little
space, no more than 2 costly lines, so I append this letter.
Just in case. I considered your focused questions as I drove north,
away from the tattooed gentiles in Cape May, the Jersey turnpike
and the unctuous winter storm coating my Volkswagen.
I was nervous, had too tight a grip on the wheel. *Unanticipated
consequences of this research?* I could skid under a trailer,
the cyber green Beetle with the German engineering I have admired

since I was 15, the "cool car, but one I shouldn't own," screeching
apart in pieces along with the German chocolate cake from the cooking
school bakery in my stomach. My interviewee in Atlantic City
bought it for us. He said on Saturdays the students sell goodies,
cheap. If you go early. We drink his good coffee—not that dirty
water from Jersey diners—in mustard lusterware cups
from Czechoslovakia (I checked the bottom). As I listen
to their stories, I drink too much crappy coffee,
eat raisin toast with margarine, bagels and jelly, fruit plates
with cottage cheese, listen to piped-in light favorites at
their local diners. I rent space with food. Sometimes afterwards,
we talk like friends. You know, we exchange book titles,
share artwork and our secrets about relationships. I meet every
Monday with Lesa, once participant, now friend, to eat bagels.
Positive consequence, would you agree? Did I mention
the car I drive to meet participants? *Is this an unanticipated
negative consequence?* What about the consent form?
I know we have to cover our asses, but the signature line
creeps me out, them signing their names on an official page
like a hit list. I want to ask you these questions, even if they smack
of academic drama. What they really want to know about me
is not there, on your consent form. I have rewritten it:
*Bisexual of German/English/Scottish Ancestry who grew
up in Atlanta with Yankee parents seeks LGBTQ Jews
for conversation. Has experience with Jews.*
They like to hear my stories of exes, mentors, all of the Jews
in my life, why I'm interested in their lifework. I guess
the personal connection. Sometimes, what really matters is this.
L'chaim, Dr. S. Faulkner

Faulkner, 2015

I wrote *Poetry as Method* (Faulkner, 2009) after finishing this identity project
as a way to understand, describe, and critique the use of poetry in qualitative
research. And frankly, it was a way to legitimize and steer my work in the direction
where I wanted it to go. Since the identity project and publication of that volume
in 2009, there have been many formal and informal conversations about the use
of poetry as/in/for research, including Arts-Based Research (ABR) practice (see
Galvin & Prendergast, 2016). I was invited to the first *International Symposium on
Poetic Inquiry* (ISPI) in 2007 and found an international community engaged with
poetry and the use of poetry in research (see Prendergast, Leggo, & Sameshima,
2009 for the proceedings). The ISPI symposium is a biennial gathering of international poets, researchers, students, and community members interested in the use
of poetry as a research method, methodology, or approach. I found a community

of poets and researchers who value Poetic Inquiry and seek out the fun and difficult conversations about what poetry can do in our work.

Motherhood, Mothering, Narrative, and Interpersonal Communication

I continued to use poetry in my scholarship, teaching, and writing about mothering, motherhood, and feminism as a way to critique and resist middle-class White motherhood (Faulkner, 2012a, 2014a, 2014b, 2017c, 2017d), marriage and the status quo (Faulkner, 2016a), to show the interplay between the private and the public, and as a critical lens in the examination of family and interpersonal communication by focusing on power structures (Suter, 2018). Poetic Inquiry offers a way to engage with the public-private dialectic to collapse this false dichotomy (Baxter, 2011). One of poetry's strengths is the ability to position dialectics and refuse easy resolution. "A poem asserts itself as poetry by being in dialogue with what it resists" (Young, 2010, p. 38). Another strength of poetry rests in the kinds of truths that can be presented. For example, I use mother-poems to lay naked the taken-for-granted assumptions and social structures around mothering to stretch the binaries with a focus on the multiple and complicated truths of personal family intimacies.

In the critical autoethnography, *Bad Mom(my) Litany: Spanking Cultural Myths of Middle-Class Motherhood*, I wrote about loving my child but abhorring the mother role by juxtaposing new motherhood experiences with being a scholar who studies close relationships (Faulkner, 2014b). I critique cultural advice and expectations of what being a good mother means and use Poetic Inquiry to question entrenched myths about motherhood as seen in the next poem.

Instructions for Surviving Infant

Remember the stubborn latch
clown purple mouth of gentian violet
your own face melted off
from exhaustion, say no thanks
to the OB at the 6-week cry
because you must remember
remember not to have another
do not get over it
do not cherish this
no taking something to ease your face
all ears that ear plugs can't stop up.

Forget which onesie you put
on the 9 week old you have to pick up,
panic when you must identify her
on the floor in the infant room

because all the White babies look alike
rows of drool encrusted chins
clumsy arms in the nursery
don't tell them her first sentence:
Dad-Dee needs more beer.

My super power means
even lactation consultants
are not safe from the arch of spray,
pure power, pure stubborn,
no bonding here
you contested and I persisted
like daughter like mother
give away the parent manuals
offer no cloak of citations.

When I was 7 weeks old
I went back to teach, to speed up
the insufferable infancy,
the mothering work I suck at.
Sit your boots in the chair
Baby Doo, Ms. Baby
first word: dog, ball, ockpuss
other first sentence: More cookie, please.

Faulkner, 2015

I use narrative and confessional poetry to question expectations about middle-class family life, the mother role as the most important, the expectation of mothering as self-abnegation, and the medical system as the expert in child rearing.

> This focus on the personal acts as an interrogation into the expectations of middle-class motherhood and the concomitant disappointments of never being good enough. I argue that the engagement with the embodied experiences of mothering can alter attitudes and create social change through the visibility of stigmatized identities (e.g., bisexual feminist, ambivalent mother) and the refusal to create false separations between the domestic and public.
>
> *Faulkner, 2017c, p. 106*

In the poetry collection, *Knit Four, Frog One* (Faulkner, 2014a), I wrote family narratives in different poetic forms (e.g., collages, free verse, dialogue poems, sonnets) to tell the stories of grandmother-mother-daughter relationships, women's work, mothering, family secrets, and patterns of communication in close relationships. I wrote and rewrote family stories to reveal patterns of interaction and to tell better stories and offer more possibilities. Feminist poet, Victoria Chang (2018) speaks to this potential in poetry:

Poems are like time machines. They travel through time as a medium for individual memory and, as a genre, they engage historical time, collective cultural memory. But I think poems also activate a simultaneity of past, present, and future. A poem's rhythm moves us forward in time; the imagination a poem (hopefully) sparks posits futurities, a constellation of potentialities. Considering the nexus of verb tenses versus the present tense of the reading experience, a poem has already happened, is always happening right now, and will soon happen again.

Chang, 2018, para. 12

I incorporate dialectical thinking into the collection of family stories as verse to give voice to the both/and. For example, the following poem considers family trauma, pregnancy, coupling, and the everyday business of relationships as something more than a dichotomous private relating versus public persona choice.

Make Two

With two needles and a ball of string,
we learn the art of multiplication—

2 couplets, lovers, dyads, pet rats,
not twins like in my preggo horror movie.

Two tickets to a concert, a table for 2.
Not my favorite number-the rent is past due.

II, 2, two ways to write the number, my favorite
curvy because you can lie

in the bottom, the bowl. The number of bites
you need to share, a joint account. Two.

The usual number of cake layers, the pieces
of toast you get with eggs, the # of eggs

in the daily special, my good and bad side,
dichotomy, either or (not both/and),

one part of a compound sentence. Two sides
to the bed, two dimensions, two favorite colors,

the number of legs Dad once had,
knit in front and back=M1, 2 stitches,

what you need to erase a day, not the number
after birth, 2 parts water, 2 ounces of bourbon.

Faulkner, 2015

Mother-poems lay naked the taken-for-granted assumptions and social structures around mothering with a focus on personal family intimacies. In a series of collage poems composed from family artifacts, feminist research, and systematic recollections, I queer staid understandings of White middle-class mothering with MotherWork collages that act like a queer Pinterest scrapbook to

> critique and interrogate expectations and attitudes about what mothers should do, think, and feel. Good mothers in a pro-natalist culture should channel their creativity into things like making scrapbooks of their progeny. Spending time developing identities other than mother—such as poet, academic, and partner—makes fulfilling the normative role of the "good mother" impossible.
>
> *Faulkner, 2017d*

Reactions to Poetry as Method

My Poetic Inquiry and move to the narrative and lyric side of qualitative research has elicited bipolar reactions in the academic world:

> *Why does the author use poetry when her prose is so articulate and well written?*
> (a reviewer on my *Poetry as Method* book)
> *Where are the Chi-Squares reporting differences between groups?*
> (the review that got my narrative work on being Gay and Jewish rejected)
> *I wouldn't call the work here poetry.*
> (the reviewer who didn't see my found poetry email as poems)
> *In my relationship, feminism and romance coexisted. Feminist identity can be romantic. Why don't you address this?*
> (a reviewer who argued my critique of personal experience was wrong and who didn't get that the use of personal experience in poetry can connect to the universal, and dare I write—generalizable).

I prefer the other end of the spectrum descriptions that paint my work as "innovative" and marked by "crisp analysis." And what my friend, colleague, and witness to my wedding, Bernadette Calafell, considers nuanced positions and other valuable ways of practicing feminism than only variable analytic work that includes x as something to correlate with y.

> *Faulkner ("That Baby") has further complicated discussions of motherhood through the lens of ambivalence and agency.*
>
> *Calafell, 2014, p. 268*

I live here at that end of the rainbow as an "end-of-spectrum qualitative scholar": "*When you think of full-on-qualitative people, those [Sandra Faulkner and Carolyn Ellis] are the ones I think are at that end of things*" (Sahlstein, 2014, p. 113).

I am a full-on-qualitative researcher. I am a full-on Poetic Inquirer. I am a full-on-qualitative partner. I live a full-on qualitative life. I invite you to consider how Poetic Inquiry can be a powerful tool in your methodological box of research methods as we continue to consider poetry as research method.

Defining Poetry

> The art of poetry is not about the acquisition of wiles or the deployment of strategies. Beginning in the senses, imagination senses farther, senses more … Poetry is the honeymoon of my eyes, and when the honeymoon is over, I am even more at home in the world … And why do we write the poems too? For the refreshment of the courage of the good.
>
> *Revell, 2007, pp. 12, 99*

We can think of poetry as a distinct form of writing defined by alliteration, form, image, language use, line, metaphor, meter, rhythm, simile, structure, and syntax. Some people are frightened by or dislike poetry because of ideas that poetry is too difficult, esoteric, and ambiguous. Others laud the power of poetry because of its ability to present embodied experience, to be fun and political, lyrical and narrative, and to be a tool for social justice. Because poetry can be straightforward and twisting, refined and rough, full of jargon and simple, yes and no, either/or, both/and, all of the above, and none of the above, it makes defining poetry and Poetic Inquiry challenging.

Nevertheless, I begin with B. H. Fairchild's (2003) definition of poetry because it stirs me to read, write, and listen to poetry: "A poem is a verbal construction employing an array of rhetorical and prosodic devices of embodiment in order to achieve an ontological state, a mode of being, radically different from that of other forms of discourse" (p. 1). Fairchild's definition highlights the importance of poetry as embodied presentation (as opposed to representation) that "depends on discovering, moment by moment, ways of being: improvisation, not recitation" (Buckley & Merrill, 1995, p. xi). Parini (2008) states: "A poem, for me, is an interrogation of the world of spirit in nature" (p. 179). Poetry is about showing, not telling, our (in)humanity and all of its mysteries. Carl Leggo (2008a), poet-educator-scholar, defines poetry with many similar sentiments:

> Poetry … creates or makes the world in words. Poetry calls attention to itself as a text, as rhetorical device and stratagem. Poetry does not invite readers to consume the text as if it were a husk that contains a pithy truth … Poetry invites us to listen. Poetry is a site for dwelling, for holding up, for stopping … Poetry is about rhythm … Poetry creates textual spaces

that invite and create ways of knowing and becoming in the world. Poetry invites interactive responses, intellectual, emotional, spiritual, and aesthetic responses, Poetry invites ways of uniting the heart, mind, imagination, body, and spirit.

Leggo, 2008a, pp. 166–167

Leggo (2012) considers poetry to be pleasure, prayer, presence, performance, and prophecy.

Other poets focus on poetry as a distinct form of writing defined by form, structure, and in particular, the line. Longenbach (2008) offered this: "Poetry is the sound of language in lines. More than meter, more than rhyme, more than images or alliteration or figurative language, line is what distinguishes our experience of poetry as poetry, rather than some other kind of writing" (p. xi). He continued by explaining that line has no meaning in a poem except in relation to other poetic elements, especially sentence syntax. Vander Zee (2011) also argues for the importance of the line. "More than ever, the line *is* poetry, the radical against which even alternate and emerging poetic forms that foreground the visual or the auditory, the page or the screen, can be distinguished and understood" (p. 6). In contrast, Annie Finch (2005) defines poetry based on structure because otherwise everything can be poetry. For her, a poem is more than line, it is "a text structured (not merely decorated) by the repetition of any language element or elements." These elements of repetition may be aural (e.g., number of beats/accents), visual (e.g., line breaks), and conceptual (e.g., pun and riddle). She argued that repetition pulls us into a pre-literate body with child-like pleasure.

Qualitative researchers use poetry in their work precisely because of its slipperiness and ambiguity, its precision and distinctiveness, its joyfulness and playfulness. "The poet makes the world visible in new and different ways, in ways ordinary social science writing does not allow. The poet is accessible, visible, and present in the text, in ways that traditional writing forms discourage" (Denzin, 2014, p. 86).

Defining Poetic Inquiry

The labels that researchers have used for poetry in qualitative and ABR work varies; some terms include poetic transcription (Richardson, 2002), ethnographic or anthropological poetics (Behar, 2008), narratives of the self (Denzin, 1997), investigative poetry (Hartnett, 2003), research poetry (Faulkner, 2007, 2009; Lahman & Richard, 2014), lyric inquiry (Neilson, 2008), interpretive poetry (Langer & Furman, 2004), autoethnographic poetry (Faulkner, 2014a), found poetry (Butler-Kisber, 2002), performance poetry (Denzin, 2005), to (just) poetry (Faulkner, 2005). Langer and Furman (2004) define research poetry as poems that utilize a participant's exact words in a compressed form, excluding explicit reference to the researcher (what some would call poetic transcription), whereas interpretive poetry includes the researcher's subjective responses for a fusing of the researcher and participant perspectives (what I would call narrative poetry).

Regardless of what we call poetry used as/in qualitative research, all of these labels describe a method of turning research interviews, transcripts, observations, personal experience, and reflections into poems or poetic forms. In an annotated bibliography of 182 entries of poetry as/in qualitative research from 1918 to 2007, Prendergast (2009) gives us 29 ways of looking at Poetic Inquiry: as a form of qualitative research across disciplines—"**Poetic inquiry is** a form of qualitative research in the social sciences that incorporates poetry in some way as a component of investigation." (p. xxxv)—to a version of narrative inquiry—"**Poetic inquiry is**, like narrative inquiry with which it shares many characteristics, interested in drawing on the literary arts in the attempt to more authentically express human experiences." (p. xxxvi)—to an interdisciplinary effort between the social sciences, humanities, and fine arts—"**Poetic inquiry is** the attempt to work in fruitful interdisciplinary ways between the humanities [literature/aesthetic philosophy], fine arts (creative writing), and the social sciences." (p. xxxvi)—concerned with craft and quality—"**Poetic inquiry is**, along with arts-based inquiry approaches, deeply concerned with aesthetic issues around quality, qualifications, preparedness, elitism, and expertise" (p. xxxvii).

In 2012, Prendergast and Clement updated the bibliography with an additional 129 sources (for a total of 311 sources), which Prendergast (2015, p. 683) further sorted into the following categories:

Vox Theoria/Vox Poetica – Poems about self, writing and poetry as method
Vox Justitia – Poems on equity, equality, social justice, class, freedom
Vox Identitatis – Poetry exploring, self/participants' gender, race, sexuality
Vox Custodia – Poetry of caring, nursing, caregivers'/patients' experience
Vox Procreator – Poems of parenting, family and/ or religion.

In the past, I advanced the term "research poetry" to reference poems used in the research context, but I now use the label Poetic Inquiry, given the rise in popularity of the term (Faulkner, 2017a; Vincent, 2018). James (2017) traced the use and prevalence of the term in books from 1900–2008 with Google's Ngram Viewer finding a surge in 1948 after the Second World War and another in 2008, both times of political, economic, and social change. Thus, I offer the following definition of Poetic Inquiry while acknowledging that a uniform and fixed definition of Poetic Inquiry does not exist (see Vincent, 2018):

"Poetic inquiry" is the use of poetry crafted from research endeavors, either before a project analysis, as a project analysis, and/or poetry that is part of or that constitutes an entire research project. The key feature of poetic inquiry is the use of poetry as/in/for inquiry.

Faulkner, 2017a, p. 210

This definition is broad enough to include work that uses Poetic Inquiry as both a method and product of research activity.

Poetic Inquiry in Qualitative Research

Q: What does it mean to use poetry in research?

A: Poetry in research is a way to tap into universality and radical subjectivity; the poet uses personal experience and research to create something from the particular, which becomes universal when the audience relates to, embodies, and/or experiences the work as if it were their own.

Faulkner, 2017a, p. 210

Why Use Poetry?

Poetry is a valuable research tool and method for researchers and practitioners in fields such as anthropology, communication, education, nursing, psychology, sociology, and social work who wish to channel the power of poetry into their work. "Poetry has been used to engage participants in aspects of a range of qualitative methods and analyses, to bear witness, and ... to ... usefully enliven professional and public engagement with research findings" (Galvin & Prendergast, 2017, p. xiii). Poetic Inquirers who use poetry in their research offer compelling and varied reasons; most are "writing poetry for greater purpose and intent than solely for self-expression" (James, 2017, p. 25). Researchers have used poetry in their work for quite a while to meld the scientific and emotive, to understand and comment on "changes in physical, social, and psychic environments," and to embrace uncertainty; "Perhaps uncertainty is the catalyst that turns attention to poetry as a way to find what we missed with our other discursive approaches to understanding" (James, 2017, p. 26).

The practitioners of PI, from various fields of practice, choose to use poetry in their studies for particular purposes and in particular ways, but the underlying reason is that they wish to interact through language in ways that are not commonly accepted in more traditional qualitative research methods and seek different ways of knowing.

Vincent, 2018, p. 51

"Through the use of consciously applied meter, cadence, line length, alliteration, speed, assonance, connotation, rhyme, variation and repetition, poetry can evoke embodied responses in listeners and readers by recreating speech in ways that traditional research prose cannot" (L. Richardson, 1997b, p. 143). Jane Hirshfield (1997) believes poetry has an ability to clarify and magnify our human existence. She writes that "each time we enter its word-woven and musical invocation, we give ourselves over to a different mode of knowing: to poetry's knowing, and to the increase of existence it brings, unlike any other" (p. vii). Longenbach (2004) contends that the power of poetry lies in its cultural marginality and how it resists itself; the fact that poetry resists itself means we can experience wonder, rediscover pleasure in our inability to make the world intelligible. "A poem's power inheres less in its conclusions than in its propensity to resist them, demonstrating their inadequacy while moving inevitably toward them … Rather than asking to be justified, poems ask us to exist" (pp. 10–11). These observations about poetry as a means to enlarge understanding, resist clear undemanding interpretations, and move closer to what it means to be human elucidates the reason some researchers use poetry as a means of representing research.

The way we use language in poetry demonstrates and discloses the human mystery allowing us to "find ourselves in poems" (Richardson, 1998, p. 459), making it a viable alternative to prose.

> As a language adequate to our experience, poetry allows us to articulate matters of concern in such a way that they become physical, tangible, and immediate. Indeed, the finest poems become indestructible objects in their own right, taking on a life beyond the immediate circumstances of the poet to create them.
>
> *Parini, 2008, p. 25*

Neilsen (2008) furthered this argument through her use of the term "lyric inquiry" to reference the union of the lyric with research. Lyric inquiry, as a process and a product, focuses on the poetic functions of language and the idea that "aesthetic writing is the inquiry" with the goal of creating a relationship between that of the knower and known through ethical engagement. Poetry is part of a reflective practice wherein we can acknowledge bias, expectations, and power differences between researcher and participants. "Poetry … allows the researcher … to enter into an experience in the only way any researcher can (regardless of method)—as herself, observing and recording. She does not presume to speak for another" (Neilsen, 2008, p. 97). Poetry is a way to tap into universality; the poet uses personal experience to create something, which is universal or generalizable because the readers see the work as if it were their own (Furman et al., 2007). "A reader comes away with the resonance of another's world" (Neilsen, 2008, p. 96).

My colleagues and fellow Poetic Inquirers, John Guiney Yallop and Sean Wiebe, and I asked one another questions about Poetic Inquiry for a special issue of *in education*—what it is, what we use it for, and what distinguishes Poetic Inquiry from other qualitative methods (Guiney Yallop, Wiebe, & Faulkner, 2014):

What Does Poetic Inquiry Mean to You?

JJGY: Poetic inquiry is a way in for me. There are other ways in, but for me, I had to reawaken the poet to become a researcher, or at least, to continue to become the researcher I needed to become in order to do the work I needed to do, that is to explore my own identities and the communities in which those identities were located.

SF: I consider poetry an excellent way to (re)present data, to analyze and create understanding of human experience, to capture and portray the human condition in a more easily "consumable," powerful, emotionally poignant, and open-ended, non-linear form compared with prose research reports. Poetry constitutes a way to say things evocatively and to say those things that may not be presented at all.

SW: Poetic inquiry invites me into the in-between space between creative and critical scholarship. Such a space is reflexive and critical, aware of the nexus that is both self and other, both personal and public.

Guiney Yallop, Wiebe, & Faulkner, 2014, p. 3

How Do You Use Poetry in Your Academic Work? What Does Poetic Inquiry Help You Do?

SF: I use poetic inquiry in/for/as social science research to accomplish three goals: (a) to connect social research and poetry, (b) to effect social change through a focus on the aesthetic, and (c) to use poetry/poetic inquiry as a pedagogical tool.

JJGY: I use poetic inquiry to help me get up close—up close to the work I am doing. Interestingly, poetic inquiry also helps me step back from my work. I can step back and look at the poem. I can put the poem away for a while. The poem, however, continues to call me closer, to have a closer look. I use poetic inquiry in all of my research, in autoethnography as well as work with participants, with documents, and with memories—my own and the memories of others.

SW: Lately, I've been trying out an idea, thinking that in poetic inquiry there is an interweaving relationship among three ways of being in the world: fierce, tender, and mischievous. Thinking of the various intersections and blends of these habits of mind and heart enriches, for me, those discussions of poetic inquiry that are more methodological. What can be learned from the poet's fierce/mischievous openness to the aesthetic qualities of human experience?

Or, how might a poet's tenderness enhance the pursuit of knowing human experience more deeply?

Guiney Yallop, Wiebe, & Faulkner, 2014, pp. 3–4

What Distinguishes Poetic Inquiry From Other Arts-Based Qualitative Research Methods?

SW: I think it is a sustained and contemplative love of language. Susan Walsh (2012) describes her poetic inquiry process as being present and dwelling with particular artifacts rather than analyzing or interpreting them (p. 273). She says this involves listening to the text, asking what it wants her to do (p. 274). Eisner (2005) writes that "As we learn to think within the medium we choose to use, we also become more able to raise questions that the media themselves suggest" (p. 181). It seems to me that each medium, each form, has within it a slightly different kind of thinking, and that this thinking—which provides direction for how to proceed with representing the knowledge—does not become apparent without sustained contemplation.

SF: Poetry embodies experience to show truths that are not usually evident. For example, our deeply ingrained ideas about gender and culture and class and race, the seemingly natural ways of being are easier to unravel in verse.

JJGY: For me, it's like the Matryoshka dolls; poetic inquiry goes further inside to the hidden, or waiting, treasure that the first, or second, glance does not give access to.

In summary, poetry may be considered a "special language" that researchers want to access when they feel that other modes of representation will not capture what they desire to show about their work and research participants (Faulkner, 2005; Reale, 2015a), when they wish to explore knowledge claims and write with more engagement and connection (Denzin, 1997; Pelias, 2005; L. Richardson, 1997a), when the researcher's story intersects or entwines with research participants' lives (Behar, 2008; Krizek, 2003), to mediate different understandings (Leggo, 2008b), to present embodied experience (Ellingson, 2017; Faulkner 2018c; Snowber, 2016), and to reach more diverse audiences (L. Richardson, 2002). "Poetic Inquiry offers (a) the possibility of participation, participative writing and transcendence of disciplinary boundaries (b) engagement in more aesthetic ways of knowing and (c) honoring of the 'relational realities of the presence of phenomenon'" (Galvin & Prendergast, 2016, p. xiii).

Poetic Inquiry as Feminist Methodology

Perhaps the main reason I am drawn to Poetic Inquiry is its ability to be embodied methodology. Embodiment is an important concept in feminist theory, research, and praxis, and many qualitative researchers call for a methodology that is attentive to bodies and bodily knowledge (see Ellingson, 2017; Snowber, 2016). Feminist poetry and Poetic Inquiry offer a means of doing and showing embodied inquiry. Brady (2004) believes that poetry returns researchers back to the body in order to demonstrate how our theories arise out of embodied experience;

> meaning is made in that way, not found, and in its making it gets anchored in what *appeals* to the senses, the sensual, including bodies themselves … Science does not give us ordinary reality, the world we live in as we live it through our senses and our culturally programmed intellects.
>
> *Brady, 2004, pp. 624, 632*

My main goals in using poetry in my research and teaching are to agitate for social change, to show embodiment and reflexivity, to collapse the false divide between body and mind, public and private, and as a feminist ethical practice. I use poetry as a feminist methodology to crank up the feminism. In poetry, I show my embodiment as a feminist, as a scholar, and as a teacher who feels their way through research with mind AND body.

> Poetry can help us see our relationships bleeding out, hemorrhaging from the invisible inside, spilling outside the neat axioms of theory. Poetry is theory. Poetry can have us experience the social structures and ruptures in situ as we read, as we listen, as we hold our breath waiting for the next line. Poetry is bandage and salve. Poetry lets me goodwill my secure cloak of citations, argue in verse that there is space for critical work and personal experience in the study of close relationships.
>
> *Faulkner, 2017b, p. 149*

I have also discovered that using poetry in the classroom makes for more engaged teaching practice; students respond to poetry, both their own and others. For example, in a feminist theory class I taught, my students and I composed Centos—a poetic form made up of lines from texts and poems by other poets— from our class texts as a way to engage with and highlight the theory we were studying. The use of poetry helped us condense difficult theory to essential nuggets that spoke to us with the music of found poems. Here is a Cento composed of lines from a feminist theory reader that makes the argument for poetry as teaching tool.

Feminist Theory Class Cento

Poetry is feminist practice:
movement comes first
the central focus a radical body of thought.

The individual   is the problem,

theories between a division of the sexes
a matter of fitting women:

lesbians must become feminists
feminists must become lesbians
the triple threat—racism   imperialism   sexism.

Concerned with women's bodies,
poetry was consciousness-raising;
poetry was theory,
        private and public
        emotion and intellect.

Interlocking women's bodies, systems
of oppression, what we believe—
black feminism as logical:

        we struggle together.

Romanticism works as a cultural tool
        love corrupted sex class   a diseased form of love
the citadel of privacy pulls women.

Who decided the norm?

Women's organizations heard
population   and   family planning
negating class   and   race.

We struggle together
        against racism
        about sexism,

the patriarchal bargain shaping relations
gender ideology as classical patriarchy:
the infractions of demands to choose our own self-definitions.

Faulkner, 2017e

    Feminist scholars, women of color, and practitioners have been interested in embodiment, experiential knowledge, and theories of the flesh for quite some time (Collins 2000; Moraga & Anzaldúa, 1981); Poetic Inquiry and feminist poetry are examples of how we can engage in embodied inquiry to emphasize the importance of storytelling and narrative in the representation of knowledge and everyday experience. Poets can use their work to give voice to gendered experiences as a form of political activity and consciousness-raising (Reed, 2013). Strine (1989) notes, "poetic discourse is quintessentially a site of personal and ideological struggle within the ongoing cultural dialogue" (p. 26). Poetry as research method is one means to theorize using the body and to disavow the mind-body split still present in much academic work. Poetry lets us "come in through the backdoor with the feeling, the emotion, the experience. But if you start reflecting on that experience you can come back to the theory" (Anzaldúa, 1981, p. 263).

I argue that Poetic Inquiry offers a feminist research methodology because of the focus on embodied experiences and attention to breath, line, form, and emotion— all things that speak to the body. More specifically, I contend that poetry is a way to refuse the mind-body split and demonstrate embodiment. Feminist scholars and poets have been using poetry as a means to represent their bodily experiences. As Reed (2013) argued, "poetry is particularly well equipped to challenge crucial dichotomies: the separation of private and public spheres, and the split between emotion and intellect ... Poetry was theory. Poetry was feminist practice" (p. 89). For example, Adrienne Rich's *Diving into the Wreck: Poems 1971–1972* and *The School among the Ruins: Poems, 2000–2004* engage with a feminist ethics to show a radical feminist take on racism, identity, sexuality, and politics (Poetry Foundation, 2012).

Poetic Inquiry and poetry are still feminist practice and theory. Reilly and colleagues (2018) used found poetry of women's experiences with breast cancer to describe their existential and posttraumatic growth experiences, because "poetry has the potential to uplift the human spirit to a vision of another's reality" (p. 21). The researchers transformed interviews into poetry as a means to evoke rich and meaningful experience of participants' voices and bodily experiences. LaFollette (2018) makes an argument for women's poetry as feminist activism by using her own poems about resisting traditionally gendered female subjectivities:

> Poetry confronts dominant social structures like patriarchy and uses language to question and break down ideologies that have oppressed women throughout history. In doing so, poetry acts as a "blueprint" for social action and change; women can articulate the issues, push back against the oppression, and create space for activist movements.
>
> *LaFollette, 2018, p. 179*

Feminist poetry uses personal, embodied experience to make larger claims about systems and structures of oppression. "Good poetry makes personal experience available to others by giving it an outward form" (Reed, 2013, p. 86).

Feminist Ethnography

Ethnographic Poetic Inquiry offers a means to develop theoretical insights, to advocate for social change and justice, and to critique the false separation between science and art through nuanced demonstrations of how the poet/researcher reflects on field experiences and reframes them through poetry (Behar, 2008; Denzin, 2005). "Using poetry in an ethnographic project is a way to demonstrate anthropological insights, to tell a story about fieldwork through the telling, retelling, and framing of embodied experiences with a poetic sensibility" (Faulkner, 2018c, p. 112). Brady (2004) uses poetry to make his ethnographic insight transparent, critique Western perceptions, and demonstrate the limitations of language for conveying experience by always placing his work in context. Richardson (1998) considers poetry to be useful when we experience epiphanies in fieldwork that show humanity, and we wish to relive the instant, to show a moment of truth. Ethnographic poetry focuses on specific cultures and highlights definitions of the term culture by resonating with cultural insiders, by wrestling with differences and similarities, and by engaging in the tension between community insiders/outsiders. González (2002) writes poetic ethnography as a way to adhere to ethical considerations and answer the question "Will my study accomplish what I intend without distorting the nature of what others have shared with me, or the relationships I developed" (p. 388)? In her three-year ethnography on non-Indians seeking to adopt Native American spiritual practices, González used poetry to represent the ethnography because of concerns for the anonymity of the people she was writing about and the shared nature of the spiritual practices and ceremonies; traditional academic writing could distort real experience of the dialectic tensions of positive and negative, strong and weak, admirable and shameful.

Ethnopoetics pay careful attention to language in an attempt to decrease distance between researchers and those researched, between mind and body, and to critique colonialism and representations of non-Western cultures through a focus on aesthetic differences between Western literary traditions and indigenous orality (Brady, 2000). Poetry is a way to say things effectively and say those things that may not be presented at all: "Ethnographic poets meditate on the ethnographic experience or focus on particulars arranged to elicit themes of general humanity that might apply cross-culturally" (Brady, 2000, 2004, p. 630). Poetry makes writing conspicuous and pays attention to particulars in opposition to transparent invisible scientific writing that focuses on comparative frameworks. In his work, Brady (2005) does the following: (1) tells us how he arrived at his understanding in personal and epistemological terms; (2) is present (i.e., grounded in the body using imagination, bodily experience, and educated analogy as evidence); (3) studies "tribal" poetries, myths, and written texts for worldviews that are embedded in orality while being careful of Western perceptions and the limitations of language for conveying experience; the work is always placed in context.

In the chapbook, *Postkarten aus Deutschland*, I map a three-and-a-half-month feminist ethnography on embodiment in Germany through ethnographic poetry and self-made photo-postcards (Faulkner, 2016b). I use a feminist lens in my DIY (Do-It-Yourself) poetry chapbook to show the interplay between power and difference. The poems and images I present demonstrate the full-body experience of learning another language and engaging in culture through language (mis) acquisition; I focus in on the concept of embodiment and what it means to learn a language and culture through attention to the senses and the full body ability to feel a language, to notice the "eye" of others when you don't quite get it, to running along the Rhine river, to the use of public transportation, ordering food, holidays and the usual activities, and to travel as a middle-aged white female body with a kindergartner plus male spouse.

Using poetry in feminist ethnography gives us a flexible and sophisticated way to show fieldwork and theorizing with no easy, determinate answers. I found using Poetic Inquiry in ethnographic work to be a process that mirrors how and why I ask particular research questions, and a means to show my bodily engagement with participants and research ideas. In a feminist ethnography on women and running, titled *Real Women Run*, I wrote: "I'm finally doing the research project I've thought about for years, and I don't give a shit if it fits into my academic program of research. I'm running toward the feminist ethnographer I want to be" (Faulkner, 2018c, p. 38). I wrote these lines to show how I used Poetic Inquiry as feminist ethnography to understand, describe, and query embodied experiences in everyday relational life, of which running and the interplay between physicality, emotional life, and intellectual life is a part for women who run. In this project, I articulated on the page what I had been feeling, thinking, and doing the past decade when using poetry in my research and in my classroom. I cranked up the feminism through a two-and-a-half-year ethnography on women's embodied experiences of running—a poetic analysis of 41 interviews with women-identified runners, an autoethnography of my participation in the road races at the 2014 Gay Games, and a critical content analysis of web sites and blogs targeted toward women who run. Poetic Inquiry in this ethnography worked as a form of feminist embodied analysis through running as poetic practice and poetry as running logs. This meant the use of poetry as research analysis. This meant paying attention to "the smells and textures and bodily movements" in running to shift "away from discourse ... to include more emphasis on materiality" (Ellingson, 2017, p. 83; Faulkner, 2018c, p. 113).

I used Poetic Inquiry—narrative poetry, haiku, poetic transcription, and poetic analysis—as feminist inquiry. Because my running practice is tied to my writing practice, I could not talk about a poetic analysis of women and running without talking about running and writing, running as poetic practice.

> Writing is not a disembodied activity. Writing about running proved to be an embodied experience; I worked out structural, content, and theoretical issues as I ran. And my running became a problem to work out in my writing ... I can't pinpoint an exact moment when I recognized that poetic inquiry was the key to organizing and demonstrating this project as a feminist embodied ethnography. Most likely, the pieces were sweat out, sorted, and rearranged during runs. The problems of writing and running were tangled together for me in this project.

> ***Writing Problems***: *How do I make running interesting to non-runners? How do I connect women's embodied experiences to the idea of running as a feminist act?*

Running Problems: How do I keep running? How do I keep running despite my maladies?

Faulkner, 2018c, p. 108

Poetry can not only show embodiment; it can be an embodied experience. The use of poems to help show what running feels like "becomes *embodied experience* when audiences feel *with*, rather than *about* a poem; they experience emotions and feelings *in situ*" (Faulkner, 2017a, p. 226). Using poems about running can be an embodied experience for the audience "to have you feel like you are running with me and other women, to feel our gasps and intake of breath, to breathe in rhythm with the words" (Faulkner, 2018c, p. 116). When I present the running research and perform the poems, audience members tell me that they feel like they are running with me and my participants.

Haiku as Running Log

Woman, Runner
a woman runner
is a woman who runs is
a woman runner

Run Body
thunder with your thighs
running is like being born
saying yes to cheese

Cat Calls
don't call us a girl
don't call us a girl jogger
fierce women running

Body is Mind
I am all body
aching arthritic hip feet
keep run-run-running

PR: Personal Record
you become body
you become your body you
become your body

Women Running
safety dressed in form
Caution: RUNNERS on the road
dogs cat call danger

Feminist Run
run as strategy
physical mouthed resistance
strong-sweat out the shoulds

You are
if you run, you are
see yourself as a runner
athlete woman run

Faulkner n.d.

I used Poetic Inquiry, specifically haiku as field notes, found poetry and poetic transcription of interviews with women runners, and narrative poetry of my embodied experiences of running to demonstrate my analysis process, to show the rhythm of running, and to connect writing as embodiment to ethnographic practice.

> In my field notes, I found poems. I wrote many entries in my field notes as poems, and constructed many poems while running. When I think about what makes poetry, I typically think of the line: "Poetry is the sound of language in lines … Line is what distinguishes our experience of poetry as poetry, rather than some other kind of writing" (Longenbach, 2008, p. xi). And when thinking of the line, I think of breath. For me, running is also about breath; breathing in the pleasure, breathing out the hurt. Breathing in who I want to be, breathing out lesser versions of self. Trying to breathe in through the nose and out through the mouth to catch my pace during a run. "The body is rooted in breath, rhythm, and poetry …" (Snowber, 2016, p. xv).
>
> *Faulkner, 2018b, p. 115*

"Poetry promises to return researchers back to the body in order to demonstrate how our theories arise out of embodied experience" (Faulkner, 2017a, p. 214). This project represents a more physical feminism as I presented women's running experiences, highlighting their bodily experiences as connected to cultural practices through narrative, poetry, and poetic transcription; poetry as analysis, as representation, and as embodiment (McCaughey, 1997: Velija, Mierzwinski, & Fortune, 2013). The use of Poetic Inquiry expands "our understanding of ethnography by considering how we do embodiment" and how "our participants do embodiment" (Ellingson, 2017, p. 81). *Real Women Run* paces readers through women's embodied running experiences; identities in motion, the inseparable mind-body connection, and running as social and solitary, pleasurable and painful, dangerous and empowering. "An embodied ethnography defies the mind-body split; a feminist ethnography pays attention to the material and the discursive by taking up emotional, physical, and ideological space" (Faulkner, 2018c, p. 113).

Identity Work and Poetic Inquiry

Poetic Inquiry is also an excellent method for projects focused on identity and identity negotiation. In a poetry manifesto (Faulkner, 2017e), I made the claim that

> the personal is poetry ... Poetry of personal experience is vital. Poetry has the power to highlight slippery identity-negotiation processes and present more nuanced views of marginalized and stigmatized identities, to demonstrate embodied experience and to be social research and autoethnography.
>
> *Faulkner, 2017e, p. 93*

Poetry may resonate with readers to have them experience the poetry as "evocative mediators" of painful relational experiences and to recognize and tell their own stories (Todres & Galvin, 2008, p. 571). For example, Kidd (2016) used poetic autoethnography to present "the embodied experiences of ethnicity for white skinned Māori" (p. 135).

> As I produce poetry for my colleagues to experience, I ask them to understand that I am more than I appear to be, but less than I want to be ... poetry provides a subversion, a space that allows me to re-define and re-present my struggle in ways that make my world accessible to others.
>
> *Kidd, 2016, p. 139*

Poetic Inquiry has helped me represent and understand identity negotiation in close relationships in a collaborative project on feminist identity in romantic relationships (Faulkner & Ruby, 2015), as a feminist ethnographer living in Germany on sabbatical (Faulkner, 2016b), and as a White feminist critiquing White Feminism (Faulkner & Squillante, 2018). The use of poetry as a research method helped me accomplish goals of collaborative action, cultural critique and resistance.

> Poetry, in particular, makes me a better social scientist. When you read poetry, my poetry, I want you to do more than think about your own life; I want you to critique how social structures scaffold your experiences of relating.
>
> *Faulkner, 2017b, p. 150*

Feminist Identity in Close Relationships

Ruby and I (Faulkner & Ruby, 2015) use collaborative autoethnography (CAE) and found poetry/poetic transcription as a feminist method to show how feminist identity in a romantic relationship influences relational discourse. The use of CAE speaks to feminist work because of the focus on personal experience, attention to reflexivity, and collaboration (Olesen, 2005). This kind of dyadic collaborative work is an example of a feminist constitutive and critical approach to interpersonal communication scholarship (see Manning & Kunkel, 2015). Our use of found poetry from a year-long series of our email exchanges acted as a critique of traditional interpersonal communication research that typically focuses on variable analytic work and one dominant position.

> We found the process of using academic research as an analysis tool an illumination of our relationship and the culture and context in which it existed; using our expertise and skill as poets and scholars demonstrates that poetic and scientific understandings of relationships can coexist. Academic discourse and romantic discourse can dialogue and potentially alter unproductive and harmful dominant discourses about romance.
>
> *Faulkner & Ruby, 2015, p. 224*

We considered how personal identities—feminist, working class, bourgeois, academic—interacted with relational processes to create a relational identity that was contested as seen in this poetic transcription:

>>*Bacon reminds me of the side of men I can't swallow.*

My truck of love came
at you hard and fast
it crushed your intellectual Volkswagen beetle.
You didn't have your seatbelt
on tight enough
now you are fucked
I feel that way everyday
i got a big cranial woody for you

I want to unfold you
you feel bad   i feel good
like that. not telling
i had a bucketful for you inside

Faulkner & Ruby, 2015, p. 214

Discourse equating feminist identity with intellect and feelings and love as connected to romance disallowed a comfortable fit for feminism in a relational culture that privileged embodied sensual experience:

the way that i feel about you
overshadows academic concepts like they don't even exist
my feelings towards you
transcend the conscious/intellectual world
my feelings are not

for grading or evaluation against technical, political or academic yardsticks

i understand the issue is how YOU feel   not how I feel.

Faulkner & Ruby, 2015, p. 215

This relational identity was seen in poetic transcription and found poems that demonstrated antagonistic discourses between feminist ethics, individual identities, and romance narratives that contributed to a conflicted relational culture because of different meanings of intimacy.

Multiple Stigmatized Identities

I used poetry to present the experiences of LGBTQ Jews in a project on negotiating multiple stigmatized identities (Faulkner, 2006; Faulkner & Hecht, 2011). Because poetry defies singular definitions and explanations, it mirrors the slipperiness of identity, the difficulty of capturing the shifting nature of who we are and want to be, and resonates more fully with the way identity is created, maintained, and altered through our interacted narratives. My goal in this project was to be an ethnographer who uses ethnographic poetry as research to show the connection between researcher and participants' identities (Krizek, 2003), a poet-researcher who provokes emotional responses, and furthers theory through the use of Poetic Inquiry.

I wrote poems from interviews, observations, and field notes to embody the experience of being LGBTQ and Jewish in ways that pay attention to the senses and offer some narrative and poetic truths about the experience of multiple stigmatized identities. "Poetry can do what other forms of thinking cannot: approximate the actual flavor of life, in which subjective and objective become one, in which conceptual mind and the inexpressible presence of things become one" (Hirshfield, 1997, p. 32). I argue that the use of poetry in this project furthers identity theories through poems that challenge stereotypes, confront prejudices, and add to the representation of LGBTQ Jews. The following poem presents the communication process of identity by portraying the reality of multiple and intersecting identities and differences in negotiation.

Reconstructionist

She thinks it's different now, and asks me how
I find the rallies, picnics, police, gay
lovers with youth who walk in open now.
She found no path, no help with the labels,
the parties of conservative newspapers
that print *Jewish activist lesbian*
as if boxes can contain her labors
to make Seders and new year with new kin.

> Now she tells mom, keeps a job, says enough
> and buys a house with oaks and shaded jade,
> makes a *minyan* and trims a holly bough
> with a Christian woman. The years they've made,
> are like the book club books read together
> for 12 years when they had nothing better.
>
> *Faulkner, 2006*

Poetic Inquiry for Social Change

> Poetry matters because it serves up the substance of our lives, and becomes
> more than a mere articulation of experience although that articulation alone
> is part of its usefulness. Mainly, it allows us to see ourselves freshly and keenly.
> It makes the invisible world visible. It transforms our politics by enhancing
> our ability to make comparisons and draw distinctions. It reanimates nature
> for us, connecting spirit and matter. It draws us more deeply into conversa-
> tion with the traditions that we feed off, modify, and extend.
>
> *Parini, 2008, p. 181*

Poetry is powerful because it helps us critique power structures. Poetry helps us
shape lives in ways that we want to live; we create and tell the stories that we
need to advocate for social justice (Denzin, 2014). Prendergast (2015) finds Poetic
Inquiry an important tool for social change and social justice.

> I am interested in social poetry as the core mandate for critical poetic
> inquirers whose work is in support of equity, human rights, and justice
> worldwide. Critical poetic inquiry invites us to engage as active witnesses
> within our research sites, as witnesses standing beside participants in their
> search for justice, recognition, healing, a better life.
>
> *Prendergast, 2015, p. 683*

For example, Hartnett (2003) combined scholarship, critical ethnography, auto-
biography, and politics in investigative prison poetry to represent social justice
through engaged activism; poems written by prisoners, poems that reference
important background readings, poems of fractured selves and self-regeneration
with paraphrased conversations and direct footnoted quotations from prisoners,
prison guards, and anonymous sources show the embodied experience of daily
life in prison, as well as serve to connect the prison industrial complex to larger
cultural, historical, and political conditions. Hartnett (2003) refers to scholarly
work and poetry combined in a persuasive way using critical ethnography, auto-
biography, and politics as investigative poetry; the goal is that of social justice
through engaged activism. "Investigative poetry is committed to a version of

synecdoche in which grand claims can be supported only through micrological analyses based on deep historical scholarship" (Hartnett & Engels, 2005, p. 1051). His work with prison populations emphasizes the transformative power of poetry through cultural political critique and research *with* and *for* those populations. Hartnett uses poems "that are laden with research, hence merging the evidence-gathering force of scholarship with the emotion-producing force of poetry" to argue that the prison industrial complex threatens America's radical experiment with democracy.

From the *Pendleton Poems* (p. 25; pp. 29–30):

I. Students

> Black separatists little Africas
> > dangling from their necks
> command the back corner

> eyeing the Muslims
> > soft-spoken Mahdi Buddy-Love
> prayer mats unrolled

II. Jailors

> It's easy to pretend
> > I don't pay rent
> to the conspiracies

> yet I must confess
> > no greater satisfaction
> than fleeing that shit hole

> dungeon gulag factory
> > of *falling grief of unpleasure*
> designed to humiliate

From *Love and Death in California* (p. 122):

III. Thankful

Balancing the joys of teaching in prison with the terrors of having to spend time in them has left me confused. I am sympathetic with those prison activists who refuse to set foot in prisons, yet cannot begin to convey how joyous it is to watch men who have never before been validated in ideas, writing, and speech come to life, come to power, come to self-realization through learning.

Hartnett (2003) presents poems written by prisoners, poems that implicitly and explicitly reference other texts to suggest background readings for the audience, and poems that deal with terror, fracturing of the self and self-regeneration with paraphrased conversations and direct footnoted quotations from students, prison guards, and anonymous sources in hopes of celebrating the embodied experience of daily life *as well as* connecting to larger cultural, historical, and political conditions that give these acts deep meaning.

Kimberly Dark (2009), a performance poet and sociologist, emphasizes the performance of sociological poetry to emphasize the role of the audience in our Poetic Inquiry:

> There is a mystery in poetry, the discovery, rhythm, the importance placed on breath and pause that is not so strong in other forms of writing. Research-poetry represents an ability to bring what truly connects people into the forefront while the social critique remains an ever-present backdrop. Rather than asserting the writer's superior knowledge of the topic, the poem can invite the audience in to find meaning and join the dialogue about the things found there. The readers/listeners may even take collective action based on the ways their new understanding interacts with their life experiences and social abilities. This form of inspiration to act toward social change is as non-linear as social change itself.
>
> *Dark, 2009, p. 184*

The act of listening to a poem can bring in the audience through the non-linear expression, the rhythm and cadence, in ways that traditional social science writing with its "mumbling, passive voice, and long sentences" cannot.

Poetry as Political Response

> Poetry and politics are both matters of verbal connection.
>
> *Orr, 2008, p. 409*

> Students and audience members will take what they will from poetry. This is perhaps part of the traditional researcher's fear.
>
> *Dark, 2009, p. 175*

Poetry is political. Poetic Inquiry can be an active response to social inequities. Writing, performing, and publishing poetry is important political activity. Jay Parini (2008) wrote that poets' work is politically powerful because the language of poetry provides deep understanding in ways that other writing does not. Many poets engage politics through their writing, bypassing stifling social structures (Orr, 2008). Poets represent marginalized groups and positions in nuanced, sensitive, and myriad ways (Archambeau, 2008; Faulkner, Calafell, & Grimes, 2009). As Fisher (2009) argued, the "political task" of poetry is "a visionary one, the work of making way for new worlds and words" (p. 984). Poetry confronts social structures to engage audiences and activate poetry's political potential; poetry engages a "political voice" (Orr, 2008, p. 416).

Poetic Inquirers harness the power of poetry for political aims. Reale (2015a, 2015b, 2015c) uses poetry and poetic transcription as critical qualitative research to speak with migrants, immigrants, and refugees in Sicily. Sheila Squillante and I (Faulkner & Squillante, 2018) remixed an intersectional approach to feminism and feminist identity through a womanifesta that uses video, images, and poetry to appeal to White feminists after reflecting on our own ignorance around the symbolism of pink pussy hats. The womanifesta is a political response to events after the election of Donald Trump as President of the USA and the Women's Marches™. We use poetic collage to invite White feminists to decenter White women in our movements, to eradicate White feminism, to reject White fragility and tears, and to "just listen." "There can be empathy between people of color and progressive, sensitive, politically aware whites … We need to create poetry, art, research, and books that cannot be assimilated, but is accessible" (Anzaldúa, 2013, p. 281). Burford (2018) uses poetry in academic practice as self-care, ritual, and political practice in an effort to transform the university:

> I have now come to see my own academic practice as using poetry both to evoke the subjective experience of political transformations to universities, as well as to identify the attentiveness poetry calls for as a possible practice for surviving inhospitable political conditions.
>
> *Burford, 2018, p. 230*

As Denzin (2014) notes, "the poet makes the world visible in new and different ways, in ways ordinary social science writing does not allow. The poet is accessible, visible, and present in the text, in ways that traditional writing forms discourage" (p. 86). Some researchers use poetry in their work to make the act of writing conspicuous by attending to particulars in opposition to transparent invisible scientific writing that focuses on comparative frameworks (Richardson, 2002). Leggo (2008a, 2008b) writes poetry to challenge dominant discourses inside and outside of the academy, to show "that everything is constructed in language; our experiences are all epistemologically and ontologically composed and understood in words, our words and others' words" (2008b, p. 166). Therefore, the epistemological question that frames Leggo's use of poetry in educational research is: "How do I know what I know?" (2008b, p. 166). He uses autobiographic poetry to "not close anything down" but to be open to process, to mystery, to fragmentation and understanding because there is much we don't know and can't possibly know and control (p. 168). Poetry is both autobiographical and scholarly. Furman (2006a), for example, used autobiographical poems as data analysis when he wrote a poem about going to the emergency room, analyzed the poem using open and axial coding, and then wrote more poems about the experience based on his analysis. "There is no separating the personal from the professional" (Leggo, 2008a, p. 91).

Sexual Harassment in the Academy

Poetry can unmask hidden cultural assumptions, which is why it is valuable in activist projects. In my chapbook, *Hello Kitty Goes to College* (Faulkner, 2012b), I wrote poetry about sexual harassment, bias, and racism in the academy using the pop culture character Hello Kitty as a way to examine taken-for-granted patterns of behavior. As Sara Ahmed (2017) writes, "making feminist points, antiracist points … is about pointing out structures that many are invested in not recognizing" (p. 158). The series of poems portray administrative and faculty reactions to the standpoints of women of color, untenured women faculty, and students' experiences and narratives of harassment and hostile learning environments through fictionalized experiences of the cartoon character, Hello Kitty (Faulkner, Calafell, & Grimes, 2009). The following poem demonstrates these goals (Faulkner, 2012b):

> *When She Passes by Her Professor's Door, Hello Kitty Spits on His Creepy Poetry.*
>
> Or she would, had she gone through with the plastic mouth surgery. That feminist class she took last semester slackened her spine in the surgeon's office. She felt like a naughty kitten dangling in big mother's jaw and left sans alteration. H.K.'s classmates sighed that *actually having no mouth* authenticates Muted Group Theory better than their final project – a duct-taped mouth protest of male language outside the football team's practice room. Still, when she passes by his elegies to dead cats, sonnets for weepy relatives and speaking proper English, she feels a tangled hair ball pushing up the back of her throat, an uncontrollable cough to exhume her fear, a sandpaper tongue that could work sick ink off the paper. H.K. fights her desire for words that would erase the taped up lines of trash, stops the professor from pressing his chair too close to her tail.

The use of a fictional pop culture icon is meant to have readers examine their implicit assumptions about academic life, because of the absurdity of a fictional character as student and professor. The use of Hello Kitty unmasks the taken-for-granted power structures and ways of being in the academy. The poems in this chapbook were part of a research journal where I wrote about my experiences with sexual harassment at the university and fighting it through institutional channels (see Faulkner, 2018d). This was the use of poetry and Poetic Inquiry as feminist theory and praxis.

> To bring feminist theory home is to make feminism work in the places we live, the places we work. When we think of feminist theory as homework, the university too becomes something we work on as well as at. We use our particulars to challenge the universal.
>
> *Ahmed, 2017, p. 10*

I wrote these poems to represent and analyze experiences of harassment, to critique the continued normalization of harassment by bringing the audience into the setting as participants through the evocation of the affective and cognitive feel of sexual harassment. The poetry in this collection shows how reactions to the presentation of standpoints are an important area to study for understanding how harassment is perpetuated and considered normal behavior in the university system.

The series of poems follows Hello Kitty as she navigates the academy as an undergraduate student, transforms into a graduate student, and then transitions into a faculty member. The title poem sets up the scene where women are not viewed as learners and equally valued members of the academic community.

Hello Kitty Goes to College

I. First Semester

Her business professor stares
at the red K sewn on the butt
of her sweats as she slinks
toward a desk in the front row.
"My best work from the self-designed line"
she confesses when he wants to know
"why K?" in the hallway
after supply chain class. He checks
attendance during her group's talk
on surplus stock. His voice makes
her whiskers vibrate, the K on her top
shrinks under his incessant gaze.
But this is just her professor
she thinks. In lecture, he makes
Tom and Jerry jokes, laughs
at how the cat always
gets into tight spots.
HK considers she's the cat
for the mouse, but she's just
a student, this is just a joke.
During office hours,
her advisor tells her
"Honey, professors are just bores
with arrested development. Learn to fit
the system, get your degree." HK takes
this advice, enjoys the library
with the stuffed couches
and row after row of shelved books

that smell like possibility. She feels
smart and hip with her good grades
and pledge to the honor society
headed by her business professor.

II. HK Discovers She's Not White

When it gets colder on campus
and snow piles around her dorm
like used kitty litter, HK takes the bus
to her only night class avoiding
salty paws and snow ball fights
with the freshmen boys who chant
as she crosses the quad. Tonight,
some men ride the bus and snicker
"A.I." as HK pushes to the back
of the bus to meet Keroppi and Jodie.
She doesn't know what it means,
talks of her new idea for school supplies.
The outside bar voices continue, "Asian Invasion.
Asian Invasion stop taking our scholarships."
HK wants to tell them she pays
her way with her own body, her line
of clothing. But her friends are faster.
"Stupid Crackers. You can't even fill out
your own applications." She just watches
the green frog and orange dog
shout back as the boys exit the bus.

III. The Visual Aid

On the power point slide,
a leukemia-ridden cat cowers
while doctors examine innards
displayed on the metal exam table.
HK pictures her own paws
tied down with twine
in the vet's office,
licks between her claws
when she hears the warning voices—
See what wearing no collar
means? How hanging out with
stray cats brings sickness
to inchoate kittens?—But HK

likes how they make their dens
wherever they please, thinks
them audacious and infinitely cool
like some kind of queer po-mo cats.
When she sees the picture
blown up on the class screen
and later taped up
in the teaching assistant's office
as an example of a great visual aid,
her hair scratches her skin,
she pants, overheated.
When no one is watching
she rips it off the wall,
shreds it with her paws
and pees on it, just in case.

Faulkner, 2012b

In another poem, Hello Kitty experiences a difficult dissertation defense with work that calls out sexist practices and defies the standard status quo. Hello Kitty, speaking for women in the academy, learns that "when you speak as a feminist, you have to deal with strong reactions ... Feminism is a sensible reaction to the injustices of the world, which we might register at first through our own experiences" (Ahmed, 2017, p. 21).

Dissertation Abstracts International
Feminist Standpoint Theory: An Examination by a Post Modern Two-Dimensional Cat with No Mouth and 22,000 Products Bearing Her Image.

Dr. H. Kitty had wanted to title her dissertation, *Ode to the University*, like a love letter to ideas, to chance and other marginal characters without traditional mouths or white teeth. Her committee balked : standpoint theory and self-narratives were quite enough. Other departments would question the methods, not tenure such love gut epistemology. During the defense, the token male member screamed her seminal argument was the "pissy cat position." HK wiped his spit off her whiskers with her camouflage hair bow, slipped a blank piece of paper down the conference room table. One by one, the members held the clean sheet as if it were a twisted student evaluation. Only the bisexual lesbian clapped, said Kitty's "right-on-response disallows the difficulty with our difference." HK considered ripping herself a mouth with her advisor's fountain pen, kicking the phantom pain in the teeth. Instead, she underlined new parts of her story with a Barbie highlighter, and let them pass her with their caveats and reservations.

Faulkner, 2012b

After getting a position at a university as a faculty member, Hello Kitty reflects on her continued work as a member in a sexist culture. "The danger of institutional sexism is that it allows us to judge and become complacent with someone else's experiences. Rather than allowing people who feel oppressed to own their stories, there is a need to discount them" (Ahmed, 2017, p. 19).

After the Faculty Meeting

HK still believed in the academy
though meetings like street brawls

left feminist cat scholar bodies piled
in naked postmodern heaps beside her chair.

She believed even when she took her standpoint
to the harassment advocate who chuckled,

told her to consider being spayed
because it would help her emotionality—

even through stories of tenured professors
having to rape in the middle of the quad

in bright daylight with a metal weapon
and maybe a drunken student party

before the possibility of firing would rise
past a personnel meeting to the provost.

After all, many skillful eligible bachelors
among their faculty deserved a date.

Jodie, the canine hire, howled
through departmental dog jokes

of chewed-up essays and sexy mailmen:
Why are dogs so obedient?

Because they sport choke collars.
Jodie started chanting in the copy room,

> Getting ass in your classes:
> one semester's pay.

> Being an ass to your colleagues:
> one year's pay.

> Getting a fair job:
> impossible.

HK preferred the department's fresh talk
of cutting edge curriculums and saucy students

though the lecherous professor leered
through her working cats research talk,

asked her to retype the departmental notes
because her cat scratch made his eyes water.

Even then, she believed in her colleagues
and the idea of them wearing stripes and bows.

Faulkner, 2012b

Conclusion

Poetic Inquiry and poetry have a history of being used as feminist practice, theory, and pedagogy, and continue to offer a robust feminist methodological choice for our work. The use of poetry in qualitative research practice offers us a way to engage in feminist and liberatory methodology through collaborative work, reflexive engagement as ethical practice, evocative critique and resistance of the status quo, and continued interplay of the private and public. Qualitative researchers use poetry in their work to make the research process transparent, to evoke specific responses in readers, to show nuanced understandings, and as a form of embodied inquiry. Poetic Inquiry can be used with other methods like ethnography, interviews, and content analysis as a kind of constitutive scholarship (Manning, 2014). We can use multiple methods to engage in metatheoretical aspects of seemingly disparate theory and models across contexts and research traditions to allow different and larger understanding than a reliance on one tradition provides. In the next chapter, I describe the doing of Poetic Inquiry with a focus on the process and craft of Poetic Inquiry and poetry as research method.

2

POETRY AS METHOD

Words can be a blanket, slightly suffocating, or a wall, dividing. The exception is poetry, which illuminates, touches down, and continues along filaments and in bright spots, or curves around us, or comes in the back door. Poetry is the way to describe and distill, but remain porous, oxygenated. Poetry lets the light in.

Aitken, 2012, p. 67

What I understand is that one can write poetry as social science (2014). What I believe in is the value of poetry as relationship research.

Faulkner, 2017b, p. 148

In this chapter, I describe the process, method, and craft of Poetic Inquiry through exemplars and discussion of how we can use poetry to represent research and the research process to address the following questions:

- What goals do Poetic Inquirers hope to achieve in their work?
- How can you transform interviews, archival research, and observations into poetry?
- How do you write poetry as research?
- How can poetry be used in qualitative analysis or even as qualitative analysis?
- How can you use poetry as political activism?

I show the doing of Poetic Inquiry through examples of different poetic forms including the lyric, narrative, long forms and poetry series, collaborative, and collage work. I open the chapter with researchers' goals for using poetry in their work to put the use of poetry in qualitative research practice in context.

Poetic Inquiry as Representation, Reflexivity, and Embodied Research Practice

Poetry can be used as a tool and method for presentation of research data, as a source of data, and as a source for data analysis. To further explore the notion of poetry as research, method, and practice, I reviewed a sample of researchers' work, their goals for using poetry, and the process they follow when constructing poetry. In Table 2.1, I summarize the goals of these researchers' work.

As you can see, many researchers consider poetry as an excellent means to present data about the human experience, to work as activism and performance, and consider poetry a compelling and ideal way to capture and present this experience in a more easily "consumable," powerful, emotionally poignant, and accurate form than prose research reports. Burford (2018) sees poetry in research as a political practice that "enables inhabitants of the university to reflect on a diverse array of political phenomena—from the structuring frame of heteronormativity to the wide scale marketization of universities across the globe" (p. 238). Reale (2015a) talks about Poetic Inquiry as a form of activism and presented her work with refugees in Sicily through poetry:

> I continue to be interested in presenting my research in ways that are easily relatable, understood, and accessible. I was not interested in presenting my research in a jargon-filled and sterile way, able only to be interpreted by the chosen few.
>
> *Reale, 2015a, p. 110*

Dark (2009) considers poetry-research to be compelling to audiences because of the performative nature of Poetic Inquiry. Ward (2011) uses poetic re-presentation as an ethical research practice and a way to bring participant voices and the research forward. Galvin and Prendergast (2016) see Poetic Inquiry as ethical, caring, and empathic practice:

> The poetic inquiry movement offers a contribution to a developing body of evidence that is not merely a third person perspective, as in conventional evidence, but is also intimate with first and second person perspectives and is thus a fertile pathway to ethical, caring and empathic work. In reading or listening to a poem we are bearing witness to the other, to the person writing the poem, or to the situation that is the subject of the poem and this is a fundamental part of caring work.
>
> *Galvin and Prendergast, 2016, p. xv*

In 2009, Prendergast forwarded the term Poetic Inquiry to encompass the diversity of poetic forms and labels researchers use. In a meta-analysis of 182 Poetic Inquiry sources, Prendergast (2009) uncovered three kinds of voices present

TABLE 2.1 Goals of poetry as/in research

Author	Goals
Brady, I. (2004)	rooted in the sensual
Burford, J. (2018)	political practice
Carr, J. M. (2003)	emotional response from reader shared experience
Dark, K. (2009)	compelling to audiences
Denzin, N. K. (1997, 2014)	cultural critique emotional verisimilitude useful to readers' lives/political change
Faulkner, S. L. (2006, 2017e, 2018d, 2018e)	re-present research process successful as poetry poetry as political response embodied inquiry feminist methodology
Glesne, C. (1997)	reader response open spirit/imagination connect reader and researcher
González, M. C. (2002)	capture integral nuance of phenomenon ethical anonymity
Hartnett, S. J. (2003)	social justice celebrate daily life seduce and empower readers
Langer, C. L. & Furman R. (2004)	emotional poignancy focus on actual content and meaning reduce data
Furman et al. (2007)	metaphorically generalizable
Leggo, C. (2008a)	open up possibilities through language
Madison, D. S. (1991, 1994, 2005)	authenticity show range of meaning
Richardson, M. (1998)	show moment of "truth" and humanity
Richardson, L. (2002)	recreate moments of experience show others how it is to feel something compression of data
Pelias, R. J. (2005)	expands disciplinary knowledge show complexities of lived experience personal = political political = personal
Percer, L. H. (2002)	understanding and articulation of craft
Poindexter, C. (2002)	understanding people and situations further empathy

TABLE 2.1 (Cont.)

Author	Goals
Galvin, K. T. & Prendergast, M. (2016)	ethical, caring, and empathic practice
Reale, M. (2015a, b, c, d)	bear witness highlight participants' voices variety in data presentation
Ward, E. (2011)	to bring research message forward ethical research practice
Witkin, S. L. (2007)	show how new realities constructed

in the poetry used as qualitative research, that of the researcher, the participants, and the literature. She argued that the majority of the work used researcher-voiced poems, which emphasized the experience of the researcher using field notes, journals, and reflective writing as data for the poems. Participant-voiced work was that solicited from research participants, written with participants, and/or taken from interview transcripts to create single- or multiple-voiced poems, and literature-voiced work entailed reacting to or using the research literature and theory as a means of creating poetry. This also included poems about the art of poetry and research inquiry. In 2012, Prendergast and a doctoral student added to the bibliography by analyzing an additional 129 sources.

> poetic inquiry is contributing to the quest of engagement with concrete experiences and in ways that point to "more than words can say", and in ways that open up participation. Poetry reveals, poetry has the power to open up the unexpected, to contribute to aesthetic depth, to bring us close to ambiguities with metaphor and image, it allows access to vulnerability, courage, and truth telling and playfully or poignantly forges new critical insight.
>
> *Galvin & Prendergast, 2016, p. xv*

Poets and Qualitative Research

> The poet *is* a human scientist.
> *Leggo, 2008b, p. 165*

Many poets' inspiration and sources for poetic projects resemble qualitative researchers' uses and considerations for Poetic Inquiry highlighting a false dichotomy between the humanities and social sciences. Further, qualitative researchers who use poetry in their work are often poets, poets who do research and use research in their poetry. Both researcher-poets and poet-researchers use process-oriented craft to explore reality, create something new, disrupt usual ways of thinking, and create embodied experience (Saarnivaara, 2003). Karen Craigo (March 23, 2016), a poet, editor, and blogger, argues that "writing poetry centers and improves a person. It creates a contemplative spirit. It adds value to the world. Even bad poetry is, in a sense, good poetry." For researchers, poetry offers a way to get back to the body, to show how our theories arise out of embodied experience. For poets, research can enhance their poetry and poetic practice. Laura Liu (2019) interviewed anthropologist *and* poet, Nomi Stone about her experiences as a researcher and a poet.

> LL: Currently, you are a post-doctorate research fellow in Anthropology at Princeton, and are also writing a book on war. What do you find most fulfilling about your pursuit of anthropology? How have you found it to enrich your pursuit of writing?
>
> NS: My philosophy of seeing as a poet is strongly inflected by the anthropologist's mandate: to make the familiar strange and the strange, familiar. In that helix of estrangement and de-estrangement, I think that the poem, through the tools of syntax and sonics and the like, can recompose the body's experience.
>
> Ultimately, becoming an anthropologist was a huge gift to my poems: a way to think hard about war in the 21st century, and the role of the lyric, documentary poem in speaking about it. Both drawing on the outside (real life) and summoning readers in, the double movement of the documentary poem "constantly courts its own collapse" according to Philip Metres. I am interested in the vertigo of this experiment, working to ethically render the dark work of history and politics on the body in an era of American Empire. Getting a PhD in anthropology gave me 7 years to read first about culture and politics, and then narrow eventually into questions of war, militarism, and violence. I spent over two of those years doing fieldwork between the Middle East and America, researching war and interviewing those whose lives have been demarcated and unmade by it. I've written in multiple ways about this research: academic articles (in *Cultural Anthropology* and *American Ethnologist*) and my ethnography (the book on war that you mention) is a now a finalist for the University of California Press's Atelier Book Series. But ultimately, it is *Kill Class*, the collection of poems, which matters most to me: a book-length, bewildered song about Empire and what it has wrought.
>
> *para 6–8*

This shows how poets and poet-researchers possess similar goals of uncovering and writing about social inequities and ills with the possibilities of exploring new and different ways of understanding. "By calling upon artful ways of knowing and being in the world, arts-based researchers make a rather audacious challenge to the dominant, entrenched academic community and its claims to scientific ways of knowing" (Finley, 2008, p. 72). Parini (2008) considers poetry to have political importance, especially when poets offer useful ways of thinking about the world that aren't like clever bumper sticker slogans, when "they offer a depth of understanding, and a language adequate to the visions they summon" (p. 116). And Finley (2008) describes arts-based inquiry "as a methodology for radical, ethical, and revolutionary research that is futuristic, socially responsible, and useful for addressing social inequities" (p. 71).

Using historical and archival texts as well as personal and relational experience as the impetus for creating poetry seems analogous to the "data" and the method that many social researchers use in their own poetic forms. Whether this takes the form of the long poem or sequence of poems devoted to the same theme, the goals, uses, and processes are worth noting since artistic practice and qualitative research can both be considered crafts as opposed to more precisely delineated stages of inquiry like in quantitative research (Leavy, 2015). The poet and social scientist share some commonalities in their approach; both ground their work in meticulous observation of the empirical world, are often self-reflexive about their work and experience, and possess the capacity to foreground how subjective understanding influences their work. The goal is to re-present meaning and make that meaning-making process explicit to an audience (Leavy, 2015). For example, how does a poet convey a clear sense of a person's personality? How does a qualitative researcher convey the essence of a research participant's story?

Doing Poetic Inquiry

> A good poem has something that is said in a way that gives us insight we haven't had before, or it invites us in to participate in an emotional way or makes us see the world again; we learn to see in art and in poems.
>
> *Ruth in Table 3.1, Chapter 3*

A primary question when deciding whether to use poetry in qualitative research is knowing when and how to use poetry. Anne Sullivan (2009) asks,

> What happens when the material is right in front of us and we have to decide what to do with it, how to make sense of it, whether or not to make poetry of it? Some materials are more welcoming of poetic rendering than others, and most of us who do this work probably recognize these materials intuitively or by knowledge so deeply internalized that it feels intuitive. We recognize the occasions for poetry as easily as we recognize a familiar road.
>
> *Sullivan, 2009, p. 111*

Sullivan (2009) considers poetic occasion to occur when we can address concreteness, voice, emotion, ambiguity, and associative logic; this is more important than a reliance on line breaks and the use of space to call our work poetic. Knowing if there is an occasion for poetry means being "alert, attentive, and attuned";

> Higher level thinking (as we like to call it) demands connections, associations, linkages of conscious and unconscious elements, memory and emotion, past, present and future merging in the processes of making meaning, these are the very processes which poets actively seek to cultivate. Material in which these kinds of complexity inhere is material to catch a poet's eye and heart, sit him or her down to work.
>
> *Sullivan, 2009, p. 118*

Researchers do not need to publish all poetry that we write; poetry in qualitative research practice may be used as a means of data analysis, reflexive practice, and thematic analysis complementing traditional social science practice. For instance, Kusserow (2008) uses ethnographic poetry as a method to engage in thick description through "fierce meditation" and the ability to "uncover layers of reality and subtlety" (p. 75). For them, "poetry and data collection became mutually informative … The act of writing a poem was a deep meditation on my field notes where I tried to focus on all of the subtleties of what I had observed" (p. 74). "Writing reflective poems helps researchers ask more focused questions, and questions they may not have considered" (Faulkner, 2017a, p. 214). The use of poetry in qualitative inquiry can makes us better researchers.

Karen Craigo (2019), poet and blogger, muses on the pleasure of writing poetry, but also on how poetry can take us to unexpected places—what I would call an occasion for publishing our poetry as research.

> Writing poetry brings one distinct pleasure, and that is the satisfaction of having written. This is a feeling that only comes when the work is viable, as there is no pleasure in "having written" garbage. When we've written something we like, it feels very nice.
>
> Beyond this satisfaction, though, is a feeling that's downright exhilarating, and these are the moments when you've written the poem and the poem writes back. You scan the piece and, improbably, you discover something—some insight you didn't plant there (or at least not intentionally). I've even found dense layers of imagery in a poem that I didn't calculate; they just sort of showed themselves upon later inspection. My own poems kind of floor me sometimes, not because they're amazing poems (although there are some I'm very proud of), but because they seem to operate independently of my consciousness. They have their own consciousness—and that's a weird and breathtaking discovery on a printed page.
>
> Sometimes we think we're writing a question, and we're actually writing the answer to that question. Sometimes we write out our fury or frustration and peace peeks through. Sometimes we're just writing along the best we

can when the poem says, "Let's show her what we can do." This is the thrill of it—when a poem is a horse that can take us into astonishing wilderness but then knows exactly how to bring itself home.

para. 7–9

Once researcher-poets have determined if poetic occasion exists, the particular doings of Poetic Inquiry—the method—are important to consider. In what follows, I discuss how poets and researchers use poetry in historical, interview, and archival work, use poetry as data analysis and research process, and provide examples of the use of narrative poetry, the lyric, poetry series, collaborative, and collage/hybrid poetic forms for Poetic Inquiry.

Archival, Historical, and Interview Research

Archival and historical research is another qualitative method in which poets and researchers use poetry to re-present their research. It is illustrative for Poetic Inquirers to examine poets' reasons for using research in their poetic work, as I argue similarities in expressed goals exist. Poets' reasons for engaging in archival, historical, and interview research as the basis for their poetry range from desiring to use and create a voice beyond the individual, wanting to explore intersections between the personal and the historical, wanting to take the role of "poet as archivist" or activist, to the use of poetry as resistance and to write what is missing or "unlanguaged" in dominant discourses. The idea being that perhaps "it isn't bad for poets to go to the library every once in a while" (Collins, 2007). Collins (2007) claimed that what truly interested her was "the tension between the fact that it is poetry and the fact that we're dealing with material that usually isn't treated poetically."

Nicole Cooley (2001) expressed interest in the intersection of poetry and research and how poetry could "explore the voice beyond the poet's individual experience" (para. 1). In her collection (2004), *The Afflicted Girls*, about Salem, Massachusetts in 1692, she explores the Salem Witch Trials, accusations, and executions from the perspectives of the accusers, the accused, and the bystanders. Specifically, she has poems that narrate individual experiences of the trials (e.g., the poem, *Testimony: The Mother*, explores the story of a four-year-old girl accused of being a witch), that incorporate colonial and American prose and verse forms like the sermon and jeremiad, that explore an idea of poet as archivist and celebrate the archival experience, and poems that investigate the effects of the Salem Witch Trials today (e.g., the Salem Witch Trials Memorial). She used a preface describing events in 1691 and 1692 in Salem, an appendix with notes about historical events and sources contained in the poems, and a chronology of the Salem Witch Trials that help the audience with the content and context of material in the poems. Cooley also uses the titles of poems and epigraphs (e.g., The poem title, *Testimony: He or His Apparition*, and the epigraph, *About noon, at Salem, Giles Corey was press'd to death for standing Mute*—Samuel Sewall, *Diary*, September 19, 1692) to indicate the source of material for the poem and as a reading guide. "Thus, the poems examine both the social structures contributing to the accusations as well as the relationships between people that were wounded or destroyed by the suspicions, convictions, and executions" (para. 2).

Katherine Soniat is another poet interested in using archival texts in poetic work and embracing the role of a poet as archivist. Soniat (1997) wrote about translating and reinventing archival texts she was using as inspiration for her poetry "without using the source verbatim" (p. 259). She was interested in writing a group of poems about place and ended up with collection of poems about John Smith and the Chesapeake Bay region entitled, *The Landing*. Soniat described reading John Smith's journals, *Travels and Works*, before a three-week stay on the Choptank River and how she was struck by "his surprisingly lyric voice":

> I was becoming aware that if I read too closely, if I took notes as conclusive blocks of information, this poetic endeavor was doomed to be coldly encyclopedic and nothing more. Smith's perceptions of the bay had a pristine, almost childlike awe about them, as if these elements of nature had never been encountered ... So, I scribbled notes, phrases, an impressionistic pastiche, as I turned through his diary, ending up with perhaps five or six pages of material.
>
> *Soniat, 1997, p. 259*

Her process was to take notes, phrases, and impressions so that she learned to think and hear in Smith's voice, though she was not researching with what she called "scholar's care." Next, she read his revised and edited dairies, which left out details such as his involvement with native women. She used the texts along with her interpretations to circle thematic divisions and create subheadings to write poems. Being in the region while writing about it as a participant-observer driving through the back roads opened up a "new imaginative landscape" for her. During this process, she noted that poems were falling into 12–20 lines and, thus, decided to use a 14-line loose sonnet form for each poem, which seemed to be an appropriate formal approach for early seventeenth-century poetics. Soniat included some of Smith's exact words (e.g., reference to Native Americans as "naturals"), but she also used imaginative engagement with Smith's work and claimed not to return to the diaries to check "authorial real estate" of who owned the words. The end result was at least one poem, *The Captain's Advice to Those Headed for the Trees: 1609*, with advice that could be "applicable beyond this prescribed setting" (p. 261). Pamela Alexander and Frank X. Walker both expressed a concern with questions of voice and authenticity when using historical texts as the basis for their poetry. The problems these poets face are similar to those of fiction writers. For example, how does a poet convey a clear sense of a narrator's personality?

Alexander (1991) wrote a series of persona poems published as *Commonwealth of Wings* using the historical accounts of John James Audubon, his journals, and especially the writing of an early biographer Francis Hobart Herrick. She noted at the end of the collection that her goals were not to write history, though she used historical accounts, but rather to make her "language take on the color of Audubon's so that the reader would find the poems seamless" (p. 59). The question of authenticity of voice, how to portray a clear sense of Audubon's character, and the culture surrounding his character were three important issues she tackled in the project. Alexander (1991), for instance, found Audubon to be an unreliable speaker and considered the process of narrative construction as similar to what fiction writer's tackle:

> Audubon could not see himself as a lazy, irresponsible, egotistical, impossible lout, but the facts in this case sort of make that a clear thing. But there were other ways to handle it. I learned to show others' reactions to him and his to them ... it felt like fiction, because I had to try to enter his life even though I tried to stick to his past and just re-invent the moments, emotionally ... so it's like an autobiography that's not auto.
>
> *Alexander, 1991, p. 59*

Alexander also indicated that she didn't want to have too simplistic a rendition of Audubon, to characterize him as only a brash person. The poems are a persona sequence of Audubon arranged in chapters titled by dates that serve to provide context for the reader. She wrote the poems with fictional incidents and thoughts, some created from a "bare fact" or historical material read and reframed in her own language. At times, she used quotations or paraphrases from Audubon and his biographers and provides a bibliography of sources and a list of direct, paraphrased, and adapted quotations in an appendix.

Resistance and a view of history as more than "facts, battles, dates, cause and effect" are important to many poetic projects based on historical work (Collins, 2007). Frank X. Walker (2008) described his desire to write a new history based on what's missing. For him, the difficulty resided in writing about York, a former slave who traveled with the Lewis and Clark expedition, from York's point of view.

> This book is about deconstructing accepted notions of history, love, marriage, and freedom while simultaneously reaffirming the power of literacy and the role of mythology and storytelling in exploration of the truth. It seeks to validate the voices of enslaved African Americans and Native peoples during a time in American history when their points of view were considered invalid. In this way, it seeks to fill a gap in the collective words about the Lewis and Clark expedition and its other important but overlooked figures.
>
> *Frank X. Walker, 2008, p. 2*

When Walker studied Lewis and Clark's expedition in school, both his teachers and readings suggested that it was only the two of them traveling and not other people, including York. The poem, *Role Call*, in the collection *When Winter Come: The Ascension of York*, a sequel to *Buffalo Dance: The Journey of York*, begins:

> To hear hero makers tell it
> wasn't nobody
> on the great expedition but captains.
> An them always mention Seaman
> Capt. Lewis's dog
> before them remembers me.

Furthermore, when you read the journals, it becomes clear that not only did York participate as a full member of the expedition party, but also he was responsible for saving their lives on many occasions (Walker, 2007). Walker (2008) "tried to look for light wherever the poetic prism led" (p. 113): documentaries, scholarly books on slavery, general sources on the expeditions, visits to the Nez Perce reservation, oral history transcriptions and archival records of the Nez Perce, and interviews with York's descendants as sources of data and contextualization for the poems. In the collection, Walker surrounds the poems with an introduction detailing the expedition and the "irrevocable and devastating changes for Native people" as well as his goals for the collection, a glossary of terms, a timeline of the expedition, and an appendix that describes Walker's interactions with York's descendants and his research and inspiration for the poems. He also uses epigraphs to some of the poems that include the person speaking (e.g., York's slave wife or William Clark) to place them into context. Interestingly, Walker (2008) detailed what I would describe as ethnographic participant observation:

> Wading through these many volumes, traveling the thousand plus miles to the ocean and back, sitting in the sweat lodge, walking the same riverbanks and staring up into same big sky that embraced York, and spending time with the same beautiful people that made a home for him is the reason these poems breathe air. I pray my own feeling and beliefs don't get in the way of the voices of the individual voices assembled here, which must speak their own truths.
>
> *Walker, 2008, p. 115*

Nelson (2007) and Collins (2007) talk about their interest in writing poetry that explores the intersection between the personal and the historical. For Marilyn Nelson (2007), the problems with this exploration center on two issues: how to convey facts and information, and how to tell stories that bring "history into poetry" with voices that sound authentic and that can bear what she wants them to say. In a book-length project on George Washington Carver (2001), Nelson contextualized the poems by including pictures (e.g., Carver's school slate, Carver at Tuskegee); a paragraph on the book jacket containing biographical information about Carver; the speaker, date, or reference in a poem below the title (e.g., Susan Carver, 1871); and postscripts to poems with factual date information and exposition (e.g., below the poem, *The Penol Cures*, is this postscript: "1933 An Associated Press story about Carver's peanut-oil massages as a treatment for polio brings throngs of polio victims to Carver's door"). Nelson (2007) read books on Carver's research, talked to researchers and scientists, and sent drafts of the poems to a scientist as a fact check; the question is whether the science she presented in the poems was accurate, authentic, and poetic. She had the problem of representing the voice of a genius and a scientist, "finding a voice to carry the information." For instance, Carver made a type of plastic out of peanuts and a type of rubber, but the language used now to talk about the production of plastics was not used when Carver conducted his research.

> I wanted to describe these two things and I would write drafts of this one poem, the part about plastics is about three lines, the part about rubber is about three lines, later in the poem. I would send drafts of this poem to this professor, and his kindness was overwhelming. He would write back and say, "That's almost right." So we were corresponding for several months with drafts of this poem until he finally said, "Well, with a little bit of poetic license, this is correct, it's acceptable." So nobody would know how much work went into these six lines, but I know if Carver read this poem he would recognize this as hard science—as real, authentic, accurate science, and that was a great victory for me.
>
> *Nelson, 2007*

She described finding the confidence to use not only characters who could talk about Carver's life and she could imagine her way into, but to actually write in Carver's voice. Though "for the most part when Carver speaks in this book he's speaking quotes from his actual life and I was just shaping the quotes because again, Carver was a genius."

Martha Collins described her passion for using history in her poetry at the 2007 AWP (Associated Writing Programs) conference:

> The most immediate source of my own book, *Blue Front,* a book-length poem, is not literature but an exhibit of postcards of lynchings I saw in New York about six months ago. Shocking images—shocking also because those postcards were souvenirs that people bought to keep or send to their friends and relatives, often with little messages on them about the celebrations that they had when they were hanging someone. But thirdly, [they were] shocking to me because I came upon a set of cards from Cairo, Illinois. Now my father was born there and lived there as a child and he

had told me at some point that he had seen a man hanged at some point in Cairo when he was a kid. But I didn't know until I saw the exhibit that this was a lynching, that there were 10,000 people there, and that my father was five years old.

Collins imagined what it would be like to be her father as a child and researched and googled newspaper accounts of the lynching. Other sources included visits to Cairo, Illinois and the U.S. Custom House museum, maps, family photos, newspaper archives in Springfield, Illinois, and general sources on lynching and responses to lynching, historical Cairo, the Ku Klux Klan, and the Civil Rights Movement. The goal of the poem is to change the way we write and think and feel about events, similar to that of investigative poetry.

> My interest in writing the book was however, not in writing a coherent historical narrative. My interest was in trying to figure out for myself what happened. I was writing even as I was doing research, the first layer of course was just what happened, the second layer was what would it have been like to be my father, a five-year-old child witnessing a lynching, as many children did, I found in my research … I'm intrigued by history, but it's this way of getting at it that has really changed, not only the way I write, but probably the way I think and feel.
>
> *Collins, 2007*

Collins (2006) used dates, places (e.g., Birmingham), word themes (e.g., drag, cut), and text boxes containing newspaper quotations and lynching postcard captions between sections of poems. The title of the poem, *The Blue Front*, references the restaurant where her father sold fruit when he was five. "My general rule has been to italicize any passage longer than a few words, as well as language of any length that is clearly interpretive. All statements presented as factual are based on newspaper and other accounts" (p. 83). Because she didn't use any voices of those involved and presented the conflicting accounts, Collins claimed to not make anything up as she had sources for it all.

In summary, as I demonstrated through the discussion of poet and researchers' work, the way, and to what extent, they conduct and use research in their poetic work, varies. Poets using historical and archival work in their poetry have raised concerns such as contextualization, authorial voice, authenticity, turgidity, and attribution (e.g., Collins, 2007). Researchers have raised similar concerns of truth, representation, aesthetics, researcher ethics, and voice (e.g., Denzin, 2014). Some poets use dates and epigraphs from historical texts in the titles of poems (e.g., Smith, 2000), include chronologies of facts and appendices with endnotes and source material (e.g., Cooley, 2004), while others use prefaces with a description of the historical event and time frame, pictures, maps, quotations, and prose exposition about the sources between sections of poetry (e.g., Hudgins, 1988).

Researchers include footnotes and end notes; use a layered text with explicit context, theory, and methodological notes surrounding poems; and sometimes, just the poems.

Andrew Hudgins (2007) described the problem of authorial voice this way:

> Who can you speak for when you're speaking for a group? What I started then was moving out of my comfort zone, the past, and even then, if you got sense of a common community of the past [it] is an illusion. So one of the ways I ended up dealing with that was to divide the speakers up and the poems, and put them in conflict with one another. Even that is its own illusion because within those groups the people are not a unified voice.

The question of whether to write in first or third person, to include the poet explicitly in the work is a decision of voice. Frank X. Walker (2007) argued he could be present by giving poems contemporary titles and, thus, remain out of the body of the poems, though admitted it "can be a challenge to stay out of the way." Writing in meter, and using language in interesting ways, including fragmentation, are important devices given that poetry and exposition are antithetical. Writing in meter, for instance, is one way to keep the lyrical and "work with information at a place where the line can bare the burden" (Hudgins, 2007). A concentrated study of poetic craft will help both poets and researchers understand the challenges with Poetic Inquiry and suggest ways for contending with these challenges (see Chapter 3).

Data Analysis and Research Process

Poetic Inquirers use poetry as a method of inquiry by presenting research as poetry, by analyzing poetry as qualitative data, using poetry to show the research process, and as a means of data analysis. We may write poems as part of a research journal and field notes, as a kind of thematic analysis, as data to subsequently analyze, as a way to ensure rigor in qualitative research (Ohito & Nyachae, 2018), and as a means to show our reflexivity and the research context. Names and techniques for these include poetic analysis (Faulkner, 2017a), poetic transcription (Madison, 1994), poetic re-presentation (Reale, 2015a), poetic reflexivity/reflective poems (Faulkner, 2017a), Black feminist data analysis (Ohito & Nyachae, 2018), and relational poetry (Witkin, 2007).

Reale (2015a) used poetry as a form of data analysis and research presentation in her work with refugees to Sicily by beginning with an autoethnographic approach, using her experience with Italians coming to America and (mostly) Africans going to Italy: "I understood that what I sought (and still seek) to understand, began with myself and the sense of my 'otherness,' but would, of course, not end there" (p. 108). She asked the questions: Who is Italian? Why do they come? Why do they stay when they are unwelcome? Reale used her personal journals wherein she wrote about cultural identity, being Italian-American and the differences between that identity marker and being Italian from Italy, and her experiences growing up in a neighborhood where most Italians and Italian immigrants came from the same town in Italy. She began with conversations with mostly White immigrants in Sicily, but did not find what she was looking for. Next, with the help of a mentor, she gained entry into a refugee community of mostly men and mostly Africans. Reale (2015a) described an organic process of scribbled notes and writing "short poems and then longer ones ... about the data ... Poetry is my habit" (2015a, p. 109). An excerpt from one of the poems demonstrates the goal of representing refugees' stories in evocative ways to affect policy.

from Suleiman

Just send me back on the street
For the sake of Allah. My mother
would hold her head in her hands
all the day if she knew of
my life like this.
Reale 2015a, p. 113

These poems from interviews are "the most truthful way I can present my research: with emotion, with sensory details and with a focus on the aesthetic. It is for me, both research and activism" (Reale 2015a, p. 113).

I created poems from narrative interviews with LGBTQ (lesbian, gay, bisexual, transgendered, queer) Jewish Americans and then analyzed the poems for themes and connections to identity theories using poetic analysis (Faulkner, 2006). Poetic analysis is a technique of using poems as data for qualitative analysis (Faulkner, 2009). This is a process of writing poems from interviews first, before coding or thematic analysis, to allow the themes of the research to emerge from the poems themselves (see Furman et al., 2007). That is, the written poems served as the data for thematic analysis. After the initial construction of poems, I transcribed the audiotaped interviews and gave them back to participants to respond to and correct in an effort to represent their narratives as they wished (Patton, 2001). The discussion of decision-making demonstrates my attention to and understanding of craft and what poetry has to offer research writing through attentiveness to form, comprehension, and aesthetics (see Chapter 3), as well as the ethics of full disclosure of methodological choices (Leavy, 2015).

I wrote some poems that re-present, query, and interpret the research process and method by showing the research story (Richardson, 1997b) and my subjective emotional processes (Leavy, 2015). They demonstrate my research/personal perspective, the integration of the social scientist and the poet, and participants' perspectives before, during, and after the "formal" interview periods. These poems highlight the difficulties of identities in the field, conducting interviews while being reflexive and conscious as well as the joy and confusion in connecting with

research participants. They show how the process of research and creating poems
furthered understanding in this study through the questions raised, the interaction
of my identities and participants' identities, and the choices made.

Method

> I don't care who you are or what you do or
> why you want to interview me or who
> you are working with or what consent form
> you need me to sign before I tell you my story
> of being gay and not so Jewish; that ad for Queer
> Jews tacked to the board at the pride center
> was evocative enough for me to talk. He tells me
>
> this over toast and eggs at the Bagel Dish.
> I wonder why I can sit and stare
> at the ketchup bottle, my half-eaten bagel
> with butter, gentile style, on this man's birthday,
> asking him to tell me more while I work out
> riddles in my head like how many more
> bottles of kosher wine I need to buy as interview thanks?
> How much explanation and toast spread with tubbed
> margarine I need to spit and swallow? Crappy Jersey
>
> diner coffee makes me think about the ones
> who need more. I recount my past and present Jews,
> ex-partner, graduate advisor, roommate, co-author—
> how he's Jewish. I'm not. I'm queer. He's not—
> how I make Hamantashen like the Kosher Korean
> Bakery in Highland Park. Though I'm not of this tribe,
> some ask how to find the others,
>
> like a gay jDate.com, like the young lesbian
> who sat in her dorm room with invisible AOL wings
> and came out to her straight roommate with only
> a whisper of keys. Even I arrange these interview
> dates online, hold my breath and type with furious fingers,
> coming out again and again as this earnest queer—
> but not Jewish-researcher from somewhere down south.
>
> *Faulkner, 2006*

The context of interviews is important, if as Richardson (1997b) argued, "Such
interviews are essentially interactional speech events created in particular contexts;
interviews themselves are examples of lived experience" (p. 141). The next poem
shows the places where these interviews occurred, the particular lived experience

of how participants invited me into their lives, homes, diners, and offices, and the food we shared. It also demonstrates the importance of food, which plays a vital and vibrant role in Jewish kin relationships, religious observances, and cultural history. The poem should be read like a menu with the daily specials highlighted by the researcher/server. It is a list poem, which consists of an itemization of things or events. Padgett (1987) argues that the list poem is good for beginning poets because of the flexibility in form as well as the authenticity derived from the use of a writer's personal experience.

The Jewish Table 31 Ways

1. Artichokes stuffed with sandy Italian breadcrumbs, beet salad with lemon zest
    leftover lunch in her student apartment post interview

2. Bagged cut carrots like knobby grade school pencils
    roll too easily from her hand to mine
    thud under her office desk, reverberate on audio tape

3. A glass of water from the non-profit agency office cooler
    by the window a small patch of rented grass,
    her computer screen saver blinks, startled

4. Iranian style chicken kabobs sprinkled with sumac, solid chocolate hedgehogs
    for the morning road, she and her partner insisted I stay,
    it would be too late, too lonely to drive away

5. A single box of tissues between us on my office couch
    his allergies flared, so sick of this undersized town,
    left with his partner for a place with "family" gym benefits

6. After Montessori school at the round, faux-wood table
    creaky chairs that sound like the teacher's pet
    who outs fidgety students and radical leftists

7. Orange oil tea, decaf house blend with a river of half and half
    Starbucks in the college district, music too hip for us, two professors

8. & 9. Chew treats for the dogs, ice water sweats lazy circles on their coffee table
    rusty earthen ware relics rest on book cases, you can touch,
    later we talk more with food at their usual place, TGI Fridays

10. Scrambled eggs splashed with ketchup, whole wheat toast, Concord grape jelly
    his birthday breakfast à la the Bagel Dish revealed
    only after the first bitter cup of coffee

11. No food at the Rabbinical School, but walls of books, comfortable chairs

> though I can't relax, after all, it's holy school,
> the Rabbi charms me until my back hurts

12. Patchouli incense, respectable office coffee smells seep into the wall tapestries,

> Jewish signs of life—menorah, Magen David—sprinkled around
> the analyst's office during the interview, or maybe my research therapy

13. Seltzer water at the rectangular kitchen table, citrus yellow walls, ticking clock

> the partner weaves out, then in, asks about the magneted grocery list,
> leaves us to go shop so we get serious about queer gender and family secrets

14. Fluffy floor pillows, glassed Bronx tap water, recorder propped on the coffee table

> 2 kids sleep in the other room with alphabet puzzles, toy dogs and blocks
> while we revolutionize gay adoption and activism

15. Creamy rice pudding with raisins, a poppy seed bagel with a smear of cream cheese

> a ritualistic after work snack
> like the weekly gay group meetings in the back of this 7th Avenue diner

16. & 19. Institutional black tea, honey and powdered creamer in chipped mugs

> we schlep up flights of stairs to the buried half-floor and the research lab
> with one-way mirrors, leather couches, and salmon colored walls

17. Garden vegetable soup with barley, sourdough bread with a pat of foil butter

> at his local Panera where he tells me of HIV and meds,
> how he loves his teenage children

18. Brewed coffee concentrate in fresh single serve containers, hamantaschen, scones

> at the Internet café that we both felt was better before,
> an antique store with the older Jewish woman who admired your purchases

20. Fruit plate with wilted, slimy lettuce, sour cottage cheese, grapes, aged cantaloupe
    at the diner where they know her name, favorite blue plate
    and we know each other's bi history like our own daily special

21. German chocolate cake created with imported cocoa, coffee with 100% cream
    in the artist's mustard luster-ware, among his ceramic art, paintings
    and two dogs leaping for love, imprisoned behind the baby gate

22. Crisp waffles (not those soggy impersonators) with real dairy butter, maple syrup
    in his Hassidic neighborhood diner, north of the hometown
    where he had lived with his cancerous wife as a semi-out gay with children

23. Her office tucked in the back behind the water pipes, like a stray piece of hair
    with a surprise view of the Nubian sunbathers on a sliver of campus

24. & 26. My usual orange rind tea, her double skim mocha latte in Squirrel Hill
    Starbucks' music too shrill and insipid to talk over, we take it
    to her ex's kosher house where she dreams of her new life, new love down South

    Iced coffee brewed double strength with cream and sugar on the dark brown leather chair
    don't put the spoon in the kosher sink
    she tells me, my arm stretched like a guilty ex-girlfriend

25. That same Starbucks, orange tea, maybe a latte, perhaps iced coffee and fake sugar
    11 years between us, we reminisce like we sang the same
    high school fight song

27. Loose leaf organic earl gray with fresh cream, peppermint infusion with simple syrup
    no paper cups here at the trendy tea house where we bartered our ideas
    of social/slash/science research just as in my shabby and chic college dream

28. Fresh brewed drip coffee with raw demerara sugar, skim milk, on the maple suede couch
    before the tour of her art, the basement studio with impaled, taped Barbie lamps

and installations, I mention my love of Duhamel who impales Barbie
 with poems

29. First, the library-too quiet to talk sex. Next, the coffee house
 with doors and one table rooms where we say sex and much more
 over chocolate chip cookies and house blend straight up

30. Double bergamot Earl Gray, black tea from India, both with brown
 sugar and milk
 at some Starbucks, somewhere in the city
 and some talk of dissertations, stirs my mood

31. Penne, sun dried tomatoes, vodka sauce, basket of mixed breakfast bread
 she orders, says no official talk at the cream linen table cloth
 or over shared cherry tart at the bakery down the street
 where she insists she pay, and I tell the story

Faulkner, 2006

Richard Hugo (1977) published a collection of 31 letter and 13 dream poems that explore issues of aloneness and the importance of place. His poems about dreams and letters to friends, old loves, and other poets work because of the personal voice and forms that allow the audience to "overhear" an important conversation like eavesdroppers. The dream poems use the word "you," which have readers ask, who is the "you" in the poems? It could be the poet. It could be the audience. I like these poems because they seem to directly address the audience, and the form allows Hugo to be didactic at just the right moments without losing the beauty of the lines. This is something I wanted to explore in my own letter and dream poems: fears and anxieties about research that include ethical considerations and the role of the Institutional Review Board (IRB) for the protection of human participants in poetic research projects (see Chapter 1 for the letter poem, *Letter to the IRB from South Jersey*).

In Your Interview Dream

On the airplane, your boyfriend teases
your best student, the one you tend
to think is Jewish. In life, she's half Mexican.
You confuse this study with the last one on Latinas'
sex talk. Your white, German nose burns like sausage
at this altitude. The plane almost smashes
into the stadium. You yank the wheel, steer left
then up, until you see your office light bright
as a highlighter pen. Your boyfriend yells in Yiddish,
though he's Catholic. Your student parachutes onto the grass.
She waves as she floats, a laugh that echoes off the wings.

You are late for the next interview. Highways, like old lies,
tangle and disappear into the clouds. The new cell phone
won't work. Wrong password. You never knew it. You
dial and dial. The operator speaks Spanish, tells you
to dial again. Your mouth opens like a hooked fish.
You smell sweat, scream, "Take me to the Pride Center."
You panic. The participant is waiting. You know he will be
angry, and your shirt is ripped. The pilot hurls your book
out the plane. You jump, and the pages ignite in the wind.

Faulkner, 2006

Bad dreams about research, nervousness and fears of participants not wanting to talk, not being who they expect me to be, and being uncomfortable are things best left unshared with an IRB, as is the real letter I was longing to write. It seemed appropriate to use the letter and dream format given that the IRB forms are anything but intimate, and they leave no room for the kinds of things that I found important during the course of this research project: How do you talk about becoming friends with research participants? How do you manage your own identity as a researcher and as a human being? The fact that the kind of life I live influences the kinds of things I notice in a research setting, the things I value, and how participants react to me as a researcher and as a person.

Lahman, Teman, and Richard (2019) also wrote IRB poems using various poetic forms, including autoethnographic, literature review, artifact, blackout, typewriter, concrete, cutout, photographic, and collage poems to speak to their frustration with the IRB review of "vulnerable groups." In the poem *risk.*, Maria Lahman used a cut-up method for creating an IRB poem using federal guidelines and the history of how those guidelines were created. Lahman et al. (2019) describe the creation of the poem:

> When creating cut-up or collage poems, the poet considers existing text reflexively or suspends their current deep understanding by repositioning and then reconsidering the text. The cut-up method is often followed by
> - cutting the text into quarters
> - labeling the section number 1 to 4 starting at the top left, moving right, and then down to the bottom left and right again
> - switching section 1 with 4, and 2 with 3
> - reading across the sections as one would normally read prose while eliminating words that do not feel salient. At this point, some poets move words or change features such as capitalization.

p. 212

Here are the first three stanzas.

risk.

research with children
cannot be permitted
legally not considered able to engage in contracts.

children are considered
vulnerable
coercion
undue influence

Child as
worthy and
capable of recognition
respect
voice

Lahman wrote this about constructing the poem:

> [I was] intrigued to see the first word on the newly arranged page was risk. with a period. The word risk in lowercase with a period following immediately resounded with [me] as the title for the poem as it seemed to reflect the tension between being a protector of children and yet advocate how powerful children are.
>
> *Lahman et al., 2019, p. 212*

The authors acknowledge that their experiences using different poetic forms allowed them to voice their experiences with IRB in new and reflexive ways and offer readers engaging poetry as they work with their own IRB and research participants in liberatory ways.

In a series of poems titled *Hello Kitty Goes to College* (Faulkner, Calafell, & Grimes, 2009; Faulkner, 2012b), I use poetry as a source of data with poems about the character Hello Kitty as a way to examine sexual harassment in the academy. These poems were written as part of a research journal for the explicit purposes of representation and analysis of harassment experiences (see Furman, 2006a). They use fictionalized accounts of Hello Kitty narrating her experiences with harassment to represent an amalgam of women's voices. The goal was to create evocative poems that represent the affective and cognitive feel of students' and faculty's experiences of sexual harassment in the academy as well as analyze the reasons for its continued normalization and bring the audience into the setting as participants and "co-discoverers" (see Krizek, 2003). The poem, *When Hello Kitty Registers for the Working Cats Conference, Security Confiscates Her Catnip*, demonstrates these goals.

When Hello Kitty Registers for the Working Cats Conference, Security Confiscates Her Catnip

She forgets the stems and buds
tucked in her red pleather briefcase,
late for the train, her presentation
on supply chains. The marketing staff
refused to accept her line of toothbrushes
with bright blue and black bristles.

Why would girls want to wash out
their mouths with colors like a fresh bruise?
What about hot-pant pink? H.K. skulked
out of the office, tossed a toothbrush
at the market and development room den,
a substitute for her silent screech and yowl.

On the train, she tracks the girls,
the up and down pistons of their mouths
crushing gum, how they clamor
over the sounds of wheel clack on track
with fresh pink vocal chords. At the hotel,
H.K. stalks past fair trade protestors

who monitor the meeting room, a guard grabs
a paw as she opens the partition,
crinkles the stash in her Ziploc.
He won't look at her mouthlessness,
instead stares at her paws, searches for more.
She can't find a pen to write a protest:

other conference goers get
their coffee, breath mints, and tobacco buzz.
As she slinks up to the podium,
she craves a familiar smell, something
to get her through. When she settles
on a stool, a colleague smiles and lights a cigar

the burning tip blazes while she plays
the projection screen. She changes
her talk to maternity benefits. Her whiskers
feel damp with smoke and heat,
as they curl away from her nose
ready, she scans the room.

Faulkner, 2012b

In my ethnography, *Real Women Run* (Faulkner, 2018c), I read the poetry in my field notes, the poems composed from field notes, and the poetic transcription of women's running stories to analyze the embodied experiences of running. Second, I used poetry to demonstrate the process of analysis. Ethnographic poetry is a way to meditate on field notes (Kusserow, 2008). The poems that represented running logs, and the poems I wrote during field work helped me to analyze women's stories of running on and offline. "Writing reflective poems helps researchers ask more focused questions, and questions that they may not have considered" (Faulkner, 2017a, p. 214). Poetry from my fieldwork ended up being part of the analysis process. This project is an example of poetic analysis, poetic re-presentation and poetic transcription, and reflective poetry.

In another example of poetic re-presentation and data analysis, Furman and his colleagues (2006) followed a four-step method for constructing research poems about social work in an international context: They wrote poems about clients, took the original poems and used open coding to analyze them for themes, considered how different poetic forms (e.g., tanka, pantoum) would represent the themes, and then used these forms to construct new poems. Here are some lines from one poem about a client and the response tanka that represents the themes discovered using open coding to analyze the original poem:

Que Que

Alone in the gray soft shadows
The scowl of caverns haunted

arms crossed silent,
and what nine year old

folds her arms in anger, but those
abandoned by death on some roadside

or in shanty shacks baking alone?

Que Que: A Tanka

scowl of caverns haunted
only communication a sound
folds nine year old arms, anger

never ready to comprehend
the reasons for being thrown away.
Furman et al., 2006, p. 5

The goal is to stimulate critical thinking about the poetry in order for policy makers to develop good decision-making skills. Using a similar technique, Witkin

(2007) uses what he calls relational poetry where a poet responds to a freestanding poem by writing another poem, and then writing a third poem that interweaves lines from the first and second poems to create something different than either poem alone. What is created is the poem, the response poem, and the interactive poem. The first stanza from the Gergen-Witkin relational poem, for example, demonstrates the interweaving of Witkin's response poem with an original poem by Gergen to create an interactive poem:

> Here am I.
> *can you see me*
> Standing before you
> *right behind you*
> Singular and solitary
> In the shadows of the light?

The italicized lines represent the Witkin response poem, and the non-italicized lines represent the original Gergen poem. This process of writing relational poetry speaks to social construction and the meaning-making process and how point of view demonstrates different interpretations. "The relational form is a way of illustrating how new realities are constructed in interaction" (p. 478).

Researchers also use Poetic Inquiry in the research process as a means to ensure rigor. Ohito and Nyachae (2018) offer poetry as a method of data analysis for feminist CDA (Critical Discourse Analysis) that is especially good for reflexive research practice and researcher triangulation. They argue that Black feminist poetry allows researchers to engage in "rigorous, expressly political critical qualitative inquiry" (p. 9). The researchers used raw data and textual artifacts from an initial analysis of programming and curriculum materials for extracurricular activities targeted toward Black working-class girls. The second nexus of data were analytic and reflective researcher memos, and transcripts of their conversations. Next, the researchers used poetry as data analysis.

> In an effort to ensure that our preliminary interpretations and conclusions were trustworthy, we turned to poetry, which we used to make more meaning of our (a) raw data and (b) prior analysis. Specifically, using poetry, we deconstructed and reconstructed our initial analysis of that data, and then constructed new analyses. Our Black feminist orientation informed our choice of the poetic forms used, and our construction of the poems themselves.
>
> *Ohito and Nyachae, 2018, p. 5*

They crafted three poems—a list poem, a multi-voiced, three-columned poem with the data and each of their voices, and a free verse poem that built on insights from the other poems—that let them show the textual techniques in their data.

They used line-by-line coding of the documents to create the list poem, *Poem About How to be a Black Girl*, choosing declarative statements to arrange in the order they appeared in the texts. Then, they rearranged the statements by theme considering repeating words, phrases, and ideas to distill their findings. For the multi-voiced poem, *Listen and Respond: A Three-Voice Poem About Black Girlhoods*, Ohito and Nyachae used language from their initial analysis of the raw data and their language from their analytic memos to create a dialogue between researchers and between researchers and data. The final poem, *Be a Bad Black Girl*, is written in free verse because the form eschews formal rules, which show their insights about how the data contained explicit advice for being a good Black girl and implicit advice on how to be an improper one.

Poetic Transcription/Found Poetry

Poetic transcription is a method of using poetry in research as representation and analysis. Many researchers have eloquently discussed using poetic transcription as a way to enter into the world of the storyteller by preserving their speaking style and capturing the spirit of a story to portray its range of meanings (Carr, 2003; Madison, 1991; Tedlock, 1983), to make the shaping of stories more evident (L. Richardson, 2002), to give "ownership of the words" to the speaker rather than the researcher, and to privilege orality (Calafell, 2004) as an ethical research practice (Ward, 2011), as well as capture the depth of indigenous performances (Madison, 1991). These poetic renderings have been called research poems, poetic re-presentation (Reale, 2015b), transcription or archival poems (Lahman & Richard, 2014), literature review poems (Prendergast, 2006), or poetic transcription. Ward (2011) chose to highlight four participants' voices in a project on students with severe disabilities in secondary school in New Zealand through poetic re-presentation and transcription to "foreground … students' stories in order to honor them and give voice to their experiences … I wanted the research text to speak to my readers and capture the stories of my participants" (p. 357). Poetic transcription allowed Ward to address ethical concerns of representing participants' stories: "I was faced with the ethical dilemmas of authorial voice and presence and the concomitant factor of power inherent in the relationships within the research" (p. 356). Tedlock (1983) wrote that people's speech, including interviewees, is closer to poetry than that of research prose. The goal is "not only to analyze and interpret oral performances but also to make them directly accessible through transcriptions and translations that display their qualities as works of art" (p. 81).

A common method of poetic transcription entails researchers highlighting participants' exact words and language from interview transcripts, cutting and pasting the essential elements in an effort to reveal the essence of a participant's lived experience. A researcher may use one transcript to tell the story of one participant, use multiple interview transcripts from the same participant, or use multiple transcripts to create a collective voice (Lahman & Richard, 2014). This method originates in feminist and women of color's work on theories of the flesh (Madison, 1991, 1994, 2005). Gee (1985), for example, used a technique of shaping poetic quatrains from participants' words in interview transcripts. Glesne (1997) began with one rule for her poetic transcription of an interview; she could use phrases from her interviewee anywhere in the transcript and juxtapose them as long as they were the interviewee's words and enough words were presented to mirror the participant's rhythm and way of speaking. Her process was to code and sort the data after reading and rereading the interview transcripts, and at the end she had themes that described different aspects of her interviewee's life. She then wrote poetic transcriptions after reading all of her interviewee's words under each theme, "searching for the essence conveyed, the hues, the textures, and then drawing from all portions of the interviews to juxtapose details into a somewhat abstract re-presentation" (p. 205).

That Rare Feeling

I am a flying bird
moving fast
seeing quickly
looking with the eyes of God
from the tops of trees.
                    p. 202

In an interview study on family vigilance at the hospital, Carr (2003) extracted phrases verbatim from a transcript "that illustrated a particular theme, idea, or situation to one participant's transcript at a time. This would result in a poem that presented the words of an individual participant only" and one of the themes wrought from the more traditional grounded theory analysis she had engaged in previously (p. 1325).

Some researchers consider this process of extraction to be like found poetry; poetry that is created by using phrases, words, and passages from other sources paying attention to spacing and/or line breaks. Using found poetry in a project can bring researchers closer to their data and even bring different insights because of the new relationship between data and researcher (Butler-Kisber, 2002). Found poetry can be a way to re-present participant voices and experiences that may be partially or totally silenced with an academic gaze (Bhattacharya, 2008). Walsh (2006) and Butler-Kisber (2002) both craft what they label found poems from interview data. Walsh (2006) followed a process similar to others using poetic transcription; she read transcripts many times while making notes and finding recurring themes. "I culled words and cut and pasted segments of conversation into specifically labeled files, then played poetically with the segments of conversation in an attempt to distill themes and write succinct versions of them" (p. 990). She would reorder phrases to offer more clarity for the audience and made sure to include only those phrases that were important to an emerging theme. Poindexter (2002) followed this method in a study on HIV-affected African American caregivers after starting with traditional transcription. She began with interview excerpts that were transcribed with pauses noted: "I was looking for unambiguous phrases, strong statements, eloquent expressions, wording that appealed to me, and portions of narrative that I felt strongly captured the person I was interviewing" (p. 708). In other words, she paid close attention to the line and transformed the initial interviews from a prose format into a poetic format.

An alternative to using traditional transcripts is to bypass transcription of the interview in prose form and instead initially create a poetic transcript. The argument resides in the tenet that "sound, as well, as the literal word, creates the experience of the oral narrative, and in many moments sound alone determines meaning" (Madison, 1991, p. 322). The placement of the words on the page should resemble the rhythm of our voices, show us as social-historical beings, and capture the depth of indigenous performances (Madison, 1991). For example, Calafell (2004) used poetic transcription rather than traditional transcription in her work on Chicana/o identity in the new Latina/o south to privilege orality and highlight meaning, speech rhythms, and word choice in the performance of identity in historically marginalized cultures. She wished to give "ownership of the words" to the speaker rather than the researcher in an effort to embody the performance of the interviews by poetically transcribing the interviews. When I analyzed women's stories about running in *Real Women Run* (Faulkner, 2018c), I only used poetic transcription. That is, I did not make traditional transcripts of the interviews. First, I listened to women's interviews on my iPod during my own runs, imagining we were running together in stride and talking. Then, I took notations on themes and used my field notes to compose poetic transcriptions by using women's exact words and language from interviews and arranging them in lines that mirrored speaking styles and breath (e.g., Butler-Kisber, 2002), arranging their words to resemble how they told their stories (Madison, 1991). I arranged the lines on the page to show how it feels to take a run, to listen to participants' stories, to follow the unfurling of their experiences; the space forces one to breath or pause or gasp. In a 2011 Poets' Forum panel on the line, Rita Dove (2012) stated

> The one thing that I find that poetry does that no other written art form can really do is that it can use the visual and use the oral to orchestrate our breathing, so that it becomes an extremely physical act to read a poem: aloud or to yourself, if you're really into it.

For example, here is a portion of one of the poetic transcriptions of my interviews with women runners with my question as the title:

"Why do you run?" I asked.

I run   because I'm competitive
               because I am a Marathon Maniac
                  to release stress
            to meditate
      to feel strong.

    I ran   because I was in Africa
              to have some control
                  to control chronic pain
                    to lose weight
                for my health and my kids
          when my husband was deployed.

       I run   to remember
                    to remember I can do hard things
                 to forget
                to get over this divorce
            to run away from family violence.

I run   to change my life
           to keep centered
              for psychological health
        so I can drink
     so I can eat
  so I can eat cheese.

Faulkner, 2018c, p. 60

Paul Ruby and I (Faulkner & Ruby, 2015) used poetic transcription of email discourse in a collaborative autoethnography on feminist identity in romantic relationships. We created poetic transcriptions of a year-long series of our email exchanges to bring us closer to our relationship "data" and to use that relationship to bring different insights than a straightforward prose presentation would allow us. We engaged in relational dialectics theory (RDT) contrapuntal analysis outlined by Baxter (2011) by thematically examining the interplay of contrasting discourses in our email exchanges. We created a PDF file of the emails and completed contrapuntal analysis using both online comment tools and by writing on paper copies of the document (e.g., highlighting words and phrases, making notes of categories and themes and theoretical memos with the sticky note function, and writing in the margins).

First, we read through the email text to get a holistic sense of the data. We asked the following sensitizing questions: "What does a listener need to know in order to render this textual segment intelligible? What socio-cultural and interpersonal discourses need to be invoked to understand what this textual segment means?" (Baxter, 2011, p. 159). Second, we generated initial codes in the margins, noting answers to the question: "What is being said or implied about relational identity?" (Baxter, 2011, p. 162). Examples of codes included emotion, time vs. commitment, needs, and trust. We made notes about manifest themes (e.g., I think of you all of the time) and latent themes (e.g., power struggle between feminist vs. other relationship paradigms) by highlighting relevant passages in the text. The passages we highlighted became part of the poetic transcription of email exchange. Third, we focused on larger systems of meaning from the initial coding. That is, we theorized about the personal and relational identities represented in the discourse and collapsed first order codes (e.g., needs, trust) into the four competing discourse themes we discovered: (1) Intellect vs. Embodiment, (2) Real Life Work vs. Other Worlds, (3) Balance vs. Giving Everything, and (4) Past Relationships vs. The Present. Fourth, we constructed poems/poetic transcriptions to show our analysis of the competing discourses and dialectical tensions in the data by paying attention to *repeating, recurring*, and *forceful* words and phrases, following Owen's (1984) description of relational themes. See Figure 2.1 for an example of the notations and some of the raw material we used to construct the poetic transcription/poem, *Should I bring a 6 pack of bud?*, representing the theme of *Past Relationships vs. The Present*. This shows how we used poetic transcription to keep the rhythm, sense, and emotional resonance of the email exchanges.

Thus, the writing of collaborative found poems/poetic transcriptions constituted part of the theoretical coding; the process of transcribing and constructing the poems helped reinforce our analysis of the competing discourses we identified. Many of the titles of poems/poetic transcriptions mirror email headings such as the *Should I bring a 6 pack of bud?* to show how we used poetic transcription to keep the rhythm, sense, and emotional resonance of the email exchanges.

Should I bring a 6 pack of bud?

From: pdRuby
To: SF
8/16/01
09:07 AM
Subject: Re: date

i have a cooler. don't dare ask for tofu
my heart or hummus at the snack stand.

watch me. feel that I want you.
want you like you are. what does
this have to do with sandra?

From: SF
To: pdRuby
Subject: Re: bud?

The vile watered down
horse piss enigma
most people like,
your tongue becomes numb
when you drink.
I shamed my roommate out
of drinking BUD light.
I am bad. Don't call me girl.

From: pdRuby
To: SF
Re: ooo

you are a dream girl, the phd lady?
the one that tells lesbian jokes-
firegirl – whiskey straight from the bottle.
yes i remember.   tsk tsk tsk

bud isn't a beer like ferrari isn't a car,
it is a personal thing
with all the grease monkeys and votech fans,
it takes me to automotive places of comfort—

i like spam and pouilly-fuisse
buying into Anheuser-Busch
chivas and key memories:
bring a 6 pack

To: pdRuby
From: SF
11:36 AM

I know symbols,
dislike bud as a reminder
that my latte will implode.
My assignments: interview people about love,
not roses but impressionistic paintings
what reminds me to throw up.

Representing the RDT analysis as found poetry/poetic transcription contributes to Poetic Inquiry by showing how systematic analysis of relational discourse speaks to larger socio-cultural issues surrounding feminism and romantic relationships. The competing discourses we presented in poetic transcriptions demonstrate how competing messages influence relational culture and identity. Based on our experience of constructing collaborative poems/poetic transcriptions, we believe that relational

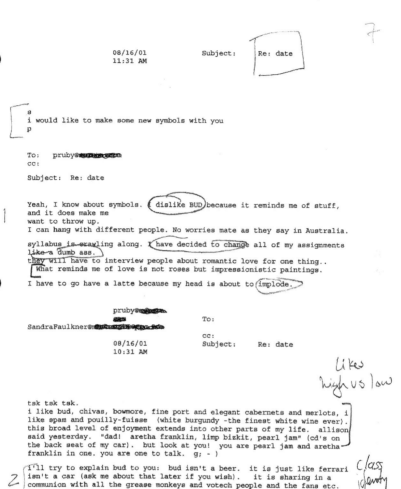

FIGURE 2.1 Poetic transcription example

partners may benefit from an analysis of their own poems or those of others to understand cultural tensions between personal and relational identities. Poetry is a vehicle for understanding and demonstrating relational transitions: "People search for poems when the occasion demands, when emotion requires the ritualized and/ or raw powers of poetry" (Young, 2010, p. 36). The use of collaborative found poems/poetic transcription connects relationship narratives to dialogic thinking.

In sum, poetic transcription is a way to ethically re-present participants' stories and answer research questions in a method that "involves crafting transcripts in a caring and relational manner to foreground ... stories, create verisimilitude and focus on the essence of the experiences, create coherent storylines, and create evocative text" (Ward, 2011, p. 355). We may use poetic transcription when we are most interested in preserving the ways in which participants tell their stories. Lahman et al. (2011) caution that poetic transcription may best be used with other forms of qualitative writing.

> Poetry and, in particular, formed poetry may be alienating to some readers who are unfamiliar with poetry or who have had largely negative experiences with poetry (e.g., Cliff notes of impregnable, dead, White men poems). Researchers should use caution in wholeheartedly embracing any one form at the expense or degradation of other forms, including traditional work.
>
> *p. 894*

Narrative Poetry

Poetic Inquirers who are most interested in narrative and the research story may use narrative poetry—poems that emphasize storytelling. Narrative poems may be short or long, written in form or not, may rhyme or not, though they are typically dramatic with a strong sense of character, plot, and narration. The use of participant narratives and self-narratives, including archival texts, as a basis for Poetic Inquiry represents human thought in context (McAdams, 1993). McAdams believes that our narratives provide, at least in part, a window into our thoughts, behavior, and experiences. Narratives allow a way to examine identities, the communicative behavior that externalizes our thoughts about identity (Faulkner & Hecht, 2011; McAdams, 1993), how we make sense of our cultural and social worlds, and how we try and create coherence (Lieblich, Tuval-Mashiach, & Zilber, 1998). In many instances, we narrate particular life experiences where there is a rift between a real and ideal self, between the self and society (Riessman, 1993). Therefore, the impulse to create poetry is the impulse toward narrative. Martha Collins (Janas, 1991) argued in an interview about the importance of poetry:

> Poetry is basically human—if it doesn't happen on one level in society, such as in the academy, it will happen on another, in bars or coffeehouses. Making music out of language is universal; it happens in all cultures; it's pre-literate.

Researchers may find the use of narrative material, especially as it connects to their lives, creates a stronger sense of connection with an audience or a universality of experience. Krizek (2003) advocates for the inclusion of personal experience in one's work when participants' stories intersect with the researcher's personal history. Prendergast (2009) argued that the best Poetic Inquiry is that which concerns itself with affect as well as intellect and deals with topics grounded in the "affective experiential domain." The poet Frank X. Walker (Bischoff, 2001) indicated in an interview that writers should be at the center of source material for their work, especially those interested in affective content, as it is difficult to make up strong emotions.

Narrative poetry is a useful tool to write about family. The poet and playwright Mary Weems (2010) wrote narrative poems about her father using the perspective of her mother, stepsister, and stepmama—those who knew her father best—as a way to let go of relational hurts.

> This sacred, poetic inquiry represents my attempt to make meaning out of a life spent in the spaces between wondering why my father didn't love me, moments when he came in and out of my life like a holiday telling me he did, and trying to maneuver the unstable landscape of relationships with men before I understood who I was and what I was supposed to be looking for in a life partner.
>
> *p. 746*

In an (auto)ethnographic project on women's work presented in verse (Faulkner, 2014a), I wrote what I call dialogue poems. These are poems that represent remembered conversation in the form of natural talk; they are ethnographic observations about daily conversations. This form is well suited for interview transcripts and/or recollected conversations. In *Knit Four, Frog One*, the dialogue poems about talk at the dining-room table represent the inclusion of narrative autoethnographic insights (Faulkner, 2014a).

Eating Dinner

Mom: If you do. not. stop. KICKING
the table, mom and dad are going to the store
and leaving you here with the dog.

Mimi: If mom and dad go to the store and leave me at home alone, I will call the police, I will dial 911. They will come and put you in jail. Then they will take me away, and I will live with another family.

Mom: And would you be sad?

Mimi: No.

Stubborn @ Dinner

Mom: If you don't eat your dinner, you are not getting ANYTHING else to eat tonight.

Mimi: I don't want dessert. Yay, no dessert for me. I'm EXCITED about no dessert.

Mom: And, you get to eat your dinner for breakfast, too.

Mimi: Can I have what you have for breakfast?

Mom: I'm having coffee.

Dinner @ the Church-House with the 4-year-old

Mom: Stop belching, Mimi. If I get a report from preschool that you were burping during lunch to make your friends laugh, I will be irritated.

Dad: Stop. Mimi.

Mimi: I could barf on my plate if I keep burping, right?

Dad: And then you would have to eat your food with the barf.

Mimi: How many more bites do I have to eat to have dessert?

Nietzsche @ the Coffee Shop

Mimi: Are Jesus and God dead?

Dad: I can't answer that.

Mom: (giving a "really?" look to Josh) It depends on whether you think they were people. If Jesus was a person, then yes.
God is more of an idea.

Mimi: (pretend reading from a book) Jesus and God died in a terrible storm. A tornado killed them. Strong winds made them die.

Mom: Okay.

Mimi: (singing) I love Jesus. I hate God. I love God. I hate Jesus. Who killed God?

Mom: Nietzsche.

Guns @ Breakfast

Mimi: Can I stay home? I don't wanta go to school today.

Mom: No. Mom and Dad have to work. Though, we could leave Buddy in charge, and you could stay here.

Mimi: He's not a human.

Mom: True, but he would tell you if anyone was outside.

Mimi:	He would bark at strangers.
Mom:	We'd lock the door, and then you would know not to answer it.
Mimi:	But what if they broke the door down? I would run away. I would take a sword and stab them. But they would have a gun.

Morning Coffee

Mimi:	When you and dad die when I am an adult, I won't mind because I will do my own stuff.
Mom:	Will you be sad?
Mimi:	I will live in this house with my baby. Will Buddy be sad when you die?
Mom:	Let's hope he dies before me. Dogs shouldn't live that long.
Mimi:	I don't like blood. Does blood come out of dead bodies?

Date Nut Muffins @ Breakfast

Mimi:	If I eat all of my breakfast, after school, can I have chocolate?
Mom:	No. You eat all of your breakfast so you can grow and get older and do all of those things you keep asking about like sliding down the big water slide at the park.
Mimi:	But I don't want to grow. Growing gives me leg cramps. By the way, I will eat lunch and snack at school and grow. And more snack after school. And I get to take a nap, and you don't.

The dialogue poem is like a social media post presented as a typical daily conversation. All of the dialogue poems were recreated from conversations between my daughter, my partner, and me. The use of dialogue poems as narrative inquiry was a way to incorporate the dialectics of family life in order to give voice to the both/and.

When we view poetry as a way to approximate life and presence, or as Charles Simic (1994) wrote, to thrive on the contradiction between word and thing, this may be the best reason for using it as a narrative tool as it "greatly upsets schoolmasters, preachers, and dictators, and cheers up the rest of us" (p. 57). The use of narrative language can show the constraints of circumstances, moral complexity, and multiple selves (Riessman, 1993). There exists resistance to narrative in poetry for some poets and schools of thought such as whether poetry and poets should be concerned with storytelling (Hoagland, 2006). We can extend this argument to Poetic Inquiry and ask whether storytelling is the reason for poetry, or whether the question itself raises a false dichotomy between a narrative and lyric impulse. David Rothman (2007) defended the narrative in poetry:

> Despite the dislocation to modern lives so frequently cited by the modernists and their prodigy narrative has been, remains, and will continue to be one of the ways we try to make sense out of the world. We seem to need it to make sense of things, and it manifests itself in every aspect of our experiences from science to sex. Anyone who disagrees with this observation can contemplate, for example, why we are in Iraq. For those who think this can be explained without resorting to storytelling, all I can say is, congratulations, you take the English Department, they'll take the White House. To discuss such things we need narratives and we need them told well. In short among other things, we need poets. Human beings are symbol-making animals, and for better or worse it would appear that narrative, with all its deceptions, problems, confusions, distortions, and illusions, will remain part of what we do.

Whatever the form—narrative analysis of poetry or presentation of poetry as narrative—the importance for many poets and researchers is storytelling. Rothman (2007) suggested that leaving this to journalists, lawyers, speechwriters, advertisers, and historians would deaden the impact. Andrew Hudgins, for example, (1988) uses a sequence of poems called, *After the Lost War*, about Sidney Lanier, a poet and musician born in 1842 in Georgia, to narrate a story about the South after the Civil War. He created the poems by imagining Lanier as a narrator. "Despite his having been dead for over a hundred years now, I'd like to thank Lanier for allowing me to use the facts of his life—more or less—to see how I might have lived if it had been mine" (p. ix). Hudgins claims that those familiar with Lanier's writing may not recognize the voice, but the goal of the collection is to narrate a lyric story.

In a project on LGBTQ Jewish Americans, I used poetry to represent participants' narratives of being gay and Jewish (Faulkner, 2006). A narrative approach to the examination of LGBTQ Jewish American identity reveals how participants make sense of their identities within their cultural and social worlds (Lieblich, Tuval-Mashiach, & Zilber, 1998) and reveal the ascribed stigma of being LGBTQ and Jewish. I used poetry rather than a standard prose format to present participants' narratives, as poetry can closely represent the way that people talk, their language use, and patterns of speech, and I wanted to privilege and recreate these patterns, syntax, words, and rhythm in lyrical ways that prose representations cannot do (Madison, 1991; Richardson, 2002). The poems are constructed to embody the experience of being LGBTQ and Jewish in ways that pay attention to the senses and offer some narrative and poetic truths about the experience of multiple stigmatized identities. Poetry may be a better choice for presenting individuals' identity narratives than other forms of writing because as Hirshfield (1997) articulates, a good poem can never be fully entered and known: "Poetry can do what other forms of thinking cannot: approximate the actual flavor of life, in which subjective and objective become one, in which conceptual mind and the inexpressible presence of things become one" (p. 32). Because poetry defies singular definitions and explanations, it mirrors the slipperiness of identity, the difficulty of capturing the shifting nature of who we are and want to be, and resonates more fully with the way identity is created, maintained, and altered through our interacted narratives. I wrote poems to embody the experience of being LGBTQ and Jewish in ways that pay attention to the senses and offer some narrative and poetic truths about the experience of multiple stigmatized identities. I argue that the use of poetry furthers identity theories through poems that challenge stereotypes, confront prejudices, add to the representation of LGBTQ Jews, and address criteria of conditionality and narrative truth (see Chapter 3).

I constructed poems from a fusion of research and poetry after exchanged conversations and emails with participants, listening to audio-tapes of interviews, and reading my research journal. The mix of forms highlights participants' narratives of identity and my own identities as researcher/participant, especially when they intersected with participants' stories (Krizek, 2003). My own identity stories are transparent throughout the research because "when researchers are open about their own personal stories, participants feel more comfortable sharing information, and the hierarchal gap between researchers and respondents formerly embraced in ethnographic work is closed" (Berger, 2001, p. 507). In addition, being reflexive in the representation of poetic projects is important to demonstrate how understanding occurred, how the researcher as human instrument influenced the research process and interpretation of participant narratives.

Thus, I used narrative poems to present participant's stories. In some narratives, I heard repeating lines and stories, different variations of the same theme throughout. A pantoum is a Malay poetic form that capitalizes on repetition through the use of quatrains; the recurring lines can be hypnotic as they weave in and out of one another, creating surprises as they work together in novel ways (Padgett, 1987). It is a slow form because a reader takes four steps forward and two steps back, making it "the perfect form for the evocation of a past time" (Strand & Boland, 2002, p. 44). I find this form enticing to represent the fact that most narratives are not straightforward, that individuals often end up back where they started working through identity issues in an anti-narrative pattern as identities change in our relationships and communities over time (e.g., Cohen, 2002). The poem, *Orthodoxy*, represents how some participants felt forced to choose between their personal level of identity (being LGBTQ and Jewish), their relationships (e.g., by being in a straight relationship), and how they enacted their identities (e.g., being closeted at work, not attending gay cultural events) because of others' ascriptions about being LGBTQ and Jewish based on communal representations of these as incompatible identities.

Orthodoxy

When I was 3, I knew I liked boys,
the interest and feelings I always carried
like ancient Hebrew script on scrolls
you could find in caves along the hills of Jerusalem.

The interest and feelings I always carried
with crushes on friends that blushed with love
in caves along the hills of Jerusalem,
relics of Judaism lying in dust,

and crushes on friends that burst into love.
I left the orthodoxy at 13
relics of Judaism lying in dust.
I had many questions I wanted to ask

as I turned from orthodoxy at 13,
mom's dream of my black hat soaked with sin.
The many questions I needed to ask
my therapist at 14 who told me "find women"

made dad's dream of me return like sin
until I found the Reconstructionists and moved.
At 17, my straight best friend showed me women.
I traveled with one, backpack and all, to see if I could.

When I found Reconstructionism and moved
I became super Jew and super Dad
with professional pack, traveled with wife and child, like I could
ignore my thoughts that men like men.

I became super Jew and super Dad
with no time to think of males with lust,
I ignored my thoughts that men like men
with hair like bears and worked out thighs.

On the Jersey turnpike, time to think of lust,
I discover at 50 on a silent retreat, thoughts
with hair like bears and worked out thighs
can make me move and renovate my love.

These thoughts in silent retreat I discover
like ancient Hebrew script on scrolls.
I move my love and reconstruct memories,
because when I was 3, I knew I liked boys.

Narratives of the self can be categorized as interpretive poetry or performative writing where the personal experiences of the researcher are connected to the ethnographic project (Denzin, 1997; Furman, 2003). Denzin (1997) described ethnopoetics and narratives of the self as "messy texts" because they are multi-voiced and no one interpretation is privileged.

> The poetic self is simply willing to put itself on the line and to take risks … predicated on a simple proposition: This writer's personal experiences are worth sharing with others. Messy texts make the writer a part of the writing project.
>
> *p. 225*

The writing vacillates between description and interpretation using voice as a means to write *for* those studied rather than *about* them. Pelias (2005) refers to this kind of writing shaped by field experience and observation as "performative writing." "My search for form is an autobiographical quest that uses the data of everyday life, real and imagined, to articulate a self, to find a self's center" (Pelias, 2004, p. 71). In a performance piece that examines the cultural pressure for hyper-masculine violence and pleasure, Pelias (2007) expressed a desire to show the researcher's involvement in cultural practices through the use of personal experience.

> I write to uncover how I have become trapped within a cultural logic that pulls me into a sadistic desire to be or identify with a person in power … I write, offering a series of life examples and disclosing perhaps more than I should, to show how being a girly man can be a resistant strategy.
>
> *p. 945*

Pelias (2007) offers the reader a collection of poems inspired by newspaper accounts where "I try to enter that world, make sense of it, by speaking from the point of view of those who do harm" (p. 950). He writes about disturbing accounts of horrible things that we do to one another, often hidden in the back pages of the newspaper, to ask questions about the place of pain in our lives, whether there exists pleasure in moving into that violent space. In the poem, *Acid Attack*, he writes,

> I guess I was blinded by love/when I hired Ruben to fling/the acid at her. But you have to/ understand. She deserved it. I do not like being there, living in that body, trying to find a logic that might explain. But I find myself over and over searching for the saving narratives we tell ourselves.
>
> *p. 950*

In his poem, *How to Watch Your Father Die* (2004, p. 74), Pelias offers the audience an example of a saving narrative in the first few stanzas:

> Come when you are called, come quickly,
> Rush, come closer, now:
>
> Notice how the muscles weaken, the body slows.
> Feel the accumulation of days.
>
> Lean in, listen when he speaks,
> Bend to his words.

Pelias writes of a need for exactness and precision as well as attention to organizing structure in his poetry:

> That desire for exactness, for closure, for opening possibilities with those I love and with those I share a language with keeps me writing in search of myself and offers constant reminders that my task can never be accomplished. It is the search that matters.
>
> *2004, p. 78*

In sum, narrative poetry and narrative forms are excellent when the researcher-poet is most interested in storytelling, re-presenting and voicing a participant's story, showing the researcher's connection to the research project, showing the field experience, and talking back to cultural experiences through performative writing. We can write research informed poetry as social commentary to great effect, bringing a social science perspective to a poem (e.g., Dark, 2009).

The Lyric

Originally, lyric poetry was accompanied by music, though in the past 500 or so years poets have written lyric poems that are not meant for accompaniment (Padgett, 1987).

> But lyric poems continue to resemble songs in three important ways: 1) they are shorter than dramatic or epic poems; 2) they tend to express the personal feelings of one speaker, often the poet; and 3) they give you the feeling that they could be sung *p. 110*

Richardson (1997a) distinguishes between ethnographic narrative and lyric poetry; narrative poetry is akin to the idea of the research poem (see Langer and Furman, 2004; Lahman, et al., 2011) and lyric poetry is that which represents actual experiences in such a way that the distance between self and other blurs, others experience and feel "episodes, epiphanies, misfortunes, pleasures" (p. 183). Simply put, narrative poetry refers to poems that are most interested in storytelling, and in lyric poetry the goal is to stress moments of subjective feeling and emotion in a short space. "Lyric poems always express some emotion …" (Padgett, 1987, p. 111). Of course, this truly is a simplistic explanation. The distinction between narrative and lyric poetry is not this clear as B. H. Fairchild (2003), for instance, points out. In fact, we can talk about lyric elements in narrative poetry and vice versa. Fairchild argues that narrative and lyric poetry are often mixed forms, and the blending of the two promises to achieve "the radical potential embedded in the language of poetry" (p. 1). Richardson (1997a) argued that lyric poetry is always ethnographic, and the task "is to represent actual experiences—episodes, epiphanies, misfortunes, pleasures—capturing those experiences in such a way that others can experience and *feel* them. Lyric poems, therefore, have the possibility of doing for ethnographic understanding what normative ethnographic writing cannot" (p. 183).

A poet constructs a lyric poem through the use of such devices as imagery, rhythm, sound, and layout to concretize feelings and give those feelings back to an audience through the creation of the experience. Richardson (1997b) provided evidence for this by sharing the consequences of poetic representation in her own life; she found herself using participants' words, speaking from participants' point of views like they were her own, and feeling more integrated. Similarly, Behar (2008) uses anthropological poetry to allow for the experience of "the emotionally wrenching ways in which we attain knowledge of others and ourselves … the most charged intellectual insights occur precisely when one's ethnographic work and one's life crash into each other in a head-one collision" (p. 63). Shidmer (2014) characterizes Poetic Inquiry as dramatic play and considers the lyric a way to write what we know and what we don't know, what we will never know:

> The lyrical quality of poetry addresses this concern because it goes beyond knowing and representing what there is to know and draws attention to the mystery and ineffability of things. Lyric also draws attention to the perishability of what there is in the world.
>
> *p. 17*

In sum, the difference between lyric poetry and narrative poetry is not as distinct as the section headings in this chapter make it. We may think of lyrical poetry as that which focuses most on aesthetics and the associations between images and feelings. "The lyrical quality of poetry and the potentialities it offers to research must be considered as important as its narrative structure and the possibilities narrative creates in research" (Shidmer, 2014, p. 13).

Chapbooks, Long Poems, and Poetry Series

The chapbook, series or cluster of poems, and longer forms of poetry are well suited for qualitative research because of the focus on sustaining a theme throughout the work (Butler-Kisber, 2012; Faulkner, 2016a). The use of connected poems or a longer poetic work enables us to show our nuanced analyses, to represent the process of our fieldwork, and to demonstrate multiple perspectives on a project and our analyses through forms that reflect and enable musing on our themes.

Chapbooks represent a part of DIY (do-it-yourself) culture and have been from inception, a medium for political action to a venue for avant-garde and new writers. Many chapbooks are made by hand—card stock sliced with paper cutter, hand sewn, bound with ribbon; they are small, self-contained entities that play with style and form. Poetry chapbooks are usually no more than 40 pages and often center on a specific theme such as Hello Kitty or family stories (e.g., Faulkner, 2012b, Faulkner, 2015). Contemporary iterations of chapbooks have been likened to DIY paperbacks and are popular again in the contemporary poetry world because of the production ease, path to other publications, and risk-taking in subject and/or style. They have changed from their past as a vehicle for the democratization of readership to a democratizing means of production for writers (Miller, 2005), especially because poetry can be difficult to sell. Noah Eli Gordan (2007) writes in *Jacket* magazine:

> it is the ease of access to the means of production that defines the chapbook's unfettering of hierarchy. The chapbook constitutes a crucial nexus of the poetry community; They provide poets a forum to publish poems as an intermediate step between magazine publication and books and in some cases, even instead of books.
>
> ¶ 11

Kimiko Hahn (2009) considers chapbooks to be like the burgeoning DIY culture, a change from past thoughts of them as solely art books or vanity publications: "Due to a true revolution in the means of production, digital technology has given writers the power to publish their own chapbooks even more cheaply than a Beat poet armed with a mimeo machine" (p. 64). Anyone can take a stapler, ribbon, tape, glue, camera, word processor, printer, or online platform and create their own chap. Gordan (2007) sums up the power and appeal of chapbooks for the poet and researcher.

> The chapbook in its current manifestation allows poets to enter into a shared life of the imagination while swerving around the dominant paradigms of economic and social space. Whether comprised of an extended sequence, a series of short poems, or a single, longer work, the chapbook, in its momentary focusing and sculpting of the reader's attention is the perfect vehicle for poetry.
>
> ¶ 11

For Poetic Inquirers, chapbooks present a compelling way to present field research and (auto)ethnography. For example, in *Postcards from Germany* (Faulkner, 2016b), I composed a digital chapbook consisting of poems, images, and sounds about my embodied experiences living, teaching, traveling, and studying in

Germany on sabbatical as a feminist ethnographer using a feminist lens to show the interplay between power and difference (Buch & Staller, 2014). I map a three-and-a-half-month feminist ethnography on embodiment in Germany through ethnographic poetry and self-made photo-postcards. From August 19, 2014 to December 2, 2014, I lived and worked in the city of Mannheim, the eighth largest metropolitan region in Germany located at the confluence of the Rhine and Neckar Rivers in the northwestern corner of the state of Baden-Württemberg, (re) learning the German language after a 21-year hiatus. I was enrolled in a German as a foreign language class (Duetsch als Fremdsprache B1: Threshold or Intermediate German) taught by two teachers from a Hochschule in Mannheim and spent Monday and Wednesday nights immersed in culture, grammar, and formal language instruction. I taught a seven-week course on Gender and Interpersonal Communication in English at the University of Mannheim where I was a visiting scholar. Many weekends, I traveled by train through Germany with my child and spouse. I ran along the Rhine river three times a week, watching the river push barges full of coal, cars, and other cargo. I spent time with a new German friend over wine, coffee, and apple cake, practicing the art of German conversation.

I presented this ethnography as a poetry chapbook that I created in a DIY spirit to pay homage to the subversive roots of chapbooks (Hahn, 2009). I used the chapbook form and the idea of atypical postcards to flaunt the false dichotomy between the domestic and public sphere, between the private and the public, and to show the interplay between power and difference. The postcard poems subvert the usual way we map trips and send the most picturesque parts to others for their consumption. In a series of 11 poems, I focus on embodiment in the experience of learning another language and engaging in culture through language (mis)acquisition in German language class, ordering food, holidays and the usual activities, and traveling with a middle-aged white female body and my kindergartner and male spouse.

The use of postkarten and the chapbook format plays with the usual way we map trips, how we try and send the most picturesque parts to others for their consumption. Mannheim, for instance, is a city where the streets are laid out in a grid pattern, leading to the nickname "Quadratestadt" (city of the squares) and a city slogan— "Leben. Im Quadrant." This slogan is plastered on city billboards, buses, and street trains. In *Poskarten aus Deutschland*, you see the not so neat and pretty parts of cultural shifts, what a city would not put on a postcard for sale. I use poetry, sound, and images about my German experience to embody an experience not found on typical postcards. The poems capture what Wanda Hurren (2009) calls postcartographia. They play with cartography, with map and card, to question what we mean by mapping, place, and position. The use of ethnographic personal poetry highlights how we can use the auto in ethnography to bridge difference. Robin Boylorn (2014) claims, "our experiences of difference and place are marked on the body" (p. 313). Here is a sequence of five connected poems (see Figures 2.2–2.6) from this project that I invite you, dear audience, to listen to and see how experiences of life in Germany marked this researcher's embodied selves (see Faulkner, 2016b for the sound).

Gefühle in Deutsch Klasse (Feelings in German Class)

1. *Die Trauer (The Sadness)*

I have two weeks left und schon I miss Mannheim,
my life, and get all like weepy American
as I scratch plus and minus signs on notebook lines
next to feelings when mein Lehrer asks, negativ
oder positiv? I pen the Gestalt wrong, all
scribbles up and down, and slash out the sad
signs my German is not prima or toll—
or any other of my Lehrer's praise—but bad.
At least I'm getting the gloom out of my way
rubbing the feelings of nostalgia
over my notes in an efficient display,
better than being a middle-aged mute und traurig
like the first *Deutsch als Fremdsprache* class all in German
-no comparing to English = I'll miss Sebastian who+
never gives in, explains German with more German.

FIGURE 2.2 *Die Trauer (The Sadness)*

2. *Die Angst* (*The Fear*)

I never give in, explain German with more German:

This place is like a Wintertraum mit Grimm magic,
not like boring Ohio where we only do mom-like
chores and homework, and the dog gets ticks.
I try to be a real Mannheimer,
like when mein Kind weint und klagt
that "I miss my dog" and "you love Germany
more than me," I speak a few words of Tratsch
arrive 10 minutes early to meet
my new German friend because I can't learn
how to speak un-American and treat
the locals to an echter Akzent as I burn
through a walk in the city's alphabet street grid
to become more German than the Germans.

FIGURE 2.3 *Die Angst* (*The Fear*)

3. *Der Stolz* (*The Pride*)

I become more German than the Germans
and don't feel Stolz in all of the American places,
not about my verstehen in class, mein Kind or Mann
who like that I can order their food in these spaces
with Kellnerin draped in Dirndls und Lederhosen,
Germans who are not proud of their nation
or their selves but show pride in gut gemacht clothes
that are more German than Germany. I get this
feeling, share this fetish for all things Deutsch
and Palatine, take my runs along the Rhein,
go places no Mannheimer knows like Bacharach
where we tourists creep along the winery
vines like a tourist blight of red, white and blue
as we dare to drink in all of these views.

FIGURE 2.4 *Der Stolz* (*The Pride*)

4. *Der Ärger* (*The Annoyance*)

Shop Windows, Mannheim

I dare to drink in all of these views—
windows with wispy women mannequins,
Dekolleté molded into Oktoberfest Dirndls,
hung over Lederhosen punked-out Männer,
displays more authentic than the Mannheimers
who sport suspenders and check-print shirts
around town, a glass of trockene Riesling in one hand,
a cigarette and a kid in the other, the dirty
smoke refracted onto the facades of shop fronts
and in my face as I stand and frown from the outside,
choke on the effluvium of cost and fashion
mutter that this is not Bavaria, outside
in English, my body warped in a hoodie,
hair frayed, jeans, disordered and strange.

FIGURE 2.5 *Der Ärger* (*The Annoyance*)

5. *Die (Un)Ordnung (The (Dis)Order)*

Disordered and strange, hair, jeans frayed,
I cannot bring mein Kind in order
as we drag along the Mannheimer Straße—
Ist alles in Ordnung? Alles klar?—
she darts like an expert frogger
onto the street and knocks a bicyclist
off his pedestal into the corner
as we snake our way to Kindergarten.
Pass Auf! He yells (and not
Ouf Pass! like a real Mannheimer).
Watch out! I yell and pull her back
to the sidewalk as the bicyclist
turns and snips: *Schlaf gut Kind!*
All of these Germans tell
us how to keep order
like the woman on the train platform
who demands, *Do you speak German?*
Because that man is taking video of your daughter.
Her last words, as she points to a suited man
with video-phone in hand, and turns away—
And I thought you should know—
mean I must clamp the fun,
bringe alle in Ordnung with mein Kind
who moves time during Bahnstreiks
by tanzen like a kleine pied piper of chaos
knocking strangers off board
the train of forgotten rules.
I have two weeks left and already I miss Mannheim.

These poems represent a riff on a crown of sonnets or a sonnet corona; a sequence of poems linked by a common theme, each poem exploring one aspect of the theme, and the final line of a poem starting the first line of the following poem. The first line of the first poem should end the last line of the final poem to bring the sequence to close. Though the poems I present are not sonnets, notice how the last line of a poem began the first line of the next poem. I used this form to explore how different situations—navigating a new city, taking a language class, socializing with new friends, traveling, shopping, and walking my child to Kindergarten spoke to negotiating my shifting identities as a researcher, mother, partner, and foreign outsider.

Poetry clusters represent a theme in a series of poems; clusters can be a series of found poems, poems by individual or multiple poets, and a cluster of poems used

FIGURE 2.6 *Die (Un)Ordnung (The (Dis)Order)*

as data representation and/or an analytical tool (Butler-Kisber & Stewart, 2009). The use of poetry clusters provides Poetic Inquirers another means to convey some kind of "truth" while concomitantly discovering something more in their research.

The "something more" is the revelation that often occurs in the unveiling of a poetry cluster. The reader, and/or author(s) herself, can see for the first time dimensions of the theme that might not otherwise be revealed. The clustering of poems that are unique and at times even contradictory allows for an up-close and granular reading of a theme and a more general reading simultaneously. This simultaneous appreciation of experience removes the need to move back and forth from the particular to the general and ... provides a richer understanding of the phenomenon.

Butler-Kisber & Stewart, 2009, p. 4

Butler-Kisber and Stewart (2009) use clusters of poems on death and dying to write about the grief of losing those close to them. They began by freewriting remembered experiences and highlighting significant words and phrases. The highlights were used to do another free write paying attention to poetic details (e.g., line breaks, rhyme, structure) to construct poems. They argue that each poem can stand alone, but when taken together, a cluster of poems around a theme provides more nuances and can amplify the effects of a good poem. And when used collaboratively (see section below), "clusters generated by a number of individuals around a single theme allow for a more multi-vocal understanding of a phenomenon than singe-authored clusters, and lend themselves to team inquiry" (p. 5).

I use a series of poems about family stories in my poetry collection, *Knit Four, Frog One* (Faulkner, 2014a), as an example of critical family communication research; through poetic forms such as collage, free verse, dialogue poems, and sonnets, I show and critique patterns of communication in close relationships in poems about mother-daughter relationships, women's work, mothering, writing, and family secrets. The poems can be considered clusters of musings on a theme; dialogue poems that show the interactions of everyday conversations at mealtime, collage poems that contrast visual family artifacts with text, sonnets about romantic relationships, concrete poems that demonstrated knitting stitches, and free verse poems that make conscious and unconscious reflections on the nature of mothering and mother's work. While I did not set out to write a series of poems, I recognized that the poetry I had been writing focused on family themes. I organized the poems by themes (parenting, writing, romantic relationships, mother-daughter relationships) and wrote new poems to further reveal the themes of relationships as women's work using the voices of grandmothers, mothers, and daughters. This series of poems helped me connect personal experience to larger cultural structures by using multiple voices and poetic forms.

In a poem series about breaking up (Faulkner, 2012c), I examine how relational dissolution provides insight into underlying values of how to do relationships, and how communication plays a role before, during, and after they end. If we think of the bevy of songs and poems that concern breaking up, we can see how this experience of ending relationships occupies our expressive imagination; I discovered that some poems in my poetry journal were about relational dissolution (i.e., breaking up). The poems were created from email, personal conversations, and journal entries like a type of found poetry.

I decided to use the poems as part of poetic analysis to make a poetry performance piece called Frogging It: A Poetic Analysis of Relational Dissolution.
Frog is a knitting term, which references the ripping out of stitches when one
makes a mistake. It is called frogging, because the ripping sound is similar to
a frog's croak. The title seemed an apt expression for breaking up. The process
I followed in this series consisted of four steps. I did a thematic analysis of nine
poems about breaking up; I read and reread the poems noting my impressions
of the poems and using characteristic words and phrases to identify themes.
Next, I used relational dissolution theory literature to connect to themes in
the poems. Then, I took the poems and my thematic analysis and juxtaposed
them with the phases in a model of relational dissolution by Steve Duck (2011).
Finally, I created the performance poem, Frogging It, by integrating prose about
the themes and the poems.

The resulting poetry piece, which I consider to be a long poem, makes an
explicit connection between poetry and interpersonal relationship dissolution
through the creation of poetry. Many poets assert that all good poetry addresses
large issues—death, silence, absence, and loss—all reasons for why relationships
end. The power of poetry to reconnect ourselves to loss, conscious and unconscious hurts that manifest in our relational interactions, offers interpersonal
scholars, educators, and those in relationships other ways of understanding. The
goal of the poetic analysis that led to the creation of the performance piece was for
audiences to experience the poetry as "evocative mediators" of painful relational
experiences (Todres & Galvin, 2008, p. 571).

In sum, a series of poems in the form of a chapbook, poetry cluster, or a long
poem is a good choice when a researcher-poet wants the audience to focus in on
the singularity of a poem while concomitantly seeing the larger work of poems
and research in a "prism-like rendition of the subtle variations of a phenomenon,
while at the same time giving a more complete overview" (Butler-Kisber, 2012,
p. 166). Representing our work in this way allows the audience to see the process
of our analyses and of our interpretation.

Collaborative Work

Many Poetic Inquirers work in interdisciplinary collaboration with poets and with
other researchers. This may take the form of mentoring others, writing poetry
from another researcher's data analysis, to working with other poets, artists, and
researchers in teams. Poetic Inquirers could alternate lines of individual poems
with or without looking at what the other has written; write a series of poems on
a research project on the same or different themes; respond to and rewrite each
other's poems; write a poem or series of poems through email or instant messenger
with agreed-upon rules and forms; intermingle lines of their own poetry with
other poet-researcher's work; or write with other poets and researchers for a set
number of hours with agreed-upon rules for form and themes. Poet-researchers

use a variety of forms for their collaborations from narrative and lyric poetry to free verse and more formal forms such as the renga, tanka, and villanelle. Collaborations may also include different art mediums (see section below).

Narrative poetry is an excellent method for (auto)ethnography and collaborative work because of the focus on storytelling, emotion, and reflexivity. Ruby and I (Faulkner & Ruby, 2015) used collaborative autoethnography (CAE) and poetic transcription of narrative to highlight the importance of emotion and flux, and "the ways in which our identities as raced, gendered, aged, sexualized, and classed researchers impact what we see, do, and say" (Jones, Adams, & Ellis, 2013, p. 35). CAE provided us with a collaborative, autobiographical, and ethnographic method wherein we could use our own relationship story as a platform for revealing and critiquing societal discourses about romantic relationships (Chang, Ngunjiri, & Hernandez, 2013). We consider the use of collaborative found poetry to speak to CAE as a feminist method because of the attention to reflexivity, personal experience, collaboration, and performance (Olesen, 2005). Creating a performative and poetic rendering enabled us to represent the experience of relational and personal identities with no one dominate position (Alcoff, 2003; Denzin, 2014).

Questions of how to engage in successful collaboration and how to consider research quality are addressed by poets and poet-researchers. When creating a research poem about a Native American woman and bi-racial identity, Langer and Furman (2004) engaged in a three-step process to ensure trustworthiness. The first author did not alter any words from the research interview transcript, but relied on her sense of the data to create stanza and line breaks, deleting any words considered unimportant to the meaning. Langer then checked the compressed work for agreement with the coding, and the researchers worked out disagreements through discussion to arrive at a consensus on the degree of accuracy and depth maintained in the content of the text. The process of constructing interpretive poems from the research interview entailed using reflective research journals to write poetry that captured core elements, images inspired by the narrative, and researcher reflections. The interpretive poems were intended to present the authors' subjective responses in a "moving and evocative manner," to show their interpretations of the research interview, and their communication about the experience through the use of poetic device.

Other poet-researchers are interested in how collaboration can bring researchers back to the body and make the academy less frigid and hierarchal. Fitzpatrick and Alansari (2018) engaged in a version of "catch and release" and juxtaposed conversations about their experiences of completing doctoral work by using Poetic Inquiry as an embodied methodology of reflection. "Using a series of poetry conversations we give voice to these experiences of the doctoral process to illuminate the emotional, affective-political experience, and engage with the neo-liberal powers of the doctoral experience" (p. 214). They juxtaposed their stories with other doctoral students' experiences and the research literature as a way to critically analyze the doctoral experience. Fitzpatrick has engaged other colleagues in using juxtaposed conversations; in a series of poems about the Orlando Pulse Nightclub shooting, the authors wrote responses to the shooting and to one another's responses through conversational poems (Fitzpatrick et al., 2018). Fitzpatrick and Fitzpatrick (2014) used poetry as a means to lessen the divide between supervisor and student by writing poems back and forth about their experiences as supervisor and supervised.

> We suggest … that introducing an explicitly artistic form of communication such as poetry into this process pushes the boundaries of research supervision and other kinds of research relationships. It opens up greater possibilities for exploring the emotional edges of the work we do. It also, at least for us, allowed us to form a stronger and more trusting relationship as we willingly exposed our vulnerabilities through our poems.
>
> *p. 50*

Pamela Richardson and Susan Walsh (2018) also used a collaborative poetic practice to heal and restore themselves as artists, educators, and researchers. They composed renga—a Japanese poetic form of linked three- and two-line stanzas with a 5-7-7 syllable and 7-7 syllable count—in conjunction with Miksang—a form of contemplative photography in which the photographer uses their camera to attend to the phenomenal world—to co-create a space of healing from their academic lives. They met monthly for five months on Skype to meditate, write, and discuss their works. Then, they used the reflective writing to create stanzas and exchange them for the construction of renga.

> The challenge and gift of the renga form is that each stanza must relate equally well with both the preceding and following stanza. As we wrote our renga, we read the verse that the other had written, contemplated the verse, and then wrote a new tercet and couplet that was responsive—and that also brought fresh perceptions, images, and ideas to the poem.
>
> *p. 154*

After creating renga, they integrated Miksang images with the poetry. "Miksang is a practice of consciously noticing the concrete details of experience and also of working with impermanence: of fully experiencing whatever arises, and then being willing to let it go" (p. 155). The renga form encourages collaboration and Miksang photography encourages contemplation, making these practices fruitful tools for poetry as contemplative and collaborative practice.

Sean Wiebe, John Guiney Yallop, Natalie Honein, and I (Faulkner, et al., 2017) created a series of villanelles around family themes by playing a game of Exquisite Corpse, which is a collaborative poetry game that has roots in Parisian Surrealism. The goal of the collaborative artistic work is to upturn usual habits of mind to create something unique and reveal a collective unconsciousness (e.g., www.poets.org/poetsorg/text/play-exquisite-corpse). Typically, players use the rule of secrecy where they do not see what the other has written until the unveiling to allow for surprise, though players decide whether to have rules around secrecy, a theme or form. We used the rule of secrecy and decided to write villanelles about family; on Mondays we emailed one another a tercet on a family theme—marriage, love, children, parenting, siblings—for five weeks, and then collectively composed a quatrain for the four surprise tercets we wrote each week, resulting in five collaborative "exquisite" villanelles. Our reflection on the process of working together was that we had different feelings and perspectives about family, "but when we put our thoughts and poetry together, they seemed to unite in essence, with little difference between us" getting at a collective unconscious (Faulkner et al., 2017, p. 92). We also recognized that the performance of the villanelles would bring forth different reactions depending on who performed the pieces, leading us to ask the following questions: "What is our work telling us about ourselves, about each other, about the collaborative creation itself, and what does it offer to others?" (p. 94). We believe that this kind of collaboration works well in interdisciplinary teams where members have different approaches and perspectives on the topic. For example, we all use Poetic Inquiry in our work, but our research expertise spans interpersonal communication, curriculum studies, literacy, narrative, and gender studies.

In work using poetry as data analysis, Furman et al. (2007) followed a four-step process to capture the contextual world of poet and subject in adolescent identity and development. First, one author wrote autobiographical poems, and then, another author used the poems as data to create research tankas (a Japanese poetic form typically written in a single line of 31 syllables). The research tankas were constructed by noting initial impressions of the poems, rereading the poems to identify themes, exploring dichotomies, mining the original poems for characteristic words and phrases, and organizing these words into lines. Next, a third author analyzed the original poems and the research tankas using a version of grounded theory analysis where she reflected on action words used in the poems and the meaning of the messages. Finally, the third and fourth authors wrote responsive poems to the grounded theory analysis and original poems. They argue that having a research team act as analysts may help minimize biases, encourage self-reflexivity, and create an environment conducive to deep understanding.

Collage and Hybrid Texts

Collage and hybrid texts, which may contain a mix of visual, audio, and textual components are useful forms for researchers who want to create multi-dimensional works digitally or in three-dimensional space. Collage comes from the French *coller*, meaning to paste or glue. In poetic texts, we may see juxtapositions or "gluing together" of different elements. Majorie Perloff (1998) writes that collage is powerful because of the potential to create double meanings:

Collage typically juxtaposes "real" items—pages torn from newspapers, color illustrations taken from picture books, letters of the alphabet, numbers, nails—with painted or drawn images so as to create a curiously contradictory pictorial surface. For each element in the collage has a kind of double function: it refers to an external reality even as its compositional thrust is to undercut the very referentiality it seems to assert. And further: collage subverts all conventional figure-ground relationships, it generally being unclear whether item A is on top of item B or behind it or whether the two coexist in the shallow space which is the "picture."

para. 2

"Collage in language-based work can now mean any composition that includes words, phrases, or sections of outside source material in juxtaposition" (Poetry Foundation, n.d.). A classic example of poetic collage is T. S. Elliot's, The Wasteland, which is composed of newspaper clippings, nursey rhymes, music lyrics, and overheard speech. Perloff (1998) points out that post-collage work has shifted from the juxtaposition of "carefully chosen statements and citations to a focus on the inherent poetic and artistic possibilities of the 'ordinary,' the 'everyday.'" Regardless of whether one is using a classic or postmodern approach to collage, Poetic Inquirers may use collage and hybrid work to queer understandings of research method and topic (e.g., Faulkner, 2017d), to present visual and aural components of their research (e.g., Faulkner, 2018), as a form of collaboration in interdisciplinary teams (e.g., Sameshima, Vandermause, & Santucci, 2012), as activist projects (e.g., Faulkner & Squillante, 2018), as part of a larger research project, and as liberatory practice (e.g., Richardson, 2017).

Some forms of collage and hybrid work include cento, found poems, cut-up, erasure poetry, and video. A cento is "a barrage of quoted fragments," an intertextual collage form created with passages from more than one poet (Drury, 2006, p. 55). I have used this form with research literature to re-present the essence and heart of scholarly arguments (see the poem Feminist Theory Class Cento in Chapter 1). Pamela Richardson (2017) used poetic erasure—poems made by erasing, obscuring, or marking out a portion of a text to make a new text— of Dorothy Dinnerstein's *The Mermaid and the Minotaur: Sexual Arrangements and Human Malaise.* "The resultant poems share experiences of conflict and dissolution, and hope for recovery and resilience in love and work as filtered through the sieves of language and meaning" (p. 121). Richardson blacked and whited out some text, and in other places used a strikethrough to keep the word visible, working with some photocopies of the text and some digital transcripts.

I used black, oil based markers, correction fluid, an MS Word for Mac font formatting functions. Working with pens, white-out, and paper was much slower and messier. The process is more frustrating. It's surfaced feelings of impatience and a sense of "this isn't working" in a way that working digitally did not. It made visible the hand doing the erasing, and made visible the gap between desire (what was imagined) and expression (what was enacted) that propels language and relationship).

p. 134

Biley (2016) uses the cut-up technique on health care texts; in one project, the researcher used a computer-generated cut-up of a short conference presentation on waking up from anesthesia after breast surgery. The resultant piece reads as a poetic transcript. The cut-up technique references manually or digitally cutting up text and rearranging it to create a new text (see Chapter 3 for examples).

In a series of collage poems about MotherWork composed from family artifacts, feminist research, and systematic recollections, I queer staid understandings of White middle-class mothering (Faulkner, 2017d). As I looked through photos my own mother gave me of family and found the not-finished scrapbook of my first 18 months, I wanted to make one for my own daughter as a kind of origin story. I never made a scrapbook of my daughter's first years, not even an attempt. I was too overwhelmed with the mother role, the expectations, and the physicality. My mother told me two children in diapers plus a five-year-old flummoxed her, and she spent her time digging a hole to breathe under a pile of dirty diapers. I juxtapose images and text from my unfinished baby book and my daughter's never begun baby book in a MotherWork scrapbook—two mothers, my mother and me, in conversation about the difficult business of never being a good enough mother. Most of the pieces I created in Photoshop, though one piece was an old-school erasure of feeding instructions with pen and stickers. I used photos, pediatrician penned instructions, my unfinished baby book, growth charts, feminist texts, sonogram photos, and autoethnographic poetry as the source material.

By re-presenting my experiences of early motherhood in collage that juxtaposes my experience and recollections with my own mother's (re)collections, I demonstrate the importance of particularized experiences in larger structures and conceptualizations of motherhood. The feminist texts, poetry, images, and poetic analysis I used to create an alternative baby book engages with Halberstam's (1998) idea of scavenger methodology.

A queer methodology, in a way, is a scavenger methodology that uses different methods to collect and produce information on subjects who have been deliberately or accidentally excluded from traditional studies of human behavior. The queer methodology attempts to combine methods that are often cast as being at odds with each other, and it refuses the academic compulsion toward disciplinary coherence.

p. 13

Taking an expected activity—scrapbook making—and queering it by naming the personal detritus of crafting as scholarship, as queer feminist praxis, and as cultural critique, blurs the lines between art, scholarship, and mothering. The baby book as queer enterprise refuses the binary of *mother* versus every other role. This project embraces the non-binary dialectic surrounding MotherWork, the dominant discourses of self-abnegation, breeding as feminine fulfillment, child as star in a mother's play, women as never good enough, and the marginalized discourses of mothering as painful, unfulfilling, and boring (see Baxter, 2011).

Collage lends itself to the spirit of scavenger methodology because of the juxtaposition of materials and ideas that seem incommensurable. For instance, in a chapter on queering sexuality education in family and school (Faulkner, 2018b), I use poetic collage as queer methodology by taking headlines of current events around women's reproductive health and justice, curriculum from liberal sexuality education, and conversations with my daughter about sex and sexuality to expand the idea of MotherWork and mother-poems.

> I engage with the meta-theoretical aspects of family talk about sex and sexuality education across seemingly disparate communication theory, models, and research traditions to allow broader understandings about communication and sexuality education than a reliance on one tradition provides: the use of my autoethnographic understandings of sexuality education in the form of dialogue with my daughter demonstrates reflexivity through the use of arts-based research methodology. The use of social science "research questions" to frame and push the poetic analysis shows critical engagement with literature on sexuality. The use of news headlines about sexuality connects personal experience about sexuality education to larger cultural issues.
>
> *Faulkner, 2018b, p. 26*

Poetic Inquirers may use collage as part of a larger research project. For example, I developed web-based material to accompany each chapter of the ethnography *Real Women Run* (Faulkner, 2018c) to present visual and aural aspects of the embodied fieldwork through sound and image in a public version of the ethnography (see Faulkner, nd). Using video, visual, and sound as components in this ethnography is a way to help readers think differently about women and running; it offers another nuanced layer of women's embodied experience of running. In addition, the soundscapes help present my embodied presence in this ethnographic project. The sounds of running—the noise, the grunts, the breathing, the encouragement, the disappointment—jog listeners through training runs, races, and the in situ embodiment of a sport women both enjoy and loathe (http://innovativeethnographies.net/realwomenrun). I used photos from races and my fieldwork along with audio and digital recordings of me running to make collage poems and a photo-essay. I crafted the photo-essay in iMovie using audio of races layered with my reading autoethnographic poems and text from the research.

The use of collage and hybrid work can also serve interdisciplinary research teams, allowing members to use their varied skills and talents. In an interdisciplinary activist project, The Women and Meth Project (www.womenandmeth.com), Sameshima, Vandermause, and Santucci (2012) used "multiple methods, media, and disciplines to provide broader, deeper understandings of the experience of methamphetamine addiction and recovery" in a reflexive inquiry (p. 188). They created and used an *Authentic Pedagogical Research Design* (APRD) focused on participants and researchers co-creating, reflecting, and engaging with research artifacts: The research team "deconstructs interview transcripts, codes, and collects salient phrases and aspect that resonate together. The team also collates key phrases and word collections, and renders these key collections into different forms (poetry, visual and digital art, narrative stories, videos, etc.)" (p. 190).

Sheila Squillante and I have been long time friends, writing collaborators, and feminist scholars. Needing to make feminist art in response to the 2016 US presidential election, we engaged in a collaborative multi-media poetry project titled *Nasty Women Join the Hive* (Faulkner & Squillante, 2018). I shared a poem about the inauguration.

> *On Inauguration Day*   *we leave our pink pussy hats home*
>
> Drape yourself in unmet resolutions,
> strap on your yak feet
> and cleat the ice scattered on sidewalk:
> Resolve to rush into the wind's season.
>
> Run where the trees have thrown off
> their bothersome fall clothes,
> hear the groan of bark on bark:
> Resolve to love with hot consent.
>
> Take the baby and throw him out
> with your dirty obligations,
> the dust balls and grit of un-mopped floors:
> Use your resolve like a steel to sharpen
>
> the needles of your feminist rage,
> knit the revolution in all hues of pink,
> wrap and turn the crooked stitches:
> Call a senator with bitchy resolve.
>
> Lick the cat clean with impatience
> as you drip cream cold from the carton
> into cheap, black coffee that tastes like work:
> resolutely step in your community walk.
>
> Always wash your ibuprofen down
> with two glasses of flat champagne

to taste the disappointment of stuck bubbles:
Resolve to dismember middle-class aches.

Throw an alcohol-free New Year's party
with too many balloons and stray kids
belch your affections into your apple cider,
you will need to be sober with resolve.

Let your food cake face and fingers
like this is your death meal,
eat without wiping your mouth:
Resolve to be a nasty woman every hour this year.

Sheila responded with a poem:

The Hive Responds

Friend, may I borrow your resolve?
I need it to feel more than frayed
and aching. My anger blooms but bruises

so easily. Spent and tender, it wilts
toward despair. I watch you
from my too-small space, hair

unwashed, face lit with flickering glow.
You scroll by, all muscle in motion
On my screen, you're signs sure and pink

And beseeching. *Wake forever
From this endless dull dumb sleep!*
I know what crowds sound like,

metallic thrum of three million
bees in the hive. I've seen parades go by.
I've seen my daughter stride down the sidewalk

to the stop, angry with more than just
her mother's loving limits. The world
wants to pin her wings to the wall. Listen,

my hair is falling out; creases deepen every day
around the stuck open scream of my mouth.
You can resist and resist and yet

still feel terror. You can weep while
you wield your best intentions, march
around your small city block. It's okay.

Grab your child by the hand and keep going.
Throw your fist in the air knowing it's just another
Word for *watch what happens when I open my palm.*

I knit 12 pink pussy hats for our local Women's Marches™. We played a game of Exquisite Corpse with themes of a Trump presidency—rape culture, misogyny, locker room talk, feminist response—and we used iMovie to create a womanifesta with text and poetry, images, video, and sound from the marches that considered how an intersectional feminism can be realized with a hive metaphor. At first, we didn't recognize the critique of pussy hats as equating women's rights to white, cis-gendered, able-bodied women's vaginas, the hats as a representation of White privilege; White women wearing pink hats and not acknowledging racism, body essentialism, and not listening to people of color, disabled, and trans★ rights activists. "We think about being White women. We think about being White feminists. We ask how we can be White feminists without White feminism" (Faulkner & Squillante 2018, p. 29). We used the critiques as part of a "call and response" and revised the piece by weaving in critiques of White Feminism as myopic and exclusionary with the symbolism of pussy hats and our own reflections on being White and feminist working toward being intersectional feminists. We crafted "A Womanifesto Invitation for White Feminists" (https://vimeo.com/230906797):

What if we leave our pink pussy hats home?

What if we listen?

What if we keep learning?

What if we

- recognize our role in allyship as one of active listening/ educating our peers?
- decenter White women?
- consider different women's experiences?
- acknowledge various realities?

Xiao, 2017

Eradicating white feminism is worth the growing pain.

Conclusion

This chapter focused on the similarities in goals and methods between poets and Poetic Inquirers, suggesting that the line between research and poetry and between science and art is blurry, and instead, may best be described as a collaborative and reciprocal enterprise. The doing of Poetic Inquiry through varied poetic forms including the lyric, narrative, long forms and poetry series, collaborative, and collage work allows researcher-poets to re-present, analyze, and show the context of their qualitative research with care, compassion, and an ethical stance. This work serves our epistemic and our aesthetic concerns, our representational and political aims, our bodies and our minds. Perhaps one of the most important aims for Poetic Inquirers is learning to live better lives by integrating the poet and the researcher, to give up feeling like "an inadequate poet and an inadequate scholar" (Leggo, 2012, p. 379). The academy needs poetry, and poetry needs researcher-poets.

The next chapter contends with issues of criteria and evaluation of Poetic Inquiry through a discussion of good and effective poetry, interviews with poets on successful poetry, *ars poetica* as one means of demonstrating attention to craft, and potential criteria by which we may evaluate Poetic Inquiry. I make the argument that a concentrated focus on craft issues promises to help us fulfill our poetic goals.

3

CONCERN WITH CRAFT

The Question of Poetic Criteria

I can't imagine poetry without criticism, or criticism without poetry.

Finch, 2005, p. 2

Concern with Craft: The Question of Poetic Criteria

If we want to write like human beings to communicate with other human beings, we need to develop our human voices. We need to show passion for what we write about, rejecting the impersonal voice and human-free zones of those who are afraid, or choose not, to reveal themselves as I or we.

Badley, 2019, p. 184

In this chapter, I wrestle with the questions of whether one should use criteria to evaluate Poetic Inquiry, and if so, what criteria would be appropriate for such an evaluation and why? I argue for the importance of considering criteria for Poetic Inquiry, and perhaps more importantly, I argue for a *willingness* to engage in dialogue about the creation and use of criteria as a concentrated focus on craft issues promises to help us fulfill our poetic goals. I present phenomenological interviews with 14 poets about craft issues, their practice of writing and teaching poetry, and ideas of good and effective poetry to pose these questions:

- What is "good" poetry used as/in qualitative research?
- What should Poetic Inquiry accomplish?
- How should we evaluate Poetic Inquiry?
- What does it mean to call poetry good or bad?
- Is there room for "good enough" poetry?

I offer ways to help us evaluate the merits of research poetry—the use of *ars poetica* (i.e., the art of poetry) and *ars criteria* poems as well as the application of poetic criteria—artistic concentration, embodied experience, discovery/surprise, conditionality, narrative truth, and transformation. Specifically, I present a discussion of the function and utility of *ars poetica* for poetic craft, a means of articulating one's own *ars poetica* and *ars criteria* poems, the implications of using poetic criteria, and the possibilities of *good enough poetry*.

Concern with Craft

Rigor Du Jour/De Rigueur

What is critical
rigor? Critical rigor?
Rigor? How do we ensure
it? Is it even possible?

What are the politics
of rigor? Why rigor? Why
rigor? Is there space

for non-rigor?

What does critical rig-
or   look like?
Is there a politics of rigor?
How do you embody

r   i   g   o   r
in your own work?
Who is responsible
for enforcing rigor?

Who are your favorite poets?
What is performance-based
rigor? What are the politics
of critique about non-rigor?

non-rigorous qualitative scholarship?
"What is good poetry?"
On what specifically, then,
should a poet concentrate?

What are they doing (in their poems)
that make you excited? Who
are your favorite researchers?
What (research) books are on your shelves

and why? What are they doing
(in their work) that makes you excited?
are you pushing yourself enough?
How are you going to tell about them?
Was my poetry that wretched?

The found poem, *Rigor Du Jour/De Rigueur*, ripe with questions of rigor and rigorous questions about qualitative research, introduces an ongoing dialogue about criteria and quality in qualitative work. I took the questions I used in the poem directly from a conference panel on "critical rigor in qualitative methods" at the 2015 International Congress of Qualitative Inquiry and the chapter on criteria and research poetry I wrote for the first edition of this text (Faulkner, May, 2015). These questions present the context and interrogation of my latest considerations of the role of rigor/criteria in qualitative research using ABR and poetry, in particular: I am working through the idea of applying criteria with rigor or adopting vigorous criteria. I have argued for quite some time about my strong belief in the importance of engaging in the debate over criteria while employing flexible criteria and demonstrating a concern with craft/method (e.g., Faulkner, 2007). I still believe in the importance of criteria for Poetic Inquiry, and perhaps more so given the increasing use of poetry in/as qualitative research in the past two decades (see Prendergast 2009; James, 2017). If poet-researchers are going to use poetry of all types in their work, we need a critical discussion about how we understand poetry, the process of using poetry in our research, and how poetry informs our work and scholarly endeavors. I believe these discussions will make our work better and help us accomplish our research, practice, and teaching goals.

My interest in poetic craft was born out of frustration with some poetry published as academic research that seemed sloppy, ill-conceived, and unconsidered. Just because research poetry is published in academic journals, read at academic conferences, or merely labeled academic, does not mean we should not consider poetic craft, especially when poets spend considerable time studying craft issues in an effort to further their aesthetics. When we consider the time that researchers invest in learning research methods, it seems that poet-researchers should study poetic craft with a similar intensity and not claim "poetic license" as a reason for unconsidered craft (cf. Cahnmann, 2003; Finch, 2005; Piirto, 2002). Or to state this in other ways: one poet I talked with about craft told me that "whatever you crap out is not a poem" and another iterated that "poetry isn't poetry until there's revision." It seems then that focusing on craft and believing in the power of revision are the first criteria for Poetic Inquirers. "The willingness, the ardent desire even, to revise separates the poet from the person who sees poetry as therapy or self-expression" (Tillinghast, 2001, p. 245). Finch (2005) argued that the idea of poetic inspiration has led to an unwillingness to revise or improve one's poems, and/or to read other poets because of a fear of damaging the inspiration, the idea of an unconscious poetic muse who can be capricious.

Of course, there are numerous poet-researchers who are intensely interested in the epistemic-aesthetic dialectic in this kind of work (e.g., Gingrich-Philbrook, 2005; Leggo, 2008a; Prendergast, 2006). Cahnmann (2003), for instance, claimed "If poetry is to have a greater impact on research, those engaged in poetic practices need to share our processes and products with the entire research community, and the terms of its use must be clearly defined" (p. 30). And in recent years, I have witnessed some Poetic Inquiry that in the words of Emily Dickinson, "blows the top of my head off." The actual quote found in a letter from Dickinson to Thomas Wentworth Higginson (1870, letter #342a) reads,

> If I read a book [and] it makes my whole body so cold no fire can ever warm me, I know *that* is poetry. If I feel physically as if the top of my head were taken off, I know *that* is poetry. These are the only ways I know it. Is there any other way?
>
> *Johnson, 1958, p. 474*

This is what I want our Poetic Inquiry to do and be.

What Makes (Good) Poetry Good

Poets contribute to the cultural, spiritual, and political health of society by writing well with music, passion, honesty, depth, and courage (Buckley & Merrill, 1995). To describe what makes an effective or good poem, however, is a seemingly impossible task; often the definitions are elusive, variable, and highly personal. Wiegers (2003) notes that poets thrive on being disagreeable, as is their nature, especially when arguing over questions of good poetry, bad poetry, and, even, over what constitutes poetry.

Poetic traditions and influences, aesthetic concerns, and definitions of what constitutes poetry differ, and often wildly so, demonstrating the quagmire of examining the idea of good and effective poetry. Tony Hoagland (2006) argued that "despite the usefulness of categories, in the blurry hybridities of aesthetic practice, many contemporary poems fall outside any designated bin" (p. 158). In a panel on relations among various contemporary poetries at the 2009 Associated Writers and Writing Program's (AWP) annual conference, poet panelists described the difficulty (and importance and fun) of engaging the connections and disconnections among different poetic schools, given the idea that schools represent such divergent aesthetics. What then is "good" poetry used as/in/for qualitative research and what should it accomplish? What can a study of poetic craft tell us about the aesthetic/epistemic dialectic in poetry as social research? What do poets and qualitative researchers consider important to their craft? The poet Katherine Soniat (1997), for instance, wrote about her desire to translate and reinvent archival texts she was using as inspiration for her poetry "without using the source verbatim" (p. 259). "I was becoming aware that if I read too closely, if I took notes as conclusive blocks of information, this poetic endeavor was doomed to the coldly encyclopedic and nothing more" (ibid.). This is an argument for using more than poetic transcription in our work as poet-researchers.

As I argued in the previous chapters, many researchers use poetic representation as a means to evoke emotional responses in readers and listeners in an effort to produce some shared experience between researcher, audience, and participant. The similarities in the goals are worth nothing: evocation, political action, understanding, connection, and emotionality. All of these researchers wish to evoke and create emotional connection through poetic means, goals that are similar to many poets. A studious concern with craft may further the poetic goals of writing research poetry and facilitate the connection between science and art. With this goal of intensely concentrating on poetics, I conducted in-depth phenomenological interviews with working poets about their conceptualizations of poetic craft. The specific question that I addressed through interviews was: How do poets perceive, describe, experience, and write good and effective poetry?

The Interviews

I used phenomenological interviews that explored the meaning and experience of "good poetry" (Moustakas, 1994). The purpose was to seek comprehensive descriptions or depictions of poets' experiences with reading, listening to, and writing good and effective poetry. I sought vivid, accurate, and comprehensive portrayals of what these experiences were like, including thoughts, feelings, behaviors, as well as situations, events, places, and people connected with poetic experiences. For example, I began the interviews by asking poets to think of a poem they considered to be good and what made it work. I audiotaped the interviews with permission; they ranged in length between one-and-a-half to three hours. The poets received transcriptions of the interviews to provide further comment and clarification.

I interviewed six women and five men ranging in age from 27–68 ($M=39$). All interview participants were published and working poets in that they actively wrote poetry, taught poetry, and/or sought publication for their poems as well as participated in poetry readings in various venues as poets and audience members. Their occupations included visual artist, former hospice nurse, director of arts programming (including writing) at a community center, instructor of poetry and composition, freelance writer, university vice president for marketing, former and current poetry editor of literary journals, and assistant director of an MFA program. Ten of the poets had an MFA (eight with an emphasis in poetry, one in fiction writing, and one in painting).

I read and reread each transcript, making notes about good and effective poetry and the poets' process of creating their own poetry. First, I marked every relevant passage and grouped the passages according to the experience, process, and descriptions of good and effective poetry. Next, I read through the passages, asking whether the moment was necessary to the experience and if there was a label that could be abstracted from it. I then clustered passages that were core themes of the experience. These core themes are represented in Table 3.1. For each participant, I wrote a textual-structural description of good and effective poetry (Moustakas, 1994).

Finally, I wrote a composite description of the essence and meaning of good and effective poetry that incorporated each poet's individual textual-structural descriptions. I present this description now.

Good and Effective Poetry

SLF: How do you teach what good poetry is?

PHIL: You bring good poems in to your students and try to get them to understand why you love them, contrast them as much as possible with bad poetry and get them to see it … If you're going to be the best jump shooter you do two things: you believe you can succeed and can take a shot whenever you get the ball, and you take lots and lots of jump shots. You work at it really hard. And I've known people who would say to themselves, "Oh, I don't think my poems affect other people." Or "I don't think my poems change the way people think about anything." Well, if you believe that how can you possibly be a great poet? How could you write a poem that I think is important by my criteria if you don't think it even matters? You have to set yourself up to succeed in a way, too. You have to be willing to be good, whatever that means. You have to say, "I'm going to write a really good poem about this, and then sit down and do it—and do the work and think, and then somehow get that onto the page."

Phil, lines 410–412, 449–454

Deep Suspicion

The more I know about poetry, the more gun-shy I am to come up with statements regarding it. If you had interviewed me when I first started writing seriously, I would have all these absolutes: Good poetry does this and good poetry does that. And the weirdest thing is now that I'm, I don't even want to say more established, but now that I'm more into it and I take it even more seriously and I've been doing it longer, I'm more reticent to be like, good poetry does this or good poetry does that.

Matt, lines 651–657

Like many of the other poets I talked with, Ruth expressed great difficulty (and reluctance and suspicion) with providing a list of definitive statements describing

TABLE 3.1 Core themes of "good" poetry

Poet	Themes
Marian	authentic, courageous and accessible, connectedness "That's what poetry is to me. It's an invitation into a moment to see what choices that poet has made at that time to honor that moment."
Farah	dialectics of ideal-real, creating-revising, emblematic "My goal is to use that (my experience) to get at something larger that more people can access—not knowing who I am and what are all the sort of things in my life that have led up to that experience or have come out of that experience—to make that experience some kind of emblem."
Phil	pushes and hones a poet's instincts, high stakes "There's a lot of effective poetry that's entertaining and wonderful in its own way, but really good poetry is risky business."
Sheila	fragmentation, discovery, the ineffable "That's what's great about poetry—it's all about words, but it's all about putting to words what you can't put into words somehow. You shouldn't be able to do this but when you can do it or when other people can do it, that's why it's so moving."
Christof	mystery, being, authenticity "There's a level at which you have to be inarticulate when you're talking about poems because I think that you can't reduce a poem to the parts that make it effective. I don't think its science at all. Either there is truly an essential mystery there or not."
Kim	visceral, daily practice, physically fit: "A good poem starts in your stomach and moves to your head."
Karen	big new ideas stated simply, good physique: "Every letter, every syllable, every word has an exact purpose and almost no other would do. So, a good poem has to have that. It has to have a certain musicality for me, a big idea, for lack of a better phrase. I keep coming back to it. You don't say ah-ha over little ideas."
Matt	good lies, fully rendered imaginary space "The visual really makes a poem … I tend to gravitate away from more cerebral poets because they're abstract … If you can reify those ideas into an image, I'm interested."
Dan	surety of voice, poetic presence, imagined reality "A good poem should combat ignorance with mystery."
Gabe	deep suspicion, memorable "I know I've heard a good poem when I can remember all of it. Maybe not the words, but I can remember 'well he started talking about this, maybe she moved into that, there was this one image.' If someone can read a poem that I can remember, in some cases, years later."
Ruth	engages the human condition "A good poem has something that is said in a way that gives us insight we haven't had before, or it invites us in to participate in an emotional way or makes us see the world again; we learn to see in art and in poems."

a good poem. However, she shared a list of questions she gave to students when teaching a drawing class as a way to think about innovation as part of a good poem: "Did it answer the problem? It should if you set yourself up. Did it look like nothing needed to be added or removed? Is it saying something? If it is simple, is it saying it in an innovative way?" Ruth described the innovative by providing an example in a poem by Ted Kooser that described washing dishes. There is an image of a grandmother throwing dishwater out of the back door that made Ruth think about washing the dishes as something new again. This newness is one standard she uses to determine good poetry, given the difficulty of having any objective standards. A poet should use visuals that put the audience there, in the poetic situation, so that the abstract becomes tangible and part of the audience's experience.

> Love, beauty, joy, terror. They don't mean anything, don't give a picture or suck you in. What you are doing (in a poem) is shooting a film in order to put people there. So think of film, close in, what are you seeing? Say great big red roses with petals falling off rather than pretty roses.
>
> *Ruth, lines 54–57*

Because a poet often falls in love with their latest work, Ruth suggested letting it lie fallow for a while before making any judgment. In addition, having another poet or critic assess one's work seems warranted, given the difficulty of judging and the need for suspicion when considering the merit of one's own work.

Gabe also felt poets should be deeply suspicious of their own work, especially if they have the feeling they are on to something and are making important claims. "Step back because that's often when you're failing. It's when you're most conflicted and you're outside your comfort zone that maybe you're actually saying something that's worth saying." The process entails knowing you have something worth saying and determining whether a poem is revisable. He likened recognition of the revisable to driving someplace you've never been; you begin to see signs and think "it has to be around here somewhere." That feeling is key:

> You've done all the driving but you don't really know you're going to get there until you're almost there. I think if you find yourself being afraid to come back to it or spending way too much time with it, that's also an indication.

Dan knows one of his poems is good if he experiences surprise and discovery at what he has written when going back to it after a few weeks. Though he labeled himself a "tinkerer" and often revises and rewrites poems, even after they are published, he obsesses about going for the right lines and words to capture the urgency of voice. "Knowing when I've written well has a lot to do with how much work I've put into the poem, how many drafts I've gone through ... I'm suspicious of poems that come off after one or two drafts." He composes poems by hand in spiral-bound notebooks as a way to slow down because he expressed that a bad poem was the poet's fault and not the poem's fault. "I compose longhand, because I really believe in the poem as a handmade object. A person with a pen and some paper made the poem, and that's hand-crafted." Everything in the poem should belong, should form a web: "It should all hang together without any loose ends or anything that isn't going to contribute to the whole."

An editor or a peer's estimation may increase one's confidence in a good poem, the way a complement on your shirt may cause you to wear it more often. A good poem speaks to tradition; others recognize experiences and "common appreciations" in a poem, such as the description in parts of Gabe's poem, *Pennsylvania* (Welsch, 2006, pp. 13–14):

> The state with the prettiest name
> and the ear of an ancient ridge—
> its runnel of stone cluttered
> with the wet trees that hold taut
> the devastating brown in winter,
> the state with air cluttered by the noise
> of more miles of road
> than any other state, its cities
> rarified by steel and freedom—//
> the state where to talk of soup is to talk
> of God and Sunday bundling and bazaars
> through the countryside and gravestones
> laid over with flags and begonias—
> the state with pierogi sales and funnel cakes
> and cheesesteaks and soft pretzels
> and the ruddy faces of corpulent railroaders—//
> We hear robins in the laurel, semis
> jake-braking into town.
> the sudden snap of deer hooves
> on tomato stakes. And always,
> highways building and seething
> with our weight, pushing on limestone,
> building and building on this softening ground.

Gabe cited this poem as good because it had been anthologized; he was the first to talk about Pennsylvania this way, and he tapped into common understandings of the state. "It responds to the poetic tradition while trying to expand it, and it has an unexpected twist in it … It's not just experimentation for experimentation's sake."

Gabe reflected on one difference he saw between social scientists and poets:

In one way, there are the researchers for whom the art is a secondary matter to the representation versus those people for whom the art is the primary and representation is secondary.

For Gabe, the poetry writing process means to first consider the art and enter the artistic dialogue; only later does he consider the subtext or epistemic concerns and audit for authenticity or genuineness. His poems about Pennsylvania are indicative of this process.

It was sort of, "I know what's out there. I'm going to grab it [the image of a foundry] even though I haven't yet experienced it," which may be something that flies in the face of some social science commitments, right? It's not representative if you haven't yourself experienced it, or your subject hasn't spoken about it. Again, in my case, because the art was first and foremost, and I wanted to enter into that dialogue, I took that image.

Narrative Connectedness

So, that's how I know a poem is authentic, when I feel like I'm a member of this community, this reaching out.

Marian, lines 15–16

Marian considers a good poem to be one that is authentic, courageous, and accessible; it shouldn't solely entertain her but rather highlight her discomfort with her own insecurities "because I'm invited into a community where I'm not alone. Where the poet is, obviously, searching for something. And I'm not looking for an answer, but I'm looking for somebody to travel with." She suggested *Healing the Mare* by Linda McCarriston (1991) as representative of a good poem because of the process of sense-making that occurs. The narrator in the poem describes her care for an injured mare as a way to understand her own abuse as a child: "As I soothe you I surprise wounds/of my own this long time unmothered." The description of making sense of the past was vital to Marian's contemplation of authenticity. The reader witnesses the transition through the past with a show of courageous vulnerability that Marian defined as "a self-imposed sensitivity and the ability to fear, anguish, angst, pain." This vulnerability honors a moment and represents "a tool that you can use to connect those dots from the past to the present to the future." The experience may not mirror every reader's experience, but it works because "It helps you to look back and see your own helplessness and you find yourself in that journey."

Authenticity is someone else's voice reaching you and mirroring your own experiences, even if the experiences are not identical. At some point others may remember a poem and link the experience to something in their own lives, and this is especially important for creating a sense of connection. As Marian stated, McCarriston was white, Irish, born in Boston, and she herself was Black. But both of them were struggling with getting respect and acceptance for who they were from others without becoming victims. Good poetry makes a connection to fear—the basic emotion—fear of being the other, learning to not fear others. Poets who can address this fear in their work accomplish authenticity by writing "from the place that doesn't want to be written," going to "where it hurts. Even if you have to go back to the time when you were personally humiliated." Marian considered this connection to fear as not giving in to victimhood; it is altering an experience by witnessing it in the present with courage: "You can go back, revisit that as a witness, and stand beside that little girl. And that is really being authentic, that little girl reaches her hand to you and you reach back. And that's how I have found my authentic voice." Ruth described the idea of connectedness as a shiver she gets when someone says something beautifully. She feels charmed by language used in new and expressive ways. "It is like watching a diver jump off a high dive board and hit the water without a splash. They make it look easy." She suggested that a poet who can do this allows the audience to feel a connection, to realize that an experience is not just singular. "It is human. The poet takes you into the moment so well that it calls the same feelings you have had in your life, and you realize this is the human condition." A good poem uses authenticity to reach out to and nourish the reader. It provides courage to keep walking, to take another step toward fear, and to keep going. Showing vulnerability as an honest human experience is important in this wrestling with fear as it lets us know that we are strong and have the power to be strong even in our weak moments. Marian said:

> And even on the days I don't want to be forgiving, I can even harness the anger, even the rage, that then propels me forward into action to help my granddaughter to be a young kid of color who has pride and self-esteem. So, these are the things that really help me, everyday. And I couldn't do it without this good poetry.
>
> *lines 51–56*

And the good poem keeps us coming back again and again. In the process, the poet does not sink to the ugliness, even if she describes the ugly in her work. This writing from pain and hurt allows a poet to use the experience both as a mirror to help others who otherwise may ignore an incident a poet writes about and to be less fearful themselves.

For Christof also, a good poem is one where the poet is authentic. The speaker is "telling me something, and I'm supposed to believe … I buy the speaker, period." He articulates this idea even further by comparing an inauthentic poem to a bad movie: "You watch a movie and just so painfully you can't suspend disbelief at all because the characters are made out of cardboard." An inauthentic poem brings out the reader's critic, whereas an authentic experience is "either invading your world or you've been invited to invade that world. It doesn't make any difference. In any case, the wall has been torn down. You are no longer looking through a glass or a window at something." Christof cited Frost's poem, *Directive*, as authentic because of the experience of reading it, being excited about the language use. "You're actually physically and metaphorically walking back into this town that is abandoned. And he takes you through that place. You see the little, discarded doll." The authentic poem is a complete experience; it doesn't just start and end power-fully, but it "creates a space that is the most exciting space for me to live in." What constitutes an authentic experience is when a reader finds a poem interesting.

Sheila likened good poetry to a punch in the stomach or, after Emily Dickinson, something that blows the top of your head off and stays with you through life. She first articulated this conceptualization of good poetry during her MFA program and cited Robert Hayden's *Those Winter Sundays* as one of the first poems she encountered that engendered this reaction for all of the reasons—rich imagery, musicality, and conciseness—she learned poetry should be good:

> In that poem it's the image of the father's hands, these large worker's hands, callused, cracked from manual labor, juxtaposed with this family life and doing these kind things for sleeping children, and a sleeping wife, perhaps. This tenderness is not sentimentalized, it's not obvious, it's just understated and there. Restraint is important to me.

She considered restraint to be saying "something without over explaining it, without descending into pathos" and the expected anticipated ending. Robert Hayden, Richard Hugo, Philip Levine, and James Wright accomplished this restraint in their work through a sense of authenticity, describing a working-class life. The draw for Sheila was the connection she felt to poetry her father would have liked even though the working-class background didn't represent her experi-ence. Authenticity, which she considered to be a horrible term because of its impreciseness and overuse, is about detail and observation and painting a place and the people inside a place; it begins with small details that start a moment.

Psychological and Emotional Effect

> What I'm looking for in a poem that I seldom find are big ideas and some-thing that strikes an emotional chord that kind of resonates. And that poem has very simple words, and the ideas are even simple, but surprising.
>
> *Karen, lines 21–23*

The grunt, gasp, exclamation "oh" or "hum" that follow a performance of a poem are typical reactions to a poem, especially because we can't produce a set of prose sentences that can exactly expose the meaning.

> Poetry is made of words. But the best poetry makes you speechless. And we have to talk about it, and every word you want to use is in the poem. The words you use are not as good as the poem.
>
> *Rita Dove, 2018*

Describing a poem may be like trying to describe music; the sonorous qualities are almost ineffable though the words may sound very similar to their meaning. There exists a tension between the explication and the disposition. According to Farah, this may be just the strength of poetry: the tension between explaining emotions that arise from a poem, what it generates and the feeling present in someone. Farah provided the example, *In the Garden*, by Louis MacNeice where he used shorter lines and rhyme at the end of one line and the beginning of the next to create an effect like dancing. This is appropriate because the poem concerns a dancer leaving her husband. "And it's just amazing to me that sound can sort of mimic an action. Or that sound can mimic something more vague or hard to pin down, which is like an emotion or psychological state."

Poetic tensions played out in Farah's conceptualization of the writing process as writing vs. analysis and ideal vs. real. She talked of a cycle of despair at not having enough time to write, being afraid to write, not writing daily, and fighting against classic ideas of what it means to be a poet. A poet sits down and writes every day, reads deeply and carefully, and imitates good writers.

> That's partly what makes me feel like a beginning writer. I'm still finding that part out about where it fits in, how it fits in, and how I make it a priority, even among these other competing priorities. And I feel like I have a lot to learn about. I mean I can talk about a good poem when you set a poem in front of me. I can say a little bit about why I think it's more or less effective than this other poem that you sat in front of me, but when you try to do it, it's kind of a different story.
>
> *Farah, lines 480–486*

The difficulty for Farah was not having consistent feedback from a group of people focused on her writing and the expectation of writing regularly as in her MFA program. She described a difference between brainstorming and "being a poet" as when she is being a poet she thinks in iambic rhythm. This marks a difference in writing and critique/analysis of poems. The necessary revision process, which is often not part of the conceptualization of what doing poetry means, requires balancing daily activities like cleaning the house with revising poems, selecting poems for a book, and sending them out for publication. When it doesn't happen, she doesn't feel like a poet. The former poet laureate, Rita Dove (2018), said that writing every day is like an athlete exercising to keep in shape: "It's as unromantic as doing your sit-ups."

Good poems have structure and are memorable while mediocre poems sound similar because of worn-out language that stands in for emotion. Farah contended that every word in a good poem is necessary, whereas in a mediocre poem you can rearrange words and achieve the same effect. With a memorable poem "you walk away, and you still have a distinct sort of sense of that poem as an individual poem whereas mediocre poems tend to sound the same after awhile." A good poem is one that is memorable, maybe even years later. Gabe cited Galway Kinnell's poem about oatmeal as one that is memorable because of the specifics, the construction of the poem, the images, resonate comparisons (the relation to a personal experience), and the hinge (where a poem takes off in a surprising direction). This is a feeling of not having wasted your time, especially when you have been to many poetry readings. Gabe described the experience as recognizing things you haven't been doing in your own work:

> The other thing that I feel in addition to relief is satisfaction. It's hard to say what one because often times you'll feel sad or happy depending on what the poem wants you to feel. I think in the aggregate after those feelings, I just feel satisfied. I often feel, inspired is not the right word, stirred, I guess. I'll leave a poetry reading feeling really good, and I'll feel like so many things are justified now. It's a very affirming quality to a reading that goes well.
>
> *Gabe, lines 112–117*

Gabe acknowledged a difference between hearing a poem and reading one on the page. Some poems may not be meant to be read aloud; there may be a character who is not a voice but the subconscious. Therefore, a conscious performance of it can be strange. His preference is for voice. One test of whether a poet is good is whether he buys the book: "I feel a call to action and that call to action may not always be to sit down and write. It may not always be to go and proclaim to the world. Sometimes it may just be I want to go for a walk, now."

Farah argued that the language in a good poem can be fun, as in experimental, but there must be a strong emotional or psychological thread through

> how the poem sets me up for its ending or how the poem sets me up for understanding the moment that the poem is trying to convey. And it tends to work for me in imagery and sound, sometimes through repetition.
>
> *lines 279–282*

A good poem begins in an experience, but it pushes beyond to be "some kind of emblem." One way to do this is to write a series of poems using different perspectives. The goal is to get beyond one particular experience, e.g., "poor me," and to examine parts of the experience that matter to be successful at confessing in poetry. This involves a tension between the specific and the universal. The dialectics of the poem are represented in the particular, not the commentary, and make a reader surprised to recognize a part of human experience they "didn't think of in that way before." Tony Hoagland (2006) echoed this sentiment: "I love poems that locate, coordinate, and subordinate, that build up a compound picture of the world. These poetic properties—of attention, proportion, and relationality—I have come to think of as Thingitude and Causality" (p. 164).

Skating just short of sentimentality is another way to conceive of making the connection between the specific and the universal. Former poet laureate, Ted Kooser (2005), cited a letter he wrote to the late Richard Hugo expressing admiration of his poems that skirted on the edge of sentimentality without falling over the edge. Farah likes poems that offer some kind of dialectic between happiness and darkness. An example of this would be her series of poems about marriage where she had incorporated some philosophical writings against the existence of God, and used that to juxtapose the exciting and decidedly boring everyday details of being married. The poems are intended to get beyond "a really bad day my husband and I had" to examine the larger role of marriage.

Pushing the Boundaries

> American poetry still largely believes, as romantics have for a few hundred years, that a poem is a straightforward autobiographical testimony to, among other things, the decency of the speaker ... Welcome to Poetry City: hurt someone's feelings—go to jail.
>
> *Hoagland, 2006, p. 197*

The frustration with too much niceness in poetry can be seen when Phil described good poetry as challenging to others, as that which can hurt feelings because "the stakes are high."

> Can you write the poem that's going to make your mother weep? ... And not because you hate your mother, not your mom who you can't stand who would never let you do anything you want to do and you don't want to be around and haven't spoken to in ten years ... But your mom who does everything for you [and] who you love talking to and adore, and you know these poems will upset her. Can you push hard enough on your work to do that because it's something you believe in and something you want to write, a story you think has to be told? And push hard enough to accomplish what you hope to accomplish with it, not let yourself off.

A good poem addresses large issues—death, silence, absence, and loss—though Phil quoted a former teacher who felt that of the four subjects in poetry, it was all about death once you examined it, regardless of what subject matter a poet claimed. Phil felt frustrated with some contemporary poetry where groups of poets are "writing about absolutely nothing" and just "fucking around with words"; a poem about your pet rat better be more than a poem about a pet rat.

This is why Phil cited Bridget Pegeen Kelly as a great poet: "Her poems are never just about the fact that her kid happened to have a funny little story she (the poet) told to him. They're about that and the end of the world."

Phil differentiated between an effective poem, a good poem, and great poem: "A good poem has to be effective, but an effective poem doesn't have to be good." "Effective" was a pejorative label according to Phil, a way to show faint praise; the effective poem works by getting across its meaning through the use of poetic sound, music, and metaphor: "It's not archaic. It has some modernity about it. It's a decent piece of work." Contrast this with the notion of a good poem as one that gives you "goose bumps," makes you smile and you can't stop smiling at the mastery as you read it, and at least, in some small way, it changes your thoughts about the poem's subject matter so that you can't look at it in "the same way again."

> I know a poem is really good when … the feeling I have in my stomach is the way I felt the night I was lying awake in my bed when I first seriously thought to myself, there's probably not really a God, is there?

A good poem is one that you come back to again for many years as opposed to an effective poem which you may read once and forget about it.

In a "really good poem by a really good poet," we will go along with whatever the poet does in the poem, such as squirrels falling from the sky, quipped Phil. This typically occurs near the end when "the poet's done their work and the rhythm is that compelling and the music of the words is compelling and whatever the poem has done thematically or metaphorically is that compelling that anything will work." In his own work, Phil has started to look for the point where he can "take the turn" to stop talking about the incident or content of the poem and begin to talk about the "big issue." In his poem, *You Are Worth Many Sparrows*, Phil (Memmer, 2008, pp. 72–73) believed he managed this as the poem begins with "a tremendously straightforward and banal, daily incident and turns it into something much more serious and important by the time you get to the end of the poem."

> At least there's this—
> I saw the blown-down sparrow's nest
>
> before I could mow it under.
> And though the two surviving birds
>
> would certainly die—barn cats
> or owls, if not the cold—
>
> at least I could carry them
> one by terrified one
>
> to the bushes edging the yard.
> Then I returned where their sibling lay

stiff in the maggoty weave,
and flinging it deep in the meadow

thought of what Matthew and Jesus said
about sparrows ... *sold for a farthing,*

and one of them shall not fall
without your Father. Hope

was the lesson—a person's
worth many sparrows—

but even with our Father
sparrows fall, many of them,

and depending on what you fear
He wills it, or fails

to stop it, or fails
to exist. Old arguments,

each one. There are others,
I'm sure. Whichever is true,

I like to think of the chicks
in my cupped palm—so small

even Jesus believed
they were meaningless—

and how they clawed at my fingers,
beating their half-finished wings.

We matter that much. We matter
that much, at the least.

The question for Phil is "how do you keep that going at the same sort of linguistic pace as the rest of the poem? Because that's the hard thing to do." A poem shouldn't sound didactic or too overtly philosophical with "tiresome explanations." Phil asserted that a poem must move us on several different levels, like Bridget Kelly's work, with

> surprising twists you'd never expect, things early on in the poem that seem
> just like wonderful details (that) turn out to be very important metaphors
> by the time you get to the end, but they creep up on you in marvelous ways.
>
> *lines 257–260*

The goal is to have a fun and interesting poem so that you can tell the audience the philosophy "and hope the rhythm will support it at that point." You get the audience to connect through the specific details of the poem and the universality to allow a few lines of telling.

The process of writing a good poem requires much work and knowledge, some luck, a trust in one's artistic instincts, and the ability to self-edit. Phil claimed that anybody could get their poems published with persistence, given the number of literary journals, but a good poet has to be willing to be good. Poets need to learn what they think is good, find their own way of writing and be able to "just know" when they've written a good poem.

> That's the secret in a way. You learn what not to throw out … the other way you write good poems is you hate your work to some extent. You keep working on it until you can't hate it anymore. A poet constantly questions the self and finds the balance between pushing hard and trusting the poetic process.
>
> *lines 297–299*

For Kim, it is important to find a reader of your poems who understands your aesthetic, but is critical enough to tell you when you are not pushing hard enough, are taking the easy way out, and what parts of the poem are superfluous to what it is truly about. Hoagland (2006) argued that we should hone the icy eye of a prosecutor in order to stop "the decay of fierce analytical thinking in our poetry" (p. 197).

Fragmentation/Flux/The Ineffable

"Each of us who writes must find a balance between restraint and expressions of feeling" (Kooser, 2005, p. 57).

Farah cited the ineffable quality of poetry, not often understanding why something gets chosen for publication and the difficulty of judging effectiveness, as the mark of a beginning poet. However, she considered a poem to be good if she could solve some technical problem or had a feeling of having accomplished something in the poem. "I was writing sonnets for awhile, so if I could write a sonnet that would fit the form, had a turn where it was supposed to have a turn, had rhymes, then I was like, 'oh, that seems good.'" Some of the difficulty in judging effectiveness stemmed from a shift in her criteria, maybe even a radical shift, after being in an MFA program and her formal study of poetry.

> I've read a little bit more, thought a little bit more about other aspects of poetry. Then when I look back on that other thing, where I was maybe trying to accomplish something in terms of form, and then I'm looking at it in terms of word choice. Then suddenly, that part doesn't feel like it's working.
>
> *lines 436–440*

Hoagland (2006) calls this self-consciousness "the necessary border crossing of craft, skill, and even of poetic ambition" (p. 62).

Sheila described her aesthetic of good poetry as in flux and bifurcated since the advent of motherhood and increasing daily responsibilities.

> My brain is broken in a profound way since having a child … I'm literally fragmented in my days because I'm trying to do a hundred things at once … I feel in chaos all the time … I tend to write, now, poems that are really fragmented. If there's a narrative, it's a broken narrative. It's a submerged narrative. It's not a narrative that's overt. It's certainly not a narrative that is identifiable as from my life. I've written a lot of collage poems since becoming a mother that are really just—I hate that word just—they are, among other things, exercises in language.
>
> *lines 175–184*

She argued that you know good poetry when you see it after years of training, having seen and read and practiced. This is the way to earn the right to bifurcation or the use of whatever works (i.e., method or school of poetry). In this spirit, Sheila hasn't put aside those previous "blow the top of my head off poets," but she doesn't return to them or confessional/narrative poetry as often. Good poetry shows a truth that the audience immediately knows and recognizes as if they had written the lines, but concomitantly it demonstrates that you "write what you're willing to discover" like the poet Yusef Komunyakaa urges. Sheila tells her students to go beyond the "old creative writing maxim: Write what you know." This is emphasized by teaching her students the importance of language and its impact, and using the advice of a former teacher who "gave her poetry in a real way" by saying he wanted poems or lines from poems you could take and put on a T-shirt.

Even though Sheila described a change in her conception of good poetry, she argued that narrative was still vital because poetry has to connect to humans and the body or it's worthless. For her, this meant changing the way she approached language and narrative in poetry. Whatever a poet does that is different for her can be labeled experimental, regardless of the form.

> So I've returned in some ways to language as a primary engine for my poetry, as opposed to a secondary engine. It was always that narrative was first, narrative was the driving force and language was important. I wanted to make sure the language was complimenting the narrative, but now I'm sort of doing it in an opposite way.
>
> *lines 186–192*

Hoagland (2006) considers the use of collage and juxtaposition as a way to create more participation in the audience. They may have to work more to discern meaning. Sheila considered her interest in collage poetry now as one of discovery and surprise and invocation of the ineffable without using clever tricks such as the poet turns out to be a barking dog at the end of a poem.

> I don't like to be told anymore … I don't prefer directness in a certain way now in poetry … It's because my life isn't direct anymore. I don't have ready answers for anything anymore. It used to be my project, truly, in poetry to try to make sense of my life and of the world because my growing up years were chaotic … but now making beautiful things is not as important to me as making interesting things.
>
> *lines 319–324*

The audience should sense layered meanings and want to return to the poem; there is something more than entertainment. Sheila asked: "Why would you want your audience to read your poem and say, wow, good poem and put it down and never return to it?" She warns not to show the audience something they already know like a Kincaid painting of cozy cottages: "The minute the poet makes her or his project to capture something in that way, I think you've failed as a poet."

Flexing the Poetry Muscle to Get a Good Physique

> Until you put boundaries on something you limit your own ability. You [don't] give readers, the potential recipients of your art … any means of understanding. Some people sniff at accessibility. Well, fine, I guess I'm hanging my hat strongly on the side of the fence that says accessibility is okay. It doesn't mean you're dumb.
>
> *Gabe, lines 196–201*

A good poem provides aesthetic pleasure, according to Dan. He quoted Robert Pinksy who considered the human body to be the medium and instrument of poetry. As such, the experience of a good poem is an adrenaline rush, perhaps like sleep deprivation or oversleeping, over or undereating. The aesthetic pleasure manifests in the feelings reading a poem provides—the way your foot moves, your tongue, and the breaths you take, the sounds.

> For me it's sort of a breathlessness, a wordlessness, a silence, pleasant contemplation. Almost a feeling of not wanting anything but those words, not wanting to explain them … Even if you don't understand them completely, (not) going to the dictionary to look them up is simply sort of abiding with the words. Enjoying the silence around them. A good line of poetry … I don't need anything but that line.

Kim exhorts a poem to be "physically fit"; it doesn't outwardly say anything but shows what it needs to say by using a turn or moment of emotional change and understanding. For a reader, the poem begins with a visceral reaction in the stomach like "a little butterfly when someone surprises you when you're reading" and then moves to an intellectual understanding of how the poem works. Kim, like Sheila, cited *Those Winter Sundays* by Robert Hayden as an illustrative poem to show beginner poetry students. "It is absolutely a tight working body. It is, as I like to say, a physically fit poem. Seriously, there's no flab on that poem anywhere." She uses this poem to appeal to students' hearts first through a relatable clear moment, and then they feel it using their heads to explore the formal background and how "it speaks to its predecessors ... (and) also makes way for the future in a very specific way with the realism." A good poem is like the development of love: "It starts in your gut when you see them walk across the room. I think when you see the poem walk across the room, and you fall in love with it, then you start to care how it's made." The poem's words have multiple meanings, specifically the description of the "blueblack" cold, which emphasizes bruises in an angry household, bitter weather, and hard sounds like chronic anger. Importantly, the poem takes a turn, like all good poems in the English language, changing from what it was originally to something else.

> It's an imaginative leap ... it's the moment where you leave behind the intellectual and make the bridge to the next thing that happens, and that is often why poems are so hard to paraphrase. Because the turn is inexplicable, it defies logic often, it moves to something else, something that's emotional or visceral but not intellectual. Sometimes it can be intellectual, but it has to be emotional on some level or it doesn't matter.

The academic or intellectual part of poetry is not as interesting to Kim because of her approach to poetry. "For me in poetry, it's as daily as laundry. You read some poems, you do some laundry, you clean your dishes, and it makes sense then that you do everything sort of the same way." She talked about flexing the poetry muscle as a daily occurrence, and she tells her students to always be thinking or percolating ideas for writing poems and understanding poems previously read. She tells them to think of this as making a toolbox of what works in good poems, so that they can use them in their daily lives (e.g., wedding toasts). "It's only when you think it's good that you respond to it and go back and think about how to keep it for yourself." Annie Finch (2005) echoed this argument with her call to beginner poets to learn the tools of poetic repetition (e.g., meter, rhyme) in order to bring poetry out of the province of the ineffable into their daily lives as writers. Kim doesn't write every day, but she believed that the planning or idea generation for a poem occurs days before the writing process. And poems have a way of coming out, even if it is through "weird dreams." This approach may be because Kim considered most poets to be beginning ones until they die since in writing and teaching one is never good enough. Therefore, all poets need to train themselves. "If you don't push the metaphor, if you don't try to tighten the story then you're never going to get good at it."

This honing of poetic instincts occurs by reading (and reading and reading), and then by studying a few poets who are great, understanding what they do specifically in their work. For Phil, the poets Bridget Kelly, Robert Frost, Emily Dickinson, and Charles Wright are the poets he can't live without and to whom he compares his own work. "I really think of myself as writing for all the great, dead masters that came before me that I admire tremendously and would want to have respect my company." Another way to learn to trust poetic instinct is not to fight against daily demands by panicking if you haven't written in three months. "I can have anything else going on in the world and if it's time for a poem to come out, I'll figure out a way to get it done." Phil fits writing in when it can happen; he often props a poem on the dashboard when driving to and from work (poeming and driving!). The trust in poetic instincts helps his writing.

> What ends up happening a lot is that because I take so many breaks in the process of writing a poem, it helps those twists and turns happen. One thing I try to do is never stop at the end of a complete sentence … if I'm going to stop writing for the day, I stop in the middle of a sentence. At the end of a line, but maybe with a stanza break coming up next. So, not only do I not know what's going to happen next, but anything could happen next.

An important part of the intellectual work of poetry is to find the form that works for the poet's project. As Kim stated, "the poem is always personified. Like if the poem wants that form, you give it to it." For instance, if you want to talk about loss a pantoum may work "because for every step forward there are two steps back" which often mirrors the process of loss in our lives. In her own work, Kim described a recent series of prose poems that use this form to accentuate the scene, characterization, and story, but not necessarily the technique. She considered the prose form as a way to help keep a reader focused on the scene.

> It's a nugget. It's like a big wad of words on the page and you pick it up and you read it. And I didn't want people pausing, necessarily. I didn't want the breaks of the lines, I wanted the continuity of the prose poem because that way you would stay in the story and wouldn't get bounced out.

A poem has to "justify the skin that it's in." Even though Gabe, like others quoted in this chapter, decried empty experimentation, he also described the idea of a good poem as one that works within set boundaries for a form. The good poem moves; it's playful, brave within form, and able to sustain itself, especially in a longer form. However, it ceases to be poetry when the form is no longer serving the poem, when the form takes over. This use of form also pays homage to the poetic tradition, those who came before and with whom one is in conversation at present.

A good poem has "big new ideas stated simply." It says exactly what it means, but there is also an exciting "jumping off point." Karen considered simply describing or telling what happened in a poem, like a still life, and expecting the reader to bring the big idea to the table as not indicative of good poetry. "I like a big, philosophical one-two punch, I guess. I want there to be something to mull over." Yet, a good poem contains simple language and is not high-blown; the ideas may be difficult but a poet needs to use accessible language. Karen discussed *The Rain* by Robert Creeley as an example of a good poem because of the way his language surprises her and makes her think of the rain in new ways.

> I guess I haven't thought about it in quite that way before. And I don't even know if I think about the rain that way. The fact that he does, I kind of link up to different things that make me feel decent and innocent and happy. So, I guess I could see rain doing that, but I can (also) think of a lot of other things that make me feel like *I'm wet with a decent happiness.*

A good poem then resonates with someone's experience, even if not directly. The idea is that a poet should make something new, "as Ezra Pound suggested … saying something we haven't heard before."

Karen mused that a good poem may be something separate from a poem that a person likes thus complicating our discussion of what constitutes good poetry.

> It's sort of a trap to think you recognize a good poem. Like there's something that exists in the world that is a good poem that is different than a poem that you like. Because I know I've liked a lot of poems that others would probably consider bad poems. Consider Billy Collins, who, a lot of people think he's just a big hat, but I think he's wonderful.

Karen continued by stating that Collins does build poetry that can stand up to critique and that reveals something meaningful. Kim had similarly suggested that most poets wouldn't acknowledge that they have a narrow version of what constitutes good poetry, ruling out entire schools. She and Karen both labeled themselves as "conservative" in their views of poetry because they considered their ideas of good poetry to be narrowly defined. Karen worried about getting stuck in an aesthetic because of possessing ideas that were maybe "too definitive about poems" and, thus, being unable to grow.

As a poetry editor for a literary journal, Karen described how she could determine visually through an examination of form what poem would be successful. "Without reading a word, I can look at the shape of it and tell by crazy-long lines that sort of don't mix in with the rest of the poem, crazy-short lines. No shape … it just doesn't have a physique." She considered form to be something unique to poetry. "It's one of the main ways it delivers its message … But, a poem that kind of looks sloppy on the page is probably not done. It's probably not been refined to death. It needs to be spruced-up." A poem that appears to be "out of shape" is almost always bad according to Karen; a good poem has a good physique, and "it's not just a messy pile of words." She asserted that "a good poem has a plan behind it, and the form follows the plan. You couldn't have a ridiculous long dog leg in a poem, because the poem's demanding a different shape, has its own sort of knees." For example, free verse doesn't mean that a poet can write anything however they want, but "it means that you're free to choose your own form." In addition to form, the language in a poem should be carefully considered and tight: "Every letter, every syllable, every word has an exact purpose and almost no other would do."

An effective poem was something lower than a good poem as it encompassed all of the things Karen considered to be important in poetry with the exception that it didn't "stir" her. "I couldn't look at some poem that everyone else acknowledges as a great poem and say, yeah that is a good poem. I could really only go as far as effective unless I had a visceral reaction to it." In her own writing, she considered good poetry to be that which moved beyond content only about personal experiences. "I think that's how you write a good poem. You move past what seems mundane and what seems too self-centered, not in the selfish way, but too centered on what your kitchen looks like." The self becomes a "jumping off point for every bigger thought." This means throwing away false starts and things that are not central and part of the poem.

Imagined Reality

> I think that's what poems are…imagined reality.
>
> *Dan, line 555*

Matt enters poetry through the visual. A good poem is one that can describe things that can't exist, such as an imaginary knife in someone's hand. "I like images that are complicated in the regard that you really have to pick [them] apart, they aren't necessarily based on something real." A good poem is like modern art in that you are blown away by it or not; it relies on someone's reaction to it through the use of images.

> What a good poem will do is it will create a world. And you can kind of go into it and you have to test: can this happen? No. Can this happen? Yes. Those rules, any relation they have to the real world is irrelevant. I really want to get in there and probe and see, is it this or is it this?
>
> *lines 86–89*

Matt's previous thinking about good poems as narrative, literal, and ending with a moral (e.g., Charles Bukowski) changed to this idea of a good poem as a fully rendered imaginary space. "I don't want a photograph or a newspaper article. I want a poem." Matt also expanded the previous statement that a good poem has no holes to sometimes a good poem has holes that keep someone coming back. Thus, good poems make you want to enter and feel them in some way. They contain images that one can enter; there are no missing walls or holes. Parini (2008) argued that preciseness and concreteness make poetic language important because these characteristics bring us closer to the material world.

In his own work, Matt often begins with a phrase and thinks of images that get at an idea. For instance, he described a series of poems taken from a Salvation Army Christmas slogan, "Hunger has No Season," where he used that phrase and subsequently imagined different seasons of hunger. It is difficult to begin with an idea because it is abstract and one has to find the images; Matt doesn't want to write poems that are abstract with a "bunch of ideas." He notes that "I'm more interested in deciphering a difficult image than being given an obtuse line in the text … I'm more interested in a thick image or a complicated image more so than the writing."

The label "poet" is even problematic as one can self-publish a book, teach poetry, and still that doesn't make one a poet. This aligns with Matt's idea that good poetry is not confessional or just an outlet for feelings. He doesn't often tell people he is a poet because of a resistance to notions of poetry as self-healing and writing as a release.

> It's me out there, but I'm picking and choosing how I'm represented and that relationship, to me, versus a videotape of me. So, I like poetry that's a little bit removed; I'm not interested in a straight boom. It's withholding a little bit, it's crafting a little bit.
>
> *lines 390–393*

A good poet can use whatever subject matter, even confessional, as long as a poem is crafted and different from a journal entry. A poet can't get away with only having a good story: "You can be a lot truer if you're not bound by the truth." You want a poem that screams: a well-crafted poem is sharp and has things cut out. A good poet learns what to cut, for instance, choosing the images that are most representative of a feeling, just the details that further the poem, and leaving out the anecdotal like the guy you passed in the street when you broke up with your girlfriend.

Another element of a good poem is surety of voice according to Dan. This voice constitutes the craft of poetry:

> There should be a tension between the syntax of the sentence and the way it flows across the page so the lines are broken and the rhythm of each line. There should be some sort of tension there, something to keep the reader from mistaking the poem for just ordinary, everyday language.

The voice should be one with urgency and uniqueness, one the audience believes, but one that is also "genuine to itself." To portray this urgency of voice, a poem must have what is essential and necessary, though this doesn't necessarily mean creating a short poem. It may take a few pages to get across what is needed.

An effective poem is "how close the poet can get to the imaginary reality of their subject." Dan argued that a poem is not a traffic report or a grocery list; an effective poem is one that is clearly different from everyday language, even if a poet borrows an interesting passage from a book. The poet adds to it through enjambment, for instance. In his own work, Dan had been writing poems from the perspective of different birds and fish, thinking about "being true to the experience of that voice." He told me that most of his poems arrive from imagined versus physical experience, and he is interested in the intermingling of those experiences because of his belief that the inner world is just as real as any physical world. Dan emphasized his process of *looking* instead of *trying* to find things to say:

> I may have an idea, title, first line or something, but when I sit down I try not to have an ending in mind, try not to have a line that I'm working towards. Like, oh yeah, that's going to be an awesome last line. Now let's write five pages to get to that last line.
>
> *lines 163–165*

The best poems are good and effective. "A good poem can give you pleasure and can maybe give you some sense of mystery that fends off your own confusion or your own blindness. It should also touch that inner world, that inner weather as Frost calls it" (Dan, lines 672-675).

Keeping the Mystery

Christof relayed the difficulty of describing good poetry—its "inherent mystery" that should leave one inarticulate. This approach, like that of Kim and Farah, focuses on the feeling in poetry rather than the intellect. "I can be critical but I'm happy not to be, and that's not my basic approach to it." Poetry can be ruined if it is used only as a vehicle for ideas. Farah claimed that explanations of poetry often fall a little flat, and Christof stated that teachers often destroy poetry with the pressure of interpretation. "It's like being outside of yourself. It's the experience of reading the poem, but at the same time you're aware of interpreting and aware of yourself as a reader interpreting the poem, and I hate that split focus." He cited total involvement and absorption in the poem as the key experience. A poet must bring everything he/she is to the experience. He said, "I don't have a special place for poetry that exists outside of my life." Christof's argument, echoed by Kim and Karen, that poetry and daily experience are fused is similar to Rose's (1990) statements about living the ethnographic life as a way to radically democratize knowledge; becoming a poet and ethnographer are not separate spheres of being.

A good image can describe something, but it must not do so with "a really sharp line that accurately describes something." Matt cited the collection, *Dismantling the Silence*, by former poet laureate Charles Simic, as good due to the fact the Soviet occupation and his past in Belgrade were dealt with indirectly. There are layers of visuals—the beautiful sheer visual imagery and the layers underneath that can be picked apart. All of this accrues into something amazing, a mystery: "There are a lot of good ways you can read it, and you're never going to be done with a book like that." The too-defined line that describes something may mean a poem is over after one is read. He said, "I don't like poems that tell me too much. I like poems that lie to me and are subversive and are hiding things." There must be some mystery in the work, the poem "isn't coming clean with something" or defining the narrator. A good poem lies: "And I think that's what a good book of poems is like … you can guess and you can get close and you can know what it's not, but you'll never know … in a good book." He cited Richard Hugo's book on writing poetry, *The Triggering Town*, and the idea that the truth often holds a good poem back. This is demonstrated by Hugo's chapter on assumptions and writing which contains contradictory facts about the description of a town. "The poem is made for the reader, and is sent out into the world to do its work the best it can, and without any intervention from the author … The truth of a poem is the *poem's* truth" (Raab, 2016, p. 22).

Christof claimed that writing poetry means that a poet necessarily wears a mask; they are adopting a self-conscious pose. "It's not the unselfconscious way you have a conversation." At the same time, the poet should be concerned with mystery. It is important to get away from ego to a child-like place where you can take a crayon and draw something weird and let others interpret it. Christof wants to get wrapped up and transported back to that world. "There's basically a kind of an immaturity in dedicating yourself and your life to making art … to me it's a really exciting, playful, childish activity that has all kinds of adult concerns attached to it, especially after the fact." Mystery is having no idea what you are going to write, not writing toward something, loving language, and not considering a set of rules for effective poetry. Even a consideration of a set of rules makes no sense because learning poetry is like learning a different language. An effective poem implies an objective, valid set of criteria, which is antithetical to poetic language, the enjoyment of poetry. "There's something weird about it (poetic language), whether it's the language itself or the way things are, the metaphorical level, or the deep structure of a thing." Different interpretations of one's work demonstrate the arbitrary nature of language, the mystery of it, and the importance of letting go of one's work. Not worrying about a correct reading or interpretation allows people to use their own interpretation.

> I like the good poem question better than I like the effective poem question because it means it is supposed to have an effect. And you're asking me to tell you what that effect should be and how it arrives at that effect.
>
> *lines 501–504*

Christof doesn't know if his own poetry is good until years later because he believes poets have useless perspectives on their own work immediately after-wards. It takes time to let go of some of the ego. At first, if he feels a poem is a "wholesale failure" he will throw it out, though maybe begin with the same idea and title. The revision works best when he is "still in the zone." When he is not, he would rather just write a new poem. His favorite audience is one willing to provide feedback, often the audience not trained in poetry or amenable to poetry readings. This observation is borne out of the sameness of poetry workshops and writing programs whose mission is to produce publishable poets.

For Dan, "a good poem should combat ignorance with mystery." This means readers should be taken out of their knowledge base, what they know, and what they are happy knowing. The poem, "should present you with a new set of questions that you're satisfied with not answering almost. That would be the mystery part." Dan continued by asserting that these may be spiritual questions as many poems inherently contend with those kinds of questions. A good poem both challenges old ideas and presents new ideas or it's "not necessarily going to be a poem I'm going to write down long hand in my notebook to get the inner workings of and understand more." A poet should bracket what they know by beginning with the knowledge, but then "plunge off into the wilderness and explore." This process echoes that of bracketing in phenomenological research (Moustakas, 1994). Dan adopted William Stafford's metaphor of a thread:

> You're looking for the end of the thread or where the thread connects to something else that's going to be the end of poem. You don't start looking for the thread; you start with the thread and sort of follow it. You're walking with the thread, but the thread also has its direction that it's going that you're following.
>
> *lines 176–180*

Following the thread through the poem is based on intuition or "memory of the future" (a line taken from Robert Graves). The process is one of letting the poem instruct a poet while writing, of being careful not to let preconceived notions of what a poem should do get in the way of writing it. A poet should have some "kind of absurd idea before you start a poem to make it interesting, something that's off the wall. A talking chair." A poet should be willing to try any weird idea to see if there is a thread to follow.

Conclusion

Writing good poetry is hard work. It takes training, much reading, and concentrated study to "know it when you see it." Beginning poets should start with an examin-ation of "bad" poetry so they can begin the process of understanding how poetic devices, like form, work to make a poem matter. This is part of honing poetic instincts; learning how to use language to describe the ineffable, to say the unsayable, and to know how to craft a poem with a good physique at the same time that a poet retains the mystery. This means that "every word counts" and that form follows content. A good poem is one that an audience remembers and comes back to read again and again.

A poem must connect to something larger than the poet and the particular moment. It should make a reader want to return to the poem again, to see things in new ways, to be surprised, and to consider what a poem has to offer over time. These characteristics of a good poem seem congruent with goals of social research. Furman et al. (2007), for instance, write about research poetry as tapping into universality:

> The goal of the poet is to transform his/her personal experience into that which is universal, or in the vernacular of social research, generalizable. In this sense, the goal of the poet is to present his/her experiences, both internal and external, in such a way that the reader may enter the work as if it were their own.
>
> *p. 303*

They argue the goal of generalizable findings can be met with poetic renderings. This belief in the ability of poetry to speak to something universal, or at least clarify some part of the human condition is why some poets write. Frost (1995) wrote in "The figure a poem makes" that a poem

> assumes direction with the first line laid down, it runs its course of lucky events, and ends in a clarification of life—not with necessarily a great clarification, such as sects and cults are founded on, but in a momentary stay against confusion.
>
> *p. 777*

The stay against confusion also has to do with the subject matter, the fact that poetic devices such as imagery and rhyme are not enough to make a poem matter, and are also not enough to show the audience that there is something important at stake. Hoagland (2006) wrote about the importance of the material in poetry as allowing him to have a personal stake in a poem's function. This echoed Marian's ultimate consideration of good poetry as that which "can take and find universality," and others' concerns for poetry that has high stakes, is emblematic, full of big ideas, and has emotional connectivity.

As a writer, you place your work in the context of those before you to demonstrate the connection. Mark Jarman (1995) considers poetry as a way to bring the past into the present in order to view what poetry can uniquely accomplish in addition to brevity, compression, and tact. When discussing writing a poem entitled, *What Only Poetry Can Do*, about a visit to Macduff Castle with his father at nine years old and again with his family at age 37, Jarman asserted, "Poetry crossed boundaries of time and space that I could not cross any other way. It did what only poetry can do" (p. 73). He was able to use poetry to do what he could not do physically, return to being nine years old, and to revisit a physical place that was inaccessible because of change. Robin Becker (1995) echoed this when she described how poets "reinvent" experience; the poet can "combine the real and ideal, the concrete and abstract" as a way to depict simultaneity, being "old and young at once" and "inside and outside personal experience." For researchers, this may be a process of bracketing as conceived of in phenomenological methods (Moustakas, 1994) where one places theory and knowledge of a topic away until the analysis phase of a project.

What researcher-poets should do with the poets' exaltations and vexations of good poetry may best be summarized by Kim, who articulated her belief that social researchers interested in poetry should remember that a researcher-poet represents at least half of the content of a poem and must "aspire at the level of language. It can't just be mimicry of the voice, of the participants." If researchers use poetry as a means of analysis in addition to representation in a project, they need to remember to be reflexive and understand that the "turn" in a poem comes from inside a poet and not from external things (e.g., Furman et al., 2007). This entails wearing "both hats," that of a poet and that of a researcher, and demonstrating some effort to understand poetry, even if one is not innately a great poet. Piirto (2002) welcomed artist-educators and novices alike to bridge worlds but cautions us to "not confuse the quality of their qualification for rendering, making marks, embodying, and distilling. Let us not confuse the seekers for the master. Let us not confuse the poetasters for the poet" (p. 443). Or to conclude with a cooking analogy about good and bad poetry which Kim offered:

> If you do it poorly, it's going to look like a veggie tray. You will have cut all the veggies and put them on the tray and they will be exactly as they were, only cut up. But baking is alchemy. You put all the ingredients together and somehow it makes a cake.

lines 928–931

The Criteria Question

Discussions about criteria for alternative research writing, including Poetic Inquiry, have been occurring for some time (e.g., Faulkner, 2007; Piirto, 2002). However, defining and deeming work "good (research) poetry" presents a potential quagmire as it creates a divisive dialectic between criteria and freedom. This dialectic of criteria restricting creativity and possibilities is not endemic to those interested in research writing as many poets convey in *ars poetica* and other statements about their craft. This section contends with these issues through an exploration of the aesthetic and epistemic dimensions of Poetic Inquiry.

I wrote the following in an article on poetic criteria in 2007:

> I should uncloak myself from my social science cape of vital citations and abstractions that talk around the issue to argue explicitly and plainly for the importance of attention to craft. As much as I enjoy wearing this cloak, let me throw it off now, for a moment, and state my personal engagement with this issue: I am tired of reading and listening to lousy poetry that masquerades as research and vice versa. And to be honest, I have written my share of such poetry and received criticisms from poets and colleagues of sentimentality, cuteness, triteness, melodrama, and especially, a "ruthless adherence to research language at the sacrifice of line."

In the 12 years since this confession, I also need to confess that I have read and listened to what I consider good—and I will boldly use the following superlative— great (research) poetry.

I have been a regular participant in poetry workshops—in person and online— since 2000, working on the aesthetics of my poetry. I have been studying and writing about poetic craft as research method for most of my career. The line between my research poetry and my personal poetry has become like a gossamer thread as I live and embody the ethnographic poet's life (cf. Rose, 1990). Consideration of poetic craft and method are part of my way of being an academic and poet.

Regardless of what we would call an effective, good, or great use of poetry in/as research, a critical issue for those interested in poetic re-presentations is the evaluation of such forms (e.g., Furman, 2006a, b; Percer, 2002). I continue to be interested in entering and weighing in on the debate over what constitutes good (research) poetry, especially after rereading poet-researchers such as Cahnmann (2003), Percer (2002), and Behar (2008) who are deeply concerned about the use of poetry in research. I still pause when reading Craig Gingrich-Philbrook's (2005) essay about the importance of praxis/craft in autoethnography and performance, and the double-bind between knowledge and aesthetics, particularly a section on poetry.

> Any serious student of poetry, however, soon recognizes the profound erasure at work in the paucity of metapoetic discourse in autoethnography's metamethodological talk. When they write about how to do autoethnography, autoethnographers rarely acknowledge, for example, different poetries, movements, conversations, controversies, or debates among poets about the risk and rewards of autobiographical poetry.
>
> *p. 308*

If we want our Poetic Inquiry to be *good*, maybe even *great*, I concur with Percer (2002) and Gingrich-Philbrook's (2005) suggestions that we engage in a critical discussion about how we understand poetry, how it informs our work and scholarly endeavors (e.g., Faulkner, 2006, 2017b; Furman, 2006). Researchers interested in poetic representation must be aware of poetic traditions and techniques and study the craft as they study research writing (Piirto, 2002). Studious concern with the craft of poetry can move us forward and keep us from underestimating and misusing poetry in the name of alterative representation. Poet Mary Oliver (1998) pointed out that "Every poem is a statement. Every poem is music—a determined, persuasive, reliable, enthusiastic, and crafted music" (pp. viii–ix). To understand this music requires some knowledge of the workings of metrical poetry as well as pleasure in it. Oliver wishes the experience of such poetry to be "comprehension accompanied by felt experience" (p. ix).

What I am arguing is that poetic truth cannot be *only* an extraction of exact words or phrases from interview transcripts or our personal experience, but rather it requires a more focused attention to craft issues. Failing to engage in artistic concentration by not considering craft seems to me a rejection of poetry as method. Finch (2005) considers this attention vital to the work of poetry; a refusal to read other poets or to revise and improve one's work because of a notion that this may disturb the muse of inspiration is damaging. It plays into the labeling of anything lyrical or graceful as poetry. Craft and inspiration are not anathema: "To work with poetic craft in a skilled and attentive way brings us full circle back out of the realm of craft and into the realm of inspiration" (p. 46). Such attention will facilitate the accomplishment of good (research) poetry and further the fusion between science and art.

Of course, attention to the aesthetic dimension of research poetry may ignore the aesthetic/epistemic dialectic (see Gingrich-Philbrook, 2005). However, I feel a pull toward the aesthetic dimensions and wish to explore Percer's assertion that "evaluation can be done most effectively when ideas about craft have been explored, implemented, and disclosed" (2002, para. 19). For example, I present the following poem as one exploration of what poetic craft means to my work and to me personally. This persona poem uses imagined conversation between Richard Hugo (1992)—a poet who wrote about the importance of imagination—using one's personal passions and making up the details if they better suit the poetry, and the poet, Faulkner.

> *Letter to Faulkner from the Fluff and Fold*
>
> Assumptions lie behind the work of all writers.
> Richard Hugo, *The Triggering Town*
>
> Dear Sandra, you know poets still believe
> in hand-crafted words, write slowly in pen
> on blank pages with spiral bound notebooks
> lifted from the coffee shop next to school.
> They never write in pen because it seeps

like a grease stain on the twelfth revision.
Poets sit in empty rooms, make it up.
They write on screen about their failed affairs
make mothers weep with all that blasphemy.
Listen Faulkner, you must fold poems like sheets
think in iambs for hours without sleep
take a crayon and scribble it all out.
Wait for weeks, the words will tumble in dreams
to the mind's ridiculous arenas.
That is how the writing is done. Love, Dick.

To highlight the value of attention to poetic craft, I will discuss how *ars poetica* can demonstrate a concern with craft and a way to read and evaluate Poetic Inquiry. I suggest that writing your own *ars poetica* can show concern with aesthetic and poetic craft issues. They are more than reflexivity statements and more than statements about one's Poetic Inquiry goals; they constitute a way we can enter into a dialogue about poetic criteria.

Ars Poetica *as*

Ars poetica is often used to introduce one to writing poetry. Many poetry workshops begin with an *ars poetica* assignment where student poets articulate what poetry means to them, their own aesthetic and process. These can be statements and definitions in prose form, or most often, poems that articulate the art. Wiegers (2003) points out that writing a poem about poetry may seem paradoxical, but this writing represents an important part of a tradition which demands a poet break tradition through the use of their art.

> To write about poetry is to believe that there are answers to some of the questions poets ask of their art, or at least that there are reasons for writing it. A poem about the art of poetry is not born out of a lack of subject matter but, rather, arises out of an excess that transcends the humanly possible; it arises out of the questions one cannot answer … This process of entering a poem leads both the giver of the gift and its recipient toward a critical engagement with the poem, and through that to a larger engagement with the world. The poet brings life to writing a poem; the reader brings life to reading it. Through this process the *ars poetica*, the poem about poetry, has helped sustain the very art it addresses.
>
> *pp. xiv–xv*

Writing (and examining) *ars poetica* provides one way of expressing poetics and practicing poetic writing because unlike research methods texts which demonstrate how to conduct and evaluate research, rarely do you see poetry writing or "methods" books that minutely detail how to write a good poem. Thiel (2001), for example, begins her book on writing poetry by telling the reader that writing cannot be taught, it is "something we must often stumble upon on our own. But the suggestions which follow will point out different paths you might follow … for when the stories and poems come in search of you" (p. 11). The advice for the beginning poet usually includes references to finding your own voice by reading widely, seeking out writers whom you admire and mimicking their style, and practicing through the use of writing exercises.

The goal is to "write like you" and focus on the pleasures of writing, rather than any intrinsic reward, in order to live the writerly life (Hugo, 1992; See, 2002). Strand and Boland (2000) consider good poems to "have a lyric identity that goes beyond whatever their subject happens to be. They have a voice, and the formation of that voice, the gathering up of imagined sound into utterance, may be the true occasion for their existence" (p. xxiv). Carl Phillips (2009) described a poem as "an enactment of individual sensibility" more than the self and what we choose to push against. Voice, or style, in a poem shows an inhabited world where we see an idiosyncratic and recognizable presence (Hirshfield, 1997). Addonizio and Laux (1997) urge poets to consider their subject matter, diction, form, syntax and grammar, and imagery when finding their poetic voice.

One entrée into writing your own *ars poetica* is to read, study, and borrow other researcher-poets' work and *ars poetica* to define, refine, and test your own conceptualizations. Who are your favorite poets? Why are they your favorite? What are they doing in their poems that make you excited? I pose these questions and offer additional ones adapted from Goodall (2000) by changing one noun: Who are your favorite researchers? What research books are on your shelves and why? What are they doing in their work that makes you excited? With whom do you want to start a conversation? Using these questions can be a good beginning for writing an *ars poetica* for research poetry.

What I see when considering a small collection of poets' *ars poetica* in prose and poetry (see Table 3.2) is the importance of embodied experience through attention to the senses, especially the imperfections that often lead to discovery and surprise. Poetry is a precise way of seeing at the same time that it is conditional and partial and interested in approximations of something akin to "truth." I also see the impossibility of articulating one vision of good poetry.

On what specifically, then, should a poet concentrate? Examining these *ars poetica* suggests to me that writing is about discipline, persistence, and attention to craft with intense concentration (e.g., Hirshfield, 1997; See, 2002). Attention to craft is attention to images, line, rhetoric, metaphor and simile, music, voice, emotion, story, and grammar. Poets use the line to speed up or slow down, for emphasis, to fulfill and thwart expectations, to create tension and relaxation. "Line determines our experience of a poem's temporal unfolding. Its control of intonation creates the expectation that thrills because it might be as easily thwarted as fulfilled" (Longenbach, 2004, p. 21). Poets use metaphors and similes

TABLE 3.2 Poets' *Ars Poetica*

Poet	Ars Poetica Statement/Poem
Andrews, T. (1995)	"I find that if I insist on my original design, then 'I lose something in the original.' Increasingly I'm interested in letting my poems engage directly this tension between my own desire to speak and the language's tendency to displace the speaker" (p. 2).
Boyle, J. (2003)	"Poets, remember your skeletons. In youth or dotage, remain as light as ashes" (from POETS, quoted by Wiegers, p. 101).
Bishop, E. (2001)	"Hundreds of things coming together at the right moment" (quoted by Thiel, 2001, p. 28).
Becker, R. (1995)	"The art of poetry allows us to fly as well as to walk, to be old and young at once, to be inside and outside personal experience. And in poetry, we may combine the real and the ideal, the concrete and the abstract" (p. 5).
Collins, B. (2004)	"Poetry, I think, is an interruption of silence. The poem makes sense largely because it has this space around it. It is inhabiting a part of this space, but leaving space around it. So a poem is an interruption of silence, an occupation of silence; whereas public language is a continuation of noise" (quoted by Stewart, 2004, pp. 146–147).
Ferris, J. (2004)	"I'm not sure if I want all of my poems to limp, but I know this: all the interesting ones do, all the lovely ones do, in one way or another" (p. 10).
Galvin, J. (2005)	"POETRY, IT'S OBVIOUS, REQUIRES NO COMMENT. AN *ARS POETICA* IS ALREADY, THEREFORE, a failure of character. To comment on an *ars poetica* would be a double failure to which, though now guilty, I am unwilling to admit" (p. 36).
Hirshfield, J. (1997)	"Every good poem begins in language awake to its own connections—language that hears itself and what is around it, sees itself and what is around it, looks back at those who look into its gaze and knows more perhaps even than we do about who and what we are. It begins that is, in the body and mind of concentration" (p. 3).
Klein, E. (2001)	"Poetry is crossing a rickety old bridge, and a plank breaks beneath you" (quoted by Thiel, 2001, p. 28).
Richardson, L. (1997b)	"A poem is a whole that makes sense of its parts; and a poem is parts that anticipate, shadow, undergird the whole. That is, poems can themselves be experienced as simultaneously whole and partial, text and subtext; the 'tail' can be the dog" (p. 143).
Margolis, G. (1997)	"A poem needs to find a way into itself" (p. 151).
McHugh, H. (1995)	"Beckett says tears are liquefied brain. Poems had better come from that same place ... One writes poems as one lives, with full attention to the partiality of things" (p. 98).

TABLE 3.2 (Cont.)

Poet	Ars Poetica Statement/Poem
Seibles, T. (2004)	"Poetry is scary because it whispers transformation—of self and world … If poetry is to be of much use to people, it must be bold and clear like a saxophone solo. I want students to understand that when you sing you don't mumble and hope to seem clever, you sing …" (quoted by Bingham, pp. 224–225).
Seiferle, R. (2003)	"Why write poetry for the people? W. C. Williams answered, because you can gawk at your neighbor's wife when she goes out in her housecoat for the morning news. Which many are dying for lack of" (from Poetic Voice, quoted by Wiegers, 2003, p. 76).

to make connections that expand and deepen our understanding (Addonizio & Laux, 1997).

The important thing about poetic craft is that skill comes with practice (Thiel, 2001), with revision, with knowing when to send work to the "toxic language dump" according to Addonizio and Laux (1997). Good poets "recognize when they've written stuff that deserves to be dumped, and load up the truck" (p. 95). Finch (2007) offered a remedy for what she called "metrical incipience" or the mixing of metrical forms that goes unrecognized by young poets because of lack of training in anything other than iambic pentameter and over-reliance on free verse. Her observations of students' poems often having the most emotional and vivid impact when meter takes over led her to prescribe a broad cure of increased awareness of other forms. This entails a development of a rich understanding of varied meters (not just iambic pentameter), so that developing poets can recognize what is going on rhythmically in their own work.

> Not only the poets, but the poems, make it clear that yearning for more accurate and empowered and conspicuous engagement with the rhythmic powers of poetry is not going away, but will most likely remain one of the growing voices in the postmodern poetic conversation.
>
> *para. 12*

These considerations illuminate my own conception of poetry as fun and messy embodiment, a way of life, necessary, and hard work. Carr (2003) claims that poetry is an effective way to present and validate lived experience "while challenging researchers to learn about their abilities to communicate qualitative inquiry in a different way" (p. 1330). In this spirit, I offer four *ars poetica* I wrote from 2001–2019 to reveal my own sense of aesthetics, and how that plays into my construction and use of poetry, and to also position myself in relation to the literature and poets with whom I am in conversation. I offer short writing stories about the *ars poetica* pieces to place my experiences and emotions into context of my writerly life and demonstrate the inspiration and constraints in operation (L. Richardson, 2000).

Ars Poetica #1

The following is the first *ars poetica* I ever consciously attempted. The spark ignited after a few poetry classes with the same poet teacher. I heard him ask the following: "Are you doing something stereotypically predictable in your work? If so, are you pushing yourself enough?" I wondered what these questions meant. Was my poetry that wretched? I did notice similar patterns in the past five poems I had written in his classes after those questions. All of the poems were about interpersonal relationships (not surprising given my scholarly interests, I thought). All of the poems were free verse. Many of them contained the word "whip" in some form (e.g., "whip out," "whipped up"). When another poet teacher began her class by asking us to write what we liked about poetry, I thought of three words and the questions from the previous class. We were to begin our articulation of what we liked about poetry by listing our words and then expanding on them. This is what I wrote:

> *Self-Discovery/Curiosity/Generosity (Spring 2001)*
>
> I like poets who can make me laugh because they are honest (or seemingly so). I like to hear about experiences that remind me of my own struggles with relationships, with work, with politics. Sometimes, I like to see in ways I haven't before—descriptions of experience that are not my own.
>
> Always, I like surprise—the turning point and/or ending that shocks and brings deeper meaning that goes beyond simply being clever. Maybe I cry.
>
> I like descriptions I can visualize and smell and taste and hear—playing to the senses so you feel a poem in your gut.
>
> I like poems that make me wish I had written something that well-crafted.

Ars Poetica #2

I wrote the next *ars poetica* in a poetry class where the first writing assignment was to define poetry. I had madly been studying and writing poetry in an attempt to recapture some artistic voice I believed had died during graduate school. I see that influence here. Notice my earnest insistence on emotion and connection and the agreement with Phil Memmer (personal communication, April 12, 2005), poet and editor, who conveyed during another poetry workshop that when poems are well-constructed, we *live* them instead of *read* them. The connection need not signal agreement, however. This point I have learned in all of these poetry workshops that now blend together like a blueberry-banana-espresso-peanut butter smoothie.

Faulkner Paints Her Nails "Must be Mink": An Ars Poetica in Prose (Fall 2001)

"I don't want to fuck, I want to feel." Eddie Vedder wails to the crowd and those of us on the cheap lawn seats at the Pearl Jam concert. Rain hits us like spit balls under the clouds crowding the Philadelphia sky (or maybe the clouds are from Camden). Garbage sacks, umbrellas, and other assorted plastic bags offer little help. The owners of the amphitheater arrange venues so that one barely has to interact with the locals. You almost don't notice the burned-out war zone feeling of the surroundings as you follow the police hands and orange flares to the parking lot safely tucked behind barbed wire.

At first, these lines about not fucking rankle my hedonistic plans. I have spent two years recovering from graduate school and concepts. I want to fuck. But maybe there is something to feeling and connection that extends beyond physicality. Those inner monsters that claw at your self-confidence—I envision them splayed out on pages in lines of poetry. Well, that is what I attempt to do when I write, to punish the demons that gnaw at my interior and those of others. The goal is to find an authentic voice, to characterize what I think of as ugly and joyous and fabulous. Some buy beer, others make pot brownies in order to anesthetize those fears, make them sit, but I like explicitly whipping them out and depicting them in lines and verses. I want poetry to be the opposite of anesthesia. It is the place to show that fractured sense of identity and play with it.

More importantly, I want to connect to others through that cry of "ah-ha" recognition. Envision that moment of connection with masses of others you haven't invited to sit on your blanket, the people who are outside the carefully orchestrated line to a concert venue in a "bad" part of New Jersey. Think of the oneness that happens outside, in the rain, bouncing to music that concomitantly jars and soothes you. I want you to feel my lines in your hips. I want to make you vibrate in your seat. I want you to read/hear my lines and experience them viscerally; maybe later you will think about them. The point is that you experience them, and you say to yourself, *I know that feeling.* And maybe, just a little, I want to fuck you.

"We don't have a language for the senses. Feelings are images, sensations are like musical sounds. How are you going to tell about them?" Anais Nin writes these lines in her journal, and I feel depressed, thinking of sex (again). Maybe we don't have language to describe sensations, but surely facsimiles melt and become part of the brain, part of our experience. Think of the Sapir-Whorf hypothesis that tells us how language shapes our thoughts, that part of how we think is determined by language. If we concur with this premise, then poetry can become experience; it can be sensation. Perhaps, it is not the same as being at the football game on the

50 yard-line or tasting the sweat of a lover, but it can evoke feeling. This feeling can become its own story and experience.

Ars Poetica #3 and #3.5

I articulated my third (and third and a half) *ars poetica* during two research projects where I discovered that poetry was the best means for me to accomplish my goals of examining how LGBTQ Jews think of and manage multiple identities (see Faulkner, 2005, 2006) and to present experiences of harassment in the academy that would disrupt a continued normalization of it (see Faulkner, Calafell, & Grimes, 2009). Obsessed with poetry that presents themes, narratives, emotions, and the tone of research at the same time it works *as* poetry, I made colleagues and poet friends read poem after poem and revision after revision of poems in these projects for three years. Comments that the poems were too "researchy" or "cute" drove me to more revisions. Hirshfield's (1997) and Hoagland's (2006) books of essays about poetic craft lay under my bed with a pencil sticking out of their spines. I loved many of Hirshfield's prose lines about poems, and wondered how I could make this vulnerability happen in my own poems: "A poem is a detour we willingly subject ourselves to, a trick surprising us into the deepened vulnerability we both desire and fear. Its strategies of beauty, delay, and deception smuggle us past the border of our own hesitation" (Hirshfield, 1997, p. 125). Hoagland's (2006) observations about a need for narrative and messy lyricism, learning and unlearning of the rules, intrigued me.

> Modern consciousness may indeed be splintered, but it is one function of poetry in our time to fasten it back together—which does not mean to deny its complexity. When poetry can name the parts and position them, when it brings us out of the speedy, buzzing fog that is selfhood and modern life, our sense of being alive is heightened and intensified.
>
> *p. 171*

I decided to include my conceptualizations about poetic craft into the published works as a means to frame and evaluate the success of the projects, to see if there were any surprises and/or beauty present. I also started a series of persona poems about imagined conversations between my poet persona, Faulkner, and poets whom I admire. Here is Tony Hoagland talking to Faulkner about his contention that "Thingitude" is an important element in poems.

Hoagland Writes to Faulkner about Thingitude

> I love poems that locate, coordinate, and subordinate, that build up a compound picture of the world. These poetic properties—of attention, proportion, and relationality—I have come to think of as Thingitude and Causality.
>
> *Hoagland, 2006, p. 164*

Your idea of poems as constructed lines,
collisions between research and aesthetics
reminds me of a stack of metaphors—
a poem equals language plus attention
thought so hard it cracks the sugared pavement—
I woke up with something else in my mind,
poets playing hockey on Nascar tracks,
critics skating with black and white jerseys
kicking ice chips with dull blades on banners
for tacos, children's hospitals, and banks.
Faulkner, tell how to stop the fracture
of poetics over the brass bars, how
to choose the war soaked news without boozy
critique? Tell me how to put myself back to bed.

Poet as Archival Activist (2003–2008)

My goal is to translate and reinvent Soniat's (1997) vision of poet as archivist into poet as archival activist (e.g., Hartnett, 2003), that is, I want to use
poetry to question and alter traditional representations of identity, to provoke
emotional responses in readers/listeners, and create a sense of connection by
"critically traversing the margin and center ... opening more and different
paths for enlivening relations and spaces" (Madison, 2004, p. 471). And as
the former U.S. Poet Laureate, Billy Collins (in Stewart, 2004), said, "Poetry
is an interruption of silence." This work breaks the silence by adding to the
representation of LGBTQ Jews.

Faulkner, 2006, p. 98

As an arguably better alternative, I can show you a recent poem I wrote for
a project on sexual harassment in the academy using the character Hello Kitty
as a voice for victims of harassment (see Faulkner et al., 2009). This follows an
important tradition of writing *ars poetica* poems, and if as Wiegers (2003) contends,
poems about *ars poetica* are the most convincing arguments for what makes poetry
art, I can't make the loudest arguments through prose statements. This poem
demonstrates my idea of poetry as an act of discovery versus one of recitation, and
the excitement of throwing away "the decorum of lines" after years of worry with
the line (Longenbach, 2008). After many revisions, I recognized that this poem
demonstrated my thoughts about the art of poetry, especially if I link writing a dissertation and the creation of art. The prose form of the poem is meant to provoke,
to shift attention from lines to the sentence as a means of holding attention; I want
the audience to stay immersed in the world of the poem and to pay attention to
the tension between outside aesthetic and audience considerations and my poet's
vision of embodiment.

B. H. Fairchild (2007) considers poetry's task of embodiment to work "by bringing the tenuous emotion or subtle state of consciousness or elusive idea into a closer relation with lived experience—with, in effect, the country of the body" (p. 55). "Poems are what you make when you experience life in a certain way. Alive to yourself in the world, observant of inner and outer reality, and connected to language" (Addonizio, 2009, p. 14). Hello Kitty's lack of mouth seems an appropriate vehicle for exploring such embodiment, especially when I consider Fairchild's (2007) argument that "when poetry moves away from the body, it atrophies" (p. 68). I chose the prose form because I wanted to do something different with syntax that my usual use of lines covered up. The original (or alternative) title of the poem was *Dissertation Abstracts International/ Feminist Standpoint Theory: An Examination by a Post Modern Two-Dimensional Cat with No Mouth and 22,000 Products Bearing Her Image.*

Dr. H. Kitty Considers Her Dissertation as Ars Poetica

She had wanted to title her dissertation, *Ode to the University*, like a love letter to ideas, to chance and other marginal characters without traditional mouths or white teeth. Her committee balked: standpoint theory and self-narratives were quite enough. Other departments would question the methods, not tenure such love gut epistemology. During the defense, the token male member screamed her seminal argument was the "pissy cat position." H.K. wiped his spit off her whiskers with her camouflage hair bow, and slipped a blank piece of paper down the conference room table. One by one, the members held the clean sheet as if it were a twisted student evaluation. Only the bisexual lesbian clapped, said Kitty's "right-on-response disallows the difficulty with our difference." H.K. considered ripping herself a mouth with her advisor's fountain pen, kicking the phantom pain in the teeth. Instead, she underlined new parts of her story with a Barbie highlighter, and let them pass her with their caveats and reservations.

Ars Poetica Redux 2019, Revising Poetry as Method

As I have reread and reworked and thrown out, renewed and plucked from *Poetry as Method*, transforming it into *Poetic Inquiry*, I have spent much time thinking about a researcher-poet's job description.

A poet:

> Reminds people they have an interior life.
> Notices the construction dust caked under finger nails.
> > "Poetry is a form of attention."
> > > > > *Revell, 2007, p. 5*

> "The creative act is continuous, before, during, and after the poem."
> > > > > *Revell, 2007, p. 6*

"By beginning to see and then continuing to see. The poem's trajectory is an eyebeam, not an outline."

Revell, 2007, p. 7

"A poem is about both the ordinary and the extraordinary at the same time."

Addonizio, 2009, p. 62

A poet:

Sees what is unseen.
Writes what is seething.
Creates and recreates the poetic line: "... if we can make it new, if we can invent, we can progress. The line in poetry must reflect—and reflect upon—those changes if it is to maintain any connection to things as they are."

Vander Zee, 2011, p. 11

Keeps writing to get that poet's high, the space where writing and revising surprise you into breaking.
"A poem lies somewhere between a determined now and an open future. This capacity to stretch beyond the extant makes poems such a difficult and necessary pleasure—this blank reserve, this attenuated power, this complex allegory of a present shaded by the past, and shading into something else still."

Vander Zee, 2011, p. 13

Lives like a Poetry Scout.   [But doesn't sell the cookies.]
Swears by the poet's motto: "enjoy the fundamentally useless, contemplative pleasure of poetry."

Doty, 2010, p. 115

Gives themselves to
Poetry's Time.

"Less a made thing, a purposively broken thing, the line is more an index of idiosyncratic feeling of a mimesis of our psychology."

Vander Zee, 2011, p. 14

Make me stop-
Suspend me
in this world

You created
with this line,
I only breathe
in time to your line
meditate with fury,
calm and frenzied
eating words
like a dog,
like a phoenix
I die in a word
fire, flaming
to become
a new line.

Ars Poetica *as Criteria*

The art of poetry provides an entry point from which we can discuss potential criteria for evaluating research poetry. Examining a researcher's goals and consideration of poetic craft through *ars poetica* suggest these criteria. These presentations may accompany research poetry as appendices in a researcher's work, be discussed explicitly during the presentation of the work, become a part of the poetry through the use of process or method poems (see Chapter 4), or be discussed in a chapter such as this. The explicit discussion of the research process can be considered to be part of a researcher's ethical obligations of full disclosure of methodological choices (Leavy, 2015). I must acknowledge that conflict exists about the role of poet-as-critic, whether we can view poets as reliable narrators on their own work and what goes into the creation of their work, given that poets have a vested interest in their own aesthetics (Pack and Parini, 1995; Parini, 2008). Hoagland (2006) suggested that it could be difficult for a student to move beyond the aesthetics of poetry teachers, mentors, and schools of influence. However, what I am arguing is that such statements about the goals of the work provide criteria by which we may judge the relative success of such work. Or as emphasized by Patricia Leavy (2009), "the success of any given research project is linked to the research purpose(s) and how well the methodology has facilitated research objectives and communicated research findings" (p. 16).

Evaluating Poetic Inquiry

The criteria suggested in my *ars poetica* are those of *artistic concentration, embodied experience, discovery/surprise, conditionality, narrative truth,* and *transformation*. These criteria may also be found in the interviews with poets on craft (see Table 3.1) and in the researcher-poets' goals for Poetic Inquiry explored in Chapter 2. Laurel Richardson (2000) argued that rigorous standards of art and science applied to poetic representations are relevant and important, and that we should continue to create criteria and new criteria for selecting our criteria: "I believe in holding all ethnography to high and difficult standards" (p. 254). Leavy (2009) argued against the use of traditional criteria, such as validity and reliability, for arts-based projects because the aims differ; we see attention to things such as "resonance, understanding, multiple meanings, dimensionality, and collaboration" (p. 16). She acknowledged that vigor is a better term that can replace the concept of rigor in qualitative evaluation of this work. I agree with these authors and others who call for attention to craft and praxis, to the idea of vigor (Carr, 2003; Percer, 2002; L. Richardson, 2002).

We can also turn to alternative research criteria by those engaged in this kind of work. For example, Laurel Richardson (2000) suggests five criteria by which to consider the scientific and artistic merits of ethnographic texts: substantive contribution to understanding social life, aesthetic merit, reflexivity, impact on emotions and intellect, and expression of a reality. Similarly, Bochner (2000) offers six things that he looks for in "poetic social science" when asked to render judgment: concrete details that include facts and feelings, complex narratives that rotate between past and present, the author's emotional credibility, vulnerability, and honesty; transformation of narrator, ethical consideration, and work that moves heart and head. Ellis (2000) plays up aesthetic concerns with her desire for good plot, verisimilitude, authenticity, showing not telling, and coherence. She also wants to know what a writer's goals are in order to ask if they are achievable. Clough (2000), Denzin (2005), Madison (2005), and Hartnett (2003) focus on social justice and political action as prime criteria. Siegesmund and Cahnmann-Taylor (2008) suggest that arts-based research should "widen the circle" and ask better questions in order to get at qualitative generalizability. The work should expand perception, inspire focused participatory dialogue and purposeful discussion; initiate, extend, and develop conversation; help understanding by attending to new dimensions of a question or problem. It should answer the question: "Does the metaphor make felt qualitative meaning more accessible (p. 242)?" Piirto (2002) requires that students desiring to engage in high stakes arts-based work (e.g., dissertation) to have taken a minimum of 20 credit hours in their art medium of choice, have peer-reviewed shows, exhibits, and products if they have no formal study in the domain; and/or have not earned an undergraduate minor or major in the art form of choice. I contend that in addition to the use of *ars poetica*, these criteria suggest some qualities by which we may judge Poetic Inquiry. These criteria blend artistic and scientific concerns to create guidelines for evaluating Poetic Inquiry as seen in Figure 3.1.

The criterion of *artistic concentration* focuses attention on considerations of the history and presence of craft in poetry (see Percer, 2002). Hirshfield (1997) writes of artistic concentration as the direct and indirect attention to the language of connection that is "penetrating, unified, and focused, yet also permeable and open" (p. 3). This concentration manifests itself in careful attention to detail (titles,

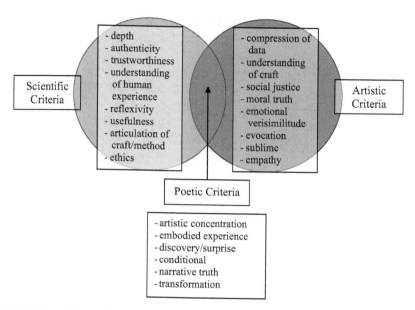

FIGURE 3.1 Criteria for evaluating poetic inquiry

lines, punctuation, sound, rhyme, figurative language, and word choice) and feeling (tone, mood); poets focus on the usual as well as the unusual details in a fresh way. It acknowledges how poets place their work within the history and craft of poetry and with whom they are conversing and resisting. Parini (2008) made a similar argument that poetry is a traditional form of art worth studying to allow for the full power of voice and metaphor to embody our work. Poets should have a solid understanding of verse, including rhythm, meter, speech, and form in order to achieve anything original; they "ignore the traditions of poetry at their peril" (pp. xi-xii). And perhaps, most importantly, a heightened focus and concentration on language is what makes poetry—a reliance on personal voice as opposed to cliché (Parini, 2008).

> Poets consistently attempt to return words to their original sense; this is one of the most vivid functions or poetry: to refresh language by drawing words back into alignment with their original pictorial, concrete, and metaphorical associations ... What will vary from poem to poem is the method used to intensify or heighten the language.
>
> *pp. 37, 25*

This concentrated study also answers a question Piirto (2002) posed: "Why is it not necessary for those who write poetry in qualitative research to have a familiarity with poetry, to study poetry?" (p. 435).

Embodied experience recognizes the need for poetry to make audiences feel *with*, rather than *about* a poem, to experience emotions and feelings in situ. "The more you practice with imagery—recording it in as much vivid detail as you can—the more likely it is that your poetry will *become* an experience for the reader, rather than simply talk *about* an experience" (Addonizio & Laux, 1997, p. 91).

> Concreteness is about embodiment ... We have to transfer something from one body to another. This is what the image is all about ... A poem without concrete particulars is a poem that is unlikely to engage the emotion of the reader. For the readers to experience the emotion that the poet wishes to embody, in particular set engage the emotions in the first place must be encoded in the poem.
>
> *Sullivan, 2009, pp. 113, 118*

A poem should use images to transform the way that we look at the world; a good image is one that brings something previously nebulous into the "realm of the expressed" (Hirshfield, 1997). This may be done by what a poem actually *leaves out*, having readers interpret what the omissions may mean. "Our continuing interest in a poem turns on its resistance to our efforts ... A poem wears its essence like a coat" (Longenbach, 2004, pp. 85, 86). The use of poetic language allows a poem to articulate human concerns in such a manner that they become concrete and immediate. We ground ourselves in poetic language as a way of grounding ourselves in physicality and the connection between mind and body or matter and spirit. "The poet quickens our sense of language, and our sense of life as well. This is why language matters in a poem, and why poetry matters" (Parini, 2008, p. 38).

Discovery means that a poem teaches us to see something familiar in new ways or ways that may be surprising; we learn something about the human condition and ourselves. Longenbach (2004) described the experience of wonder as a compelling reason for poetic language:

> Wonder contingent on inexperience and firstness can be easy to feel, and the challenge is to be wounded by "composed wonder"—wonder produced by poetry's mechanisms of self-resistance: syntax, line, figurative language, disjunction, spokenness. Without these mechanisms, poems would be vehicles for knowledge, explanations of experience that would threaten to dispel its wonder. They would be useful, then disposable.
>
> *p. 97*

Finding a way to express/inspire wonder in poetry means being dramatic versus didactic, using human language as opposed to scholarly language. The best in poetry inspires us politically and spiritually (Parini, 2008). Our pleasure in poetry resides in language, even language we may not fully understand, because of the tension between sonic and semantic aspects that good poetry embraces (Longenbach, 2004). We experience the music of language in unexpected ways.

The partiality of the story should also be recognized through poetry. Point of view is *conditional* while presenting what we may call "narrative or poetic truth." The facts as presented should ring true, regardless of whether events, feelings, emotions, and images "actually" occurred. Hugo (1992) argued that the best poetry lies. It is these lies, the use of imaginary spaces and possibilities, which recognize the contingent nature of truth. "The result *may* be quite loose in its grip on hard facts but very powerful in terms of communicating the humanity of the circumstances of the report" (Brady, 2004, p. 632). If metaphors mediate the relationship between reality and the imagination as Frost thought, then the way that poets use analogical concepts such as simile, conceit, allegory, metonymy and synecdoche, matter (Parini, 2008). Poets recognize the importance of how metaphorical thinking organizes our experience and how far metaphorical thinking can go before it breaks. "Metaphor allows for the impossible, a world in which one thing is another thing ... In this world of metaphorical alchemy, changes occur and they seem true; the poet makes them true" (Parini, 2008, pp. 76–77).

And finally, poetry should *transform* by providing new insight, giving perspective, or advocating for social change. It should ask the questions: "Why am I being told these things? What will I know by the end of the poem I did not know before? Toward what end?" (Hirshfield, 1997, p. 13). Why is there a reason for speech rather than silence? These questions contend with ethical concerns of representation. Poets "peer into dark places and speak for those who have no voice. They wander into the cities and forests, with eyes and ears open, and report on these experiences with astonishing candor and subtleness" (Parini, 2008, p. 178). The representation of research participants in a manner that honors their stories, seeks social change and new ways of being speaks to ethical issues of presentation and research participation. As Charles Simic, former poet laureate stated, a poet "reminds the reader of his or her own human predicament."

Ars Criteria *as Found Poetry as Demonstration of Artistic Concentration/Craft*

I demonstrate my commitment to the dialogue with and critique about rigor in qualitative research through the use of found poems. During NaPoMo (National Poetry Month) in April 2015, I participated in a found poetry project created by the editors of the Found Poetry Review as a PoMoSco (Poetry Month Scout) who worked with and through different exercises to create found poems (www. foundpoetryreview.com). Found poems are created by poets from existing texts such as web pages, text books, newspapers, magazines, and overheard conversations through attention to line, voice, music, and craft. A PoMoSco's charge was to act like a poet-scout and earn virtual badges by crafting a found poem a day. One of the poems I wrote, *At the intersection*, presents my consideration of and play with craft using a textbook on Arts-Based Research (Leavy, 2015). I spend many hours teaching, researching, and writing about Poetic Inquiry, so it is not surprising that *Methods Meet Art* sat next to my computer when I was scrambling to earn my "Open Book" badge. The exercise I used to generate the poem entailed selecting a source text, finding two consecutive pages, and then copying down interesting words and phrases without changing the order.

> At the intersection
> of the merging of the world
> and the Art-Science Divide,
> the points of convergence
> between polarized worlds,
> larger shifts focus new spaces,
> tools shape questions,
> our arsenal "for the sake of more."
> The value system is hybrid
> in both form and content:
> the power toward public
> is worth noting—
> grab powerful ways
> and audience members.

This poem articulates in a condensed form why I use arts-based research in much of my scholarly work and my preference for poetry, in particular.

Creating Ars Criteria Poems

When using poetry as/in/ for research à la Poetic Inquiry, I searched at the intersection between scientific and artistic criteria to offer considerations in that shaded middle space: Poetic inquiry may be evaluated on the demonstration of artistic concentration, embodied experience, discovery/surprise, conditionality, narrative truth, and transformation (see above). In the case of Poetic Inquiry, one may use *ars poetica* (i.e., the art of poetry) to establish one's aesthetic and epistemic commitments as I advocated for previously (Faulkner, 2007). In the present criteria du jour, I revisit work that speaks to what I find important when considering rigor in qualitative research, and ABR and Poetic Inquiry, through the use of found poems that I am calling *ars criteria* (the art of criteria). This is a twist on *ars poetica* as attention to craft by transforming writing about the art of criteria at the intersection between art and science.

I created the series of *ars criteria* poems, *What is qualitative criteria?*, by using an online Diastic Poem generator. This found poem technique required a source text and a seed text and is similar to an acrostic poem where the first letter of each line read downward will spell out words or each word of each line to create a message. I used chapter 3 on poetic criteria from the first edition of *Poetry as Method* as a source text and used the seed phrase, "what is qualitative criteria." The seed phrase should be 20 characters and can be related to your text, which in my case was the criteria chapter. I entered my source text and seed text into the Diastic Poem generator multiple times to retrieve six usable poems (www.languageisavirus.com/diastic-poem-generator.html). The poem generator program creates a "spell-through" of your text. For example, the program searched through my text for the first word that had "w" in the first position and added it to my word list. Next, it searched for a word that had an "h" in it and placed that word in the second position and continued in this manner until the end of my seed text was reached.

What is qualitative criteria?

I.

what:	work the reality that
is:	assignment
qualitative:	questions questions what feelings
	continued importance poetica
	grandfather observations qualitative consciousness
criteria:	craft traditional said writing
	grimes history
	attention potential

II.

what:	want the what that
is:	identity is
qualitative:	questions music stanzas taylor considerations
	semantic poetica feminist unrecognized
	qualitative demonstrate
criteria:	concentration craft spirit
	that collection
	criteria something longenbach

III.

what:	works that meant poetry
is:	is as
qualitative:	qualities dumped
	that world workings
	sensations exploration imagination
	scientific qualitative acknowledged
criteria:	connection are criteria
	poet wondered
	concerns subordinate emotional

IV.
what: with sheets craft what
is: is   is
qualitative: question buzzing   translate fully
        fulfill sensation
        persona interested inspiration
        qualitative acknowledge
criteria: circle
        ars akin   poetry statements
        better rejection performance
V.
what: wander rhythmically imagined poetry
is: is   is
qualitative: quickens fuck than goals
        qualitative attention
        poetica imagination
        qualitative alternative unrecognized
criteria: critical proportion this that failed
        requires criticism dissertation
VI.
what: when whip leads that
is: in as
qualitative: questions gut years build premise inserted disposable
        interact inspiration substantive qualitative
criteria: craft art   writes coat table rather reflexivity criteria

What I see when I examine these poem forms is a prioritization of attention to craft and the nature of Poetic Inquiry, the flexibility of fun of language to express conditional truths. When I read and reread these poems, I see the art of criteria as a vigorous exploration of what poetry as social science can do. I appreciate what Chilton and Leavy (2014) propose as criteria for arts-based research created from their careful reading of the literature: question/method fit, aesthetic power, usefulness, participatory and transformative, artful authenticity, and canonical generalization.

I am not suggesting that everyone become a PoSco (poetry scout)—though doesn't that sound like a fun undertaking?—but I am reiterating the idea of artistic concentration and concern with craft when using ABR, and poetry, in particular. Lafrenière and Cox (2012) introduce the GABRA (Guiding Arts-Based Research Assessment) framework that encompasses these ideas: training/coaching in chosen art form, application of methodological and ethical criteria, technical and artistic criteria, consideration of audience, and aspects of performance. I do not see a way out of NOT assessing the quality and effectiveness of qualitative research, and once again, choose to focus on vigorous application and transformation of craft.

Good Enough Poetry?

During the month-long process of finding source texts to create found poetry, I was struck by how the use of form and structure could be creative, how working within the constraints of form could spark and nurture the creative process and be considered like a qualitative process of criteria expanding. This notion of expanding and flexible criteria reminded me of a personal conversation I had with the poet Gabriel Welsch (May 24, 2004) about the possibilities of criteria for good research poetry.

> And the notion of vagueness is endemic to writing texts, since no one wants to go on record saying DO NOT, and therefore suffer the ignominy of some upstart winning a Pushcart doing the very thing they said not to do. SO you get vagueness, qualifiers, the kinds of things that social scientists tend to deal with in footnotes but writers wring their hands over in actual paragraphs not unlike this one. Where does that leave the enterprising ethnographer? In the same place it leaves writers: somewhere between intuition and hubris.

This raises the dialectical dilemma of proposing criteria with its stifling nature and the concomitant irony of reigning in that which is meant to expand. Can there be such a thing as flexible criteria? I transform a question posed about ABR: Does Poetic Inquiry "widen the circle" and ask better questions in order to get at qualitative generalizability (Siegesmund & Cahnmann-Taylor, 2008)? My examination of my past writing on poetic criteria through the use of *ars criteria* as found poetry offers a way to "widen the circle," to ask better questions, and to aspire to the universal.

The Poetic Inquiry Criteria I propose do focus on craft and sublime considerations, yet they are also flexible enough to be written in colored pencil, acknowledging that our conceptions of good or effective poetry may alter through time, experience, and changing tastes. Researcher-poets may need to articulate *ars poetica* or *ars criteria* with every poetic project. Or quoting the poet Richard Hugo (1992): "Ink tends to give the impression that words shouldn't be changed ... That is the advantage of making up rules. If they are working, they should lead you to better writing. If they don't, you've made up the wrong rules" (pp. 37, 43).

Some researchers have argued persuasively that criteria limit alternative forms of research writing by constraining freedom and possibility due to the connection of criteria with situated power structures (Bochner, 2000; Clough, 2000). Given these concerns, I recognize the caveat of constraint when suggesting the use of *ars poetica, ars criteria*, and *Poetic Inquiry Criteria* as potential vehicles by which to evaluate research poetry. However, I believe we need to consider the poetic process and the implications for research poetry because as Garratt and Hodkinson (1998) state:

> Such writing helps refine and develop our thinking about what doing and judging research entails, acts as an heuristic device for teaching others about these things, and represents a key part ... of the research tradition of which we are a part.
>
> *p. 535*

Writing good enough poetry in the form of found poetry or poetic transcription is another answer. Butler-Kisber and Stewart (2009) tout the benefits of using poetic transcription as found poetry.

> Found poetry not only mediates different kinds of understanding, but also enhances the relational dimensions of research. Because it relies on the words found in the data, found poetry is restricting. However, those limits can be comforting because the researcher is not compelled to find the "perfect word" ...
>
> *Butler-Kisber & Stewart, 2009, p. 4*

This may be especially helpful for beginner researcher-poets who are working on their poetic practice. Lahman and Richard (2014) suggest that good enough poetry can be revisited and edited, making revision an integral part of our Poetic Inquiry practice.

> Good enough poetry gives novice research poets the space to share their work with peers and critics in the hopes of improving and getting closer to the essence of participants' understandings, something all social science researchers hope for—poet or not.
>
> *p. 352*

Here is where the research-poet can use the nuances of data analysis and observations to highlight important parts of the research project. Good enough poetry may be that which focuses more on the epistemic dimensions of the research project. Lahman, Richard, and Teman (2019) consider poem*ish* representations to be good enough. "Poemish representations may be said to be research representations characterized by features of poetry and an effort to blend the aesthetics of poetry and science of research into something which may be said to be poem-like, ish, or poemish" (p. 215).

Consider that our work may be effective or *poemish* when it is closer to the epistemic part of the dialectic, and strive for the aesthetic side; it may be that a telling aesthetic is at work in research poetry. A focused concentration on the history and method of poetry promises to create further dialogue, help generate creativity and originality in qualitative research, and may help us create good poetry. Addonizio (2009) emphasizes the study of poetic craft as necessary and fulfilling.

> Poetry is often a misunderstood art. People think it's easy to write. They don't realize that it is as difficult to make a great poem as it is to make a great painting or blast out a virtuoso electric guitar solo. To understand poetry as an art is to understand that it is the same as every art, every discipline. It is work. Work that you struggle with and sometimes turn from in frustration or even despair. But also beautiful work you can go to in times of stress and loss.
>
> *p. 15*

I see this as an argument for making poetry a daily practice, reading other poets' and poet-researchers' work to see what you like, write in form and free verse. Read. Write. Revise. Dare to be good.

The use of *ars poetica, ars criteria*, and the suggested poetic criteria as one means of evaluating research poetry recognizes that criteria are mutable and dependant on particular communities and situations (Bochner, 2000; L. Richardson, 2000). Laurel Richardson (1997b) proposed that the "central imaginary" of validity for postmodern texts would be a crystal, "which combines symmetry and substance with an infinite variety of shapes, substances, transmutations, multidimensionalities, and angles of approach" rather than the triangle in more traditional texts (p. 92). She reminds us that crystals may alter their shape but they are not amorphous. Siegesmund and Cahnmann-Taylor (2008) make an argument for a layered conception of arts-based research, including poetry. A layered conception means allowing multiple questions and modes of evaluation. If inquiry is focused on asking questions and provoking the imagination, new, flexible methods of evaluation are needed that expand our thinking of good poetry and good research (Leavy, 2015). I adopt this crystal analogy that positions criteria as fighting nebulousness yet remaining flexible, open to critical reflection and dialogue, given that criteria and our use of it is "influenced by the nature of the research report, the standpoint and dispositions of the reader, and the socially, culturally, and historically located interaction between the two" (Garratt & Hodkinson, 1998, p. 532).

> Maybe a good enough poem is effective.
> Maybe a great poem is already in your tool box.
> Read the next chapter for ways to sharpen your focus,
> Flex and stretch your poetic muscles.

4

EXERCISING THE POETRY MUSCLE

In the beginning, you're likely to write a lot of bad poems. You will flounder around, unsure of what you're doing. You'll write lines that are perfectly clear to you that no one else understands. You'll write lines you feel are breathtaking in their beauty, only to have someone say, "That's a cliché. I've heard in a million times before." Don't worry about it. Read, write, and read some more, and you will get better (Addonizio, 2009, p. 62).

Exercising the Poetry Muscle

What remains elusive in Poetic Inquiry, as with any creative process, is the ability to really demonstrate how the poet moves from thoughts, images and sensations to the actual shaping of the words on the page. This creative process, to some extent, will always remain impervious to an articulation that is largely intuitive, and individualistic (Butler-Kisber, 2012, p. 164).

The possibilities and praxis of poetry and Poetic Inquiry for qualitative researchers lie in our skills and motivations to further poetic craft as method and methodology. This means studying poetic craft and form, developing artistic discipline, and understanding poetic inspiration as well as artistic processes of research, revision, and critique, which are similar tasks for researchers learning research methods and epistemological positions. This book has addressed the use, craft, and practice of poetry as/in/for qualitative research through an explicit discussion of the process of its construction, goals for its use, aesthetic and epistemic concerns, and criteria for good and effective Poetic Inquiry.

This final chapter acts as a heuristic, offering suggestions, questions, and challenges for Poetic Inquirers to consider in their work by focusing on poetic inspiration through the use of writing exercises intended to train the poetry muscle. I wrote this chapter to make the process of Poetic Inquiry less mysterious while concomitantly acknowledging that individual and groups of researcher-poets will find and develop their own creative processes. I address the following questions through specific and detailed writing exercises:

- In what ways can you transform research, interviews, reflections, and observations into poetry?
- How do you move from research problem to poetry?
- What are the best exercises for the type of work you want to do and your research goals?
- How can you best collaborate with other poets and poet-researchers?

I end with some reflections on how regular poetic practice may help in your poetry making through habit, mindfulness, and finding joy in the necessity of revision, and I offer selected books on craft and critique for further reference and reading.

Challenges for Poetic Inquirers

One challenge of a concentrated study of Poetic Inquiry is how this work will be labeled and accepted. Hartnett (2003) acknowledged being asked if his investigative prison poems are poetry by poets, if they are research by academics, and if poetry by activists can matter. Questions of whether Poetic Inquiry is poetry or research or whether it can make a difference may be tackled by focusing beyond an individual researcher bent on exploring questions of aesthetics *or* representation, and instead having a head-on collision between the epistemic *and* aesthetic dimensions of poetry as/in/for research. In an editorial in *Qualitative Health Research*, Janice Morse et al. (2009) discussed why they don't publish poetry as research in the journal:

> What happens when good research is presented in the form of bad or mediocre poetry? We have not been convinced by a rigorous argument that such transposition enhances the depth of analysis and richness of findings. Interpretation and analysis ought to be in the realm of theoretical construction and practical import, yet much of this poetic presentation does not even attempt to explain "what this research means" for the practice world ... So, until you convince your editors with cogent argument, we are sticking to a policy that prefers plain text, plain speak, and profound conclusions over artistic forms of data presentation.
>
> *p. 1035*

Part of the solution may be knowing when and how to use poetry in one's work to gain a wider audience. Sullivan (2009) urged researchers to understand when there is poetic occasion in their data or research context and to not rely solely on spacing and line breaks for the creation of research poetry. For Sullivan, this poetic occasion consists of five qualities: (1) concreteness or how the poem can represent and embody, (2) the potential for voice or lyric quality (which may more challenging to find in academic texts used as found poetry), (3) the tension between the intended and the accomplished, (4) ambiguity, and (5) the associative logic between relations and coherence. A good poem can show the research process and analysis in addition to making an aesthetic statement.

Another suggestion for attaining high standards in the use of poetry in qualitative research is the recognition that not all poetry need be published as part of a project. The use of poetry as a means for data analysis and reflective practice can complement traditional research practice. Kusserow (2008), for example, considers ethnographic poetry as a way to engage in thick (wild) description because of the "fierce meditation" and ability to "uncover layers of reality and subtlety" (p. 75). "Poetry and data collection became mutually informative (for me). The act of writing a poem … a deep meditation on my field notes where I tried to focus on all of the subtleties of what I had observed" (p. 74). The practice of poetry helped Kusserow ask both more focused questions during participant observation, and questions they may not have considered before they wrote poems. Other researchers advocate centering creativity in one's research to allow for artistic processes to predominate (e.g., Janesick, 2003). Poetic Inquirers can make poetry integral to the data analysis process, thus harnessing the power of poetry in their work. In addition, using the exercises I present in this chapter is a way to center creativity in the research process.

The most important difference between the poet and the Poetic Inquirer may be the ordering of the continuum, where the import of the re-presentation begins, with research or aesthetic concerns. Neilsen (2008) reminds us "our need to delineate categories prevents us from drawing upon all linguistic resources across all disciplines, allowing for the possibility of poetry, alone, for example, as being sufficient 'evidence' of inquiry and of knowing" (p. 97). This suggests that Poetic Inquirers should keep exploring questions of what poetry as/in/for research looks like, what research informed by poetry writing does, what kinds of questions poetry lets us ask, and the challenges and issues that poetry as a research genre present (Leggo, 2008a). However, many Poetic Inquirers contend that writing quality poetry and quality research means attending to criteria in both areas, persistence, and much training, especially since achieving credibility and rigor in poetry *and* research concomitantly represents a dialectical challenge. Being "true" to research experiences and data may conflict with ideas of good poetry as exposition and slavish adherence to facts are often antithetical to poetic imagination. Perhaps, striving for good enough poetry to meet one's research goals is good enough. Perhaps, we should use the crystallization metaphor; we use varied means and varied poetic forms to show the multi-dimensional nature of research. Perhaps, continued dialogue about the aesthetic and epistemic demands of Poetic Inquiry will make our work stronger on both counts. Perhaps we consider revision and reaching toward our artistic and research goals as a continuous process.

To attend to calls for quality in both research and poetry, Poetic Inquirers could not only submit their work to their research peers, but also to the scrutiny of poets. In addition to writing workshops, classes, and reading and studying poems and poets, Poetic Inquirers should consider transdisciplinary collaboration with poets. Collaboration could take other forms such as mentoring, poets writing research poetry from a Poetic Inquirer's data and data analysis, or research teams composed of poets and qualitative researchers. We can also ask ourselves reflective questions about our work to demonstrate credibility, trustworthiness, and vigor. For instance, Ohito and Nyachae (2018) offer ten questions that researchers interested in "harnessing the affordances of Black feminist poetry" may ask themselves or pose to research participants during the research process:

1. What does your poem convey about your racialized/(trans★)gendered/queer(ed)/classed, etc., identities and lived experiences?
2. Whose voices are present in this poem? Conversely, whose voices are absent? How are voices in dialogue?
3. How does your poem speak (back) to dominant discourses about identities?
4. What does your poem reveal about your data? How does the poem reveal your analyses of the data? How does the poem speak to (or with) your coresearchers' analyses of the data?
5. What deepened or different understandings about your participants, your coresearchers, and/or yourself do you have as a result of writing and rereading this poem?
6. How did you engage creativity in the construction of this poem? How does your poem reflect wordplay?
7. What word, phrase, sentence, or image in the poem most resonates? Why?
8. Did you use language that sits on the emotional and affective register? In other words, does your poem provoke feeling?
9. How did you experience the writing of this poem? Where did you feel most viscerally provoked (that is, affectively or corporeally charged) as you wrote or reread the poem? Why?
10. What segment of the poem was most/least challenging to construct? Why?

p. 9

Two final questions poet-researchers should contend with in their study of poetry as research are: How can the act of writing poetry be part of ethical research practice? How can Poetic Inquiry be part of social change and advocacy work? The altering of "facts" can protect vulnerable research participants by concealing their identities (e.g., González, 2002). Re-presenting research participants in ways that honor their stories and voice, call for social change, and offer new insight provides researchers with a means for advocating. Furthermore, the use of poetry as reflective practice can help with the acknowledgment of bias and expectations, and the intersection and power differences between researcher and participants. "Poetry ... allows the researcher or scholartist to enter into an experience in the only way any researcher can (regardless of method)—as herself, observing and recording. She does not presume to speak for another" (Neilsen, 2008, p. 97). Ethical issues of re-presentation may also be related to the quality of the Poetic Inquiry, one of the arguments I outlined in this book. With this thought, I conclude by offering exercises aimed to produce poetry for Poetic Inquiry by having you "flex the poetry muscle."

Poetic Inquiry Exercises

The Dramatic Monologue (Voice and Representation)

The dramatic monologue is a poem interested in characterization, "developing personality, motive and viewpoint" (Bugeja, 1994, p. 249). It is a poem "spoken by a character or through a persona, rather than by the poet or an unidentified speaker" (Drury, 2006, p. 78). The Victorian poet Robert Browning's dramatic monologues, *My Last Duchess* and *Soliloquy of the Spanish Cloister*, represent models of the form. The character in a dramatic monologue may be human or animal, identified though not necessarily named—a real, imaginary, historical, or literary figure (Drury, 2006). Using a persona may help when thinking about representing research participants, especially those who seem inscrutable or when describing difficult situations and actions. Robert Hayden, for instance, wrote a dramatic monologue, *Night, Death, Mississippi*, that adopts the point of view of an aging Klan member. This form of poetry is good for allowing the audience to reach conclusions and to do the analysis, given that the poem usually doesn't provide this overtly.

This exercise is a mixture of a dramatic monologue and an expression of your beliefs regarding poetry:

- Look at some poetry collections that use persona poems for ideas about how you can take a persona: for example, Frank X. Walker's (2008) collection, *When Winter Come: The Ascension of York*, in which he writes persona poems about York who traveled with the Lewis and Clark expedition; Cornelius Eady's (2001) persona poem collection, *Brutal Imagination*, about Susan Smith, a Texas mother who drowned her children and claimed a young African American man had kidnapped them before confessing; Andrew Hudgins' (1988) sequence of poems called, *After the Lost War*, about Sidney Lanier, a Georgia poet and musician born in 1842; Paul Zimmer, a poet who has written persona poems about Zimmer himself as a persona (e.g., *The Great Bird of Love*).

- Try the persona poem as a form of *ars poetica*. Imagine your research self as a persona in conversation about your poetic aesthetics with a research participant, a poet, or another researcher. You could include a conversation, choose the persona of the other to characterize; the goal is to think motive, personality, and viewpoint. Use any form. The poems, *Hoagland Writes to Faulkner about Thingitude* and *Letter to Faulkner from the Fluff and Fold*, presented in Chapter 3 are examples.

Ekphrastic Poetry

Poetry that responds to nonliterary art, especially the visual, through imitation, description, critique, dramatization, and/or reflection is called ekphrastic poetry. We can expand the idea of ekphrastic poetry with the use of poems as literature reviews, responding to the literary (see Prendergast, 2006).

> Ekphrastic poetry is a vehicle that allows the writer to enter into an imagined conversation with the artist. When Ekphrasis is practiced as a dialogue with the work of art this may lead to a process of discovery in which the poet explores some essential question of his or her own life through the lens of that work of art and an inquiry into the experience of making it. Embedded in these interpretations is the idea that any artist in any era might address certain timeless aspects of the human experience—birth, growth, maturation, love, loss, jealousy, grief, joy—each expressed in the vernacular of its moment of origin.
>
> *Gulla, 2018, p. 24*

We can use ekphrastic poetry as response to visual objects in fieldwork, and as a form of reflective research practice. Often the subject of ekphrastic poetry is not the artwork itself, but rather the poet's response and transformation as a result of the art. For research poetry, using a visual or literary source as the starting point for a poem is one method for presenting the tenor of the project, for presenting a different and broader understanding of the phenomenon, and/or for having a creative trigger. Oughton (2012) considers responding to an art work as a form of phenomenology: "when a poem is the vehicle for exploration, anything it encounters is significant" (p. 77). We bring ourselves and our sensibilities to the process, we are writing about ourselves and the process, and this can be an act of reflexivity.

> The metaphor that speaks to me about writing a poem in response to a painting is the mirror that is also a one-way window, such as in police interrogation rooms. Think of the painting is a window, albeit not perfectly transparent, into the artist's world. But it is also a mirror of the observer: why does this particular work speak to me, capture my attention? Some paintings I am

content to view for a few seconds; others grab me with almost physical force, compelling me to experience them in depth. What in me makes me respond?

Oughton, 2012, p. 77

Aitken (2012) makes an argument for poetry as one form of nonliterary art that complements visual art. Thus, ekphrastic poetry may be an occasion for words and a good way to re-present our research and research process.

- For this exercise, use a transcript from an interview, seven sources from a litera-ture review, and/or a photograph from fieldwork as the basis for your poem.
- Be aware that as Drury (2006) has argued, "The poem that merely replicates the painting (or other visual work) seems flat indeed. It should add something in its language that takes off from the picture, or talks back to it" (p. 86).
- Answer the following questions: What themes do you see? Note these portions of the interview or parts of the image. What do these themes feel, smell, and taste like? How can you describe these themes using more than one sense, especially if it is a sense you usually ignore?
- Keep this quote from T. S. Eliot in mind: "Immature poets imitate; mature poets steal; bad poets deface what they take, and good poets make it into something better, or at least something different."
- One variation of this exercise if you are interested in poetry as data analysis and openly conversing with poetic/research influences is to adapt Witkin's (2007) idea of relational poetry and Eliot's idea of what good poets do. First, choose a poem/passage that you admire. Second, write a poem in response to your admired poem/passage. You could be contesting or agreeing with something, writing an ode to the poet, etc. Third, write a poem that interweaves lines from the first and second poem, creating an interactive poem. This process demonstrates social construction and meaning-making, how point of view demonstrates different interpretations. Most likely, you will revise this third poem and "ditch the evi-dence" by ridding the poem of the stolen phrases or altering them.

Poetic Transcription

This exercise uses variations on poetic transcription to create what we may call a "found poem," or a poem created from "text discovered in a nonpoetic setting … removed from its context and presented as a poem" (Drury, 2006, p. 109). This found poem represents writing/research that was not intended as poetry, but you will declare it such through your choice of "found" parts in your research.

The closer the original intent of the language comes to that of poetry, the less likely it is to qualify as true found poetry … The poet does not enjoy the license to change, add or omit words, a rule often broken.

Padgett, 1987, p. 82

Padgett (1987) claims that one must only pay close attention to "exceptional" use of language, poetic stories, or those that create a strong affective response and decide on line breaks and the poem's limits.

Select a few research interview transcripts and some research literature from a project for the following variations:

1. The Found Poem

• Read a transcript and highlight words and passages that represent the interviewee. Arrange them in a poem that illustrates a theme, idea, or situation. Consider how line breaks and enjambment can help the tension and sense of poetic language. As Drury (2006) noted, enjambment is key to "mark the rhythmic flow of a poem ... enjambment is like musical syncopation; instead of pausing, the musical phrase pushes ahead" (p. 93). This is a found poem. You may want to read the poem out loud while you compose to help you hear line breaks, enjambment, and rhythm.

> When a poet creates relationship between the syntax and the lines of her poems, she is trying to organize the language on the page so that it corresponds to what she hears in her head. The poet may speak the lines out loud while composing the poem, but she generally does this to test what is on the page against what she hears—much as a composer turns to the piano not to discover the melody but to confirm it ... Reading a poem out loud helps us to hear that relationship, the poetry is not literally need to be spoken in order to exist primarily as a sonic work of art.
>
> Longenbach, 2008, p. 14

• For a variation on the above point, try creating a found poem that uses a form other than free verse, for instance, a sonnet. Find themes in the interview transcripts. You may use a version of open coding akin to grounded theory where you review transcripts line-by-line and make notes of descriptive codes, then selective coding where first level codes are condensed and recategorized (Glaser, 1978). Read the interviewee's words under each theme, "searching for the essence conveyed, the hues, the textures, and then drawing from all portion of the interviews to juxtapose details into a somewhat abstract re-presentation" (Carr, 2003, p. 205). The resulting poems can then be analyzed using theoretical coding where you search for conceptual relationships between the categories represented in the poems (Glaser, 1978). If you wish, create another poem that includes the themes from the theoretical coding.

2. The Investigative Poem

- Prendergast (2012) urges Poetic Inquirers to turn to the "social work of poetry":

> Over the millennia, poets have spoken the truth as they have seen it about themselves and the world around them, and oftentimes those truths have been challenging to speak and in difficult times and places. Visionaries and revolutionaries throughout history have known the power of the arts in general and of poetry in particular to speak the most beautiful (even if beautifully harsh) truths to the most awful of those in power.
>
> *p. 489*

She suggests examining Carolyn Forché's 1993 anthology collection *Against Forgetting: Twentieth Century Poetry of Witness*, wherein poets respond to war, authoritarianism, and genocide, and Muriel Rukeyser's *Book of the Dead* about a West Virginia coal mining town's lung disease for inspiration as a social poet. I like Julia Kasdorf and Steven Rubin's (2018) *Shale Play: Poems and Photographs from the Fracking Fields* as another example of poetry as political action and poet as witness and activist. It is also an excellent example of a collaboration between a visual and a literary artist.

To Try: Create an investigative poem in the spirit of being a poetic ethnographer, a poet of witness. Read the transcripts, but don't read too closely (i.e., don't make any notes until *after* you have read the transcripts through a few times). Take notes, including phrases, quotes, and impressions after reading the transcripts (see Soniat, 1997). Write a poem that includes: words that are important (what happened), your impressions and perceptions of what it was like, and connect the poem to a larger political context to show the personal and the historical intersection. This connection may be shown through the poem title or epigraph (e.g., Walker, 2008). You may try writing a fieldnote poem, an interview poem, and/or a transcript poem. Repeat this exercise by examining your observations in field notes, and write another poem using research artifacts (e.g., policy reports) as the source text.

3. The Surrender and Catch Poem

- Another variation of the found poem is the *Surrender and Catch* poem as articulated by Monica Prendergast (2015).

> My process unfolded organically in that I began highlighting lines, phrases, or stanzas that had some kind of resonance or made an impression on me as I read. While I tried very hard not to determine why I was highlighting what I did, in hindsight I can determine some guiding characteristics or qualities that struck me:

- Aesthetic power
- Imagery, metaphor
- Capturing a moment
- Truthtelling, bravery, vulnerability
- Critical insight, often through empathy
- Surprise and the unexpected.

p. 683

This method is an adaptation of the phenomenologist Kurt Wolff. The idea is you suspend any notions of what you expect to find—*the surrender*—and let what happens happen—*the catch*.

Use this method with your research literature, an interview transcript, or in a collaborative project with team members' research journals. Use Prendergast's guiding characteristics as you highlight words and passages.

4. Literature Review as Found Poem

The Jewish Question

> Never, no matter what kind of crisis I was going through, did it ever occur to me to be anything but Jewish. Or to be nothing.
> *D. Rogoff, in Petsonk, 1998, p. 129*

Rabbis sigh, throw up their hands: How are gay
Orthodox Jews the solution if they're
the problem? Abe says, I'm not *too* Jewish,
shut inside a double closet away from religion,
identity shoved into different boxes, passes for parents
as a devout—not queer—Jew when in *shul*.

Others tear their hair, can't be anything but at *shul*,
in the bakery buying bread with their gay
partners, can't be nothing, even if parents
eat ham paninis on *Yom Kippur*. For them,
the dusty rope that binds culture and religion
was never severed. The differences of Jewish,

the queer *Havurot* that smelts Jewish
and gay, dykes with boas at Seders, make old-school
rituals seem like mules beside reform religiosity
where we chant: I'm sexy, I'm queer, I'm gay.
This coming out song a religious duty for those
who know when to sing, apparent

heading to band practice; a drive to parenthood
collides with Jewish renewal. Leigh makes her child a Jew
because all the Christians at work, they
breathe in sin and horror, hold it. But at *shul*
her child will see Jewish, know that gays
like her wife perform *mitzvot* pride for this religion.

Reconstructionists ask: Is this homecoming, love and religion?
Rachel keeps her name, her nose, though her parents
never sent her to *shul*, like snow in July, her gayness
more than a small sigh. Religious Jews unnerve, but she's a Jew
and a lesbian, teaches by example—out at school.
Still, she grips a secret, tries to halt judgment they

could sentence. In private *not Jewish enough*, though they
would say Jew, welcome to the family. This is no religion
like Catholicism. We forgot our difference in schools
with Christians after fleeing dark ghettos with parents
who said no, yes, and why not assimilate? Our Jewish
modernity, a secular and religious stew, but being gay

brings no salty certainty, because we ask them queer
questions, the teachers and schools, religious parents
who hang our gay pictures in some new sewing room.

The Jewish Question is a sestina I use as a literature review to introduce a narrative study on LGBTQ Jews (Faulkner, 2006). This poem reflects Prendergast's (2006) idea of composing a literature review as found poems, the material for the poems taken from the body of literature framing a study. The poem incorporates research texts on LGBTQ and Jewish American identity, as well as voices from 31 narratives about being LGBTQ and Jewish I collected with a focused yet flexible interview guide (Patton, 2001). During interviews, conversations, and emails with participants and in the texts I studied about being Jewish and gay, I noticed repeated words and phrases. The sestina is a form that capitalizes on such repetition. During the course of the poem, the playful repetition builds around a pattern of six repeated words at the end of 39 lines, so that "in the end the sestina becomes a game of meaning, played with sounds and sense" (Strand & Boland, 2000, p. 22). "Gay," "they," "Jewish," "religion," "parents," and "school" were words I witnessed in the interviews and conversations, read, and experienced again and again. The use of repetition mirrors common speech and the fact that individuals tend to repeat themselves in everyday conversations (Strand & Boland, 2000). Repeated words become themes that circle back onto themselves, questioning meaning and becoming variations, representing the literature and narratives as more contested, uncertain, and in motion than a prose presentation (cf. Richardson, 2002).

To create a found poem as literature review:

- Take several sources from your literature.
- Do a thematic analysis by using the "surrender and catch" technique, highlighting words and phrases that feel important.
- Arrange the captured text in a way that portrays the thematic analysis. This may mean the use of formal verse.

5. The Dialogue Poem

Dialogue poems represent remembered and recorded conversation in the form of natural talk; they are ethnographic observations about daily conversations and field work (Faulkner, 2014a). This form is well suited to interview transcripts and/or recollected conversations. For example, all of the dialogue poems in *Knit Four, Frog One* (see Chapter 2; Faulkner, 2014a) are recreated from conversations between my daughter, my partner, and me. The dialogue poem is like a social media post of a conversation; the poet has captured a stirring, funny, angry, or poignant moment. Because I am a poet and a social scientist, I pay attention to everyday conversation and details, listen for moments that resonate with me and are part of larger cultural conversations that may be opportunities for poem making (Rose, 1990). Sarah Penwarden (2017), a poet-researcher-therapist, uses recued speech poetry, which is a poetic technique of listening to a person's speech during therapy and creating found poems to give back to them.

> There are a number of specific things that I am listening for in participants' speech, namely the overall narrative of the conversation, evocative phrases, metaphors, imagery, and symbols. I am also listening for re-membering. I listen with a poetic ear, both during the interview and later while I listen to the recording a number of times.
>
> *p. 228*

The dialogue poem, which we could consider a version of rescued speech poetry, is a good way to present the process of meaning-making in (auto)ethnographic work, to show the nuances and importance of everyday talk, to increase the credibility of your research, and to evoke a feeling in the audience of witnessing and being there.

To Try: 1. Recollect a conversation with a research participant, collaborator, or significant other that illustrates a theme you wish to present in your work. Use an interview transcript or your research journal if you need some help. Portray the memory using vivid language (i.e., words, details, and scene that capture something important). After you write a dialogue, ask yourself how the poem re-presents the theme you wanted to portray? The theme may become the title of the poem. Share the dialogue with the research participant, collaborator, or significant other and ask for their feedback. Write another dialogue poem based on feedback from the first poem. The poem title may be used to present the setting, the theme, or a feeling.

Poetic Analysis

One way to find themes in the interview transcripts, journals, and/or research artifacts you have is to analyze the "data" like a social scientist through poetic analysis. You may use a version of grounded theory analysis where you review transcripts and materials line-by-line and make notes of descriptive codes, then use selective coding where descriptive codes are condensed and recategorized and construct poems from the process (Glaser, 1978). See Chapter 2 for helpful details on how Rich Furman and colleagues (Furman, Lietz, & Langer, 2006) constructed research poems and how Ruby and I (Faulkner & Ruby, 2015) created found poems from a year-long series of email exchanges using RDT and contrapuntal analysis.

How To: 1. Begin descriptive coding by reading your journals/transcripts, "searching for the essence conveyed, the hues, the textures, and then drawing from all portion of the interviews to juxtapose details into a somewhat abstract re-presentation" (Carr, 2003, p. 205). Read through all of your materials to get a holistic sense of the data, and then note the themes/ideas/concepts that you see. You may wish to create a pdf file of your materials and analyze them using both online comment tools and by writing on paper copies of the document (e.g., highlighting words and phrases, making notes of categories and themes and theoretical memos with the sticky note function and writing in the margins). Ask yourself the following sensitizing questions à la Baxter (2011) and contrapuntal analysis as you read and reread your materials: "What does a listener need to know in order to render this textual segment intelligible? What socio-cultural and interpersonal discourses need to be invoked to understand what this textual segment means?" (Baxter, 2011, p. 159). Write down your initial impressions in the margins, noting answers to the question: "What is being said or implied about my research theme(s)?" (Baxter, 2011, p. 162).

2. Write a poem or poems about the themes using your coded material. The highlighted passages may become part of your poems. Use any of the other exercises presented in this chapter for ideas about form.

3. To find more themes, do a meta-coding of your work by searching for conceptual relationships between the categories you represented in your first poems. For example, in my collection of poems about mother-daughter relationships (Faulkner 2014a), I used one poem I wrote about the idea of mothering as an act of friendship as a springboard for more poems (see *Mother/Daughter*). Thus, writing poems based on my initial coding of poems

told me even more about family; I discovered in subsequent poems that mother is a verb.

The Triptych

Randall Brown, the editor of JCCA, defines the triptych as "a three-columned submission, with the piece itself in the center column ... the surrounding columns to be used in a way similar to ... the pop-ups in music videos." The poem should be a single stanza poem not exceeding ten lines or 75 words (http://matterpress. com/journal/).

I adapted the guidelines from *Compressed: The Journal of Creative Arts* to create a triptych poem titled *A.L.I.C.E. Training*, about active shooter training for

• A woman's name is an acronym for active shooter training: **A**lert **L**ockdown **I**nform **C**ounter **E**vacuate • I don't participate "in my own survival" though my university insists this training is mandatory. • Instead, I play dead in my office. • One is not supposed to play dead during a mass shooting, because a shooter may double back. • Experts don't like the term hide; they prefer "deny access." • Writers like active verbs better than passive: For example, "Keep operating if shot. Get yourself out."	Always keep your thumbs untucked Litter your purse with poems Inside the bag pack poetry like bullets Cauterize wounds with words, as if Elfin words salve riddled holes	• My daughter's school installed boots on the classroom doors. • I picture the *Vogue* fall catalogue, and not the *Guns & Ammo* Back to School issue. • The boot is a safety device also called a teacherlock. • Women as emotional Gatekeepers responsible for male anger. • The boot moves the *if* possibility of gun violence to *when*. • Mass Shooters are All Different. Except for One Thing: Most are (Angry White) Men.

FIGURE 4.1 A.L.I.C.E. Training

faculty at my university and for the teachers at my daughter's elementary school. I wrote a short acrostic poem—when the first letter of the lines, read downwards, spells a word or phrase or sentence—with the first letter of each line spelling out the acronym A-L-I-C-E. The poem is placed in the center column.

In the remaining columns, I wrote the story of the poem in bullet points:

What surprising, fascinating stuff can you tell us about the origin, drafting, and/or final version of A.L.I.C.E. Training?

My daughter is getting out of 4th grade a day early for holiday break this year, because her teachers are doing an all-day A.L.I.C.E. training. Is this real? Teachers as bullet-proof vests. I started writing this piece when I skipped the mandatory A.L.I.C.E. training at my university. I remembered Sandy Hook, and how I sat in my office crying when I heard about all of those children killed by bullets. I was paralyzed in my office as my daughter sat in preschool. Being in education is like being a target for gun violence. We still do not have sensible gun laws, and I am still shocked that we love guns more than we love people. I am certain more guns are not the answer. I am certain that me sitting in training will not prepare me to be a human shield. I turned to words, the only thing I can use as a weapon and as preparation for our sickness and obsession with guns (http://matterpress.com/journal/2018/12/).

This form is well suited to research poetry and displaying your analysis processes given the three-columned approach. You can write a poem about a research theme, and then show the analysis in the right- and left-hand columns. You could write a poem about a research participant, and write about your interaction with them in the right- and left-hand columns. You could write a poem reflecting on your research self, and write about the research context in the left- and right-hand columns.

The Short Poem

In 2005, Truth Thomas created *The Skinny*, a short form of poetry, during a poetry workshop at Howard University.

A Skinny is a short poem form that consists of eleven lines. The first and eleventh lines can be any length (although shorter lines are favored). The eleventh and last line must be repeated using the same words from the first and opening line (however, they can be rearranged). The second, sixth, and tenth lines must be identical. All the lines in this form, except for the first and last lines, must be comprised of ONLY one word.

Thomas, n.d.

The Skinny is a good form to convey a vivid image. Thomas considers the form best for reflecting "more serious concerns facing humankind," though the form can be used with any subject. This form can also be used as a series like with other forms of linked poems (e.g., haiku, senryu, tanka).

The idea of a short poem or poems as research poetry reminds me of some of the goals of lyric poetry—using condensed images, expressing personal feelings, and showing emotional context in musical lines. Randall Brown, editor of *The Journal of Compressed Creative Arts*, refers to a short, compressed poem this way:

> Skinny refers to the way it looks on the page, as well as a weightlessness. The poem should have a swift, sudden feel; therefore, lean language is imperative. Keywords are brevity, intensity, and precision. A good condensed poem should be memorable for its reading duration and its longer impression.
>
> *http://matterpress.com/journal/*

Try writing a short poem from your research journal and/or field notes. Use The Skinny as a model or consider Brown's ideas of a compressed poem as lean language and weightless feel.

The Long Poem

The long poem or series of poems connected by subject matter seems to be an excellent exercise for poet-researchers. The process of sustaining a theme or form can teach you what are "important excitements" in your poetic life (Anderson, 2001) or what Hugo called "triggering subjects" (1992). Drury (2006) writes that a long poem today may be anything over three pages, but even more likely it reaches beyond the lyric impulse. Anderson (2001) believes that writing a series of poems can indicate to you what are your personal obsessions: "you will almost certainly learn something about your habitual gestures, your extravagances, and your reticences; the places where you give up or the places where you push ahead" (p. 161). The pushing through may be helpful in honing and developing your craft skills.

- I adapt Maggie Anderson's (2001) exercise for writing a group of related poems, either in form, content, or both. First, write a proposal of what you want to do. In this, include the number of poems, the subject matter/theme, and possibly form decisions. You could decide to use a crown (or cycle or garland) of sonnets, where the last line of one sonnet becomes the first line of the next sonnet in a series of seven poems. The final line of the seventh sonnet repeats the opening line of the first sonnet, mimicking a circle or crown. A sonnet contains 14 lines and usually is written in iambic pentameter with a rhyme scheme of *abab, cdcd, efef, gg,* though a poet may not choose to follow any kind of rhyme scheme when using a crown of sonnets. See

Karen Bjorneby's (2002) crown of sonnets, *Persephone's Crown*, for an example. Alternatively, you could also choose another form for the series, such as the sestina. James Cummins' (1986) *The Whole Truth: A Poem* is a series of sestinas as detective story where he parodies the TV show "Perry Mason." Another option is to not decide on the form in the proposal stage, giving yourself more flexibility options during the writing. Use the proposal to stay focused during the construction of your poems.

Forms and Function

The use of formal forms in research poetry may help show your data analysis through the representation of themes or allow you to use poems as part of the data analysis. For example, the pantoum, a Malay form, plays on repeated lines in quatrains; the second and fourth lines of a stanza become the first and third lines of the next stanza. The recurring lines can be hypnotic as they weave in and out of one another, creating surprises as they work together in novel ways (Padgett, 1987). It is a slow form because a reader takes four steps forward and two steps back, making it "the perfect form for the evocation of a past time" (Strand & Boland, 2002, p. 44). I find this form enticing to represent the fact that most narratives are not straight-forward, that individuals often end up back where they started, working though identity issues in an anti-narrative pattern as identities change in our relationships and communities over time. The following poem from my project on LGBTQ Jewish identity (Faulkner, 2006) demonstrates this back and forth motion:

I was to be an Orthodox Rabbi

When I was 3, I knew I liked boys,
the interest and feelings I always carried
like ancient Hebrew script on scrolls
you could find in caves along the hills of Jerusalem.

The interest and feelings I always carried
with crushes on friends that blushed with love
in caves along the hills of Jerusalem,
relics of Judaism lying in dust,

and crushes on friends that burst into love.
I left the orthodoxy at 13
relics of Judaism lying in dust.
I had many questions I wanted to ask

as I turned from orthodoxy at 13,
mom's dream of me in black hat, soaked with sin.
The many questions I needed to ask
my therapist at 14 who told me to find women

made mom and dad's dream of me return like sin
until I found the Reconstructionists and moved.
My straight best friend at 17 showed me women.
I traveled with one, backpack and all, to see if I could.

When I found Reconstructionism and moved
I became a professional super Jew and super Dad
backpack and all, traveled with wife and child, like I could
ignore my thoughts that men like men.

I became super Jew and super Dad
with no time to think of males with lust,
I ignored my thoughts that men like men
with hair like bears and worked out thighs.

On the Jersey turnpike, time to think of males with lust,
I discover at 50 at a silent retreat, thoughts
with hair like bears and worked out thighs
can make me move and renovate my love.

These thoughts in silent retreat I discover
like ancient Hebrew script on scrolls.
I move my love and reconstruct memories,
because when I was 3, I knew I liked boys.

This form may be appropriate for showing broken narratives and the past because of line repetitions that disallow a linear progression. The poem represents how some participants in the study felt forced to choose between their personal level of identity (being LGBTQ and Jewish), their relationships (e.g., by being in a straight relationship), and how they enacted their identities (e.g., being closeted at work, not attending gay cultural events) because of others' ascriptions about being LGBTQ and Jewish based on communal representations of these as incompatible identities.

The epistle, or letter poem, can offer a more intimate tone because this poetic form uses plain language to discuss ideas of love, philosophy, religion, and morality (Padgett, 1987). It can allow the poet to adopt a friendly, informal tone to directly address readers (see Letter to the IRB from South Jersey in Chapter 1). A letter poem can allow Poetic Inquirers a way to reflect on the research process and show the frustrations, misunderstandings, and gaffes as well as the joy, connection, and competence. *Letter to Sol after the SSSS Presentation* demonstrates the connection between my own identities and the participants' by rooting my position in my own standpoint and history (Denzin, 1997) to show how our everyday shifting positions influence understanding and embodiment of identities. The stories of a researcher's identities intersecting with participants can help a reader understand a cultural event and illuminate it by showing a connection at a "basic level of human understanding."

Letter to Sol after the SSSS* Presentation

Dear Sol: I felt ensnared between that coffee table
littered with miniature bran muffins, squares of butter
in silver foil, and the textbook table display of the hottest
vibrators, dildos, and educational videos when you found me.
That shot of coffee I poured I needed before my talk
on gay Jews. My head hurt. Too much smiling and small
cups of caffeine (Why do those pretty scrolled ivory
things hold 3 ounces?). Too much advice taken. My Jewish
grad school advisor tells me I look mean when I think.
Smile, Sandra, she tells me. Maybe that's why you waited
to approach. That and two students with comments
about theories of identity. I remember you sat
on my right, 6 rows back or so, in the middle.
Do you think there were about 40 people? Masses
for a panel composed of new faces. But, then again, gay
topics are like hot sauce right now. That one and a half
years spent driving around New Jersey, on the subway
in New York, and in diners with margarine toast
and faux cream, I boiled down to 15 black and white
transparencies. That unnerved me. I'm still figuring
it all out. And, 15 pieces of plastic just lay there. Silent
and mind-numbing. Let me tell you, unofficially, I abhor
public speaking. Yes. I teach it when I must, but I loathe
that hot and tired wave of nervousness. I admit, I
checked out who looked gay in the audience. Sure,
it's not supposed to matter, but what and who you
are slinks in like a six-pack in the balcony.

So, there was nowhere to go when you approached,
muffin in hand, to say, "I'm a liberal Jew. What the *hell*
were you talking about with those different affiliations?"
Your question stung, made me forget if you even
introduced yourself or asked this question with muffin
in your mouth. I was like a 1st year graduate student
lost in a master theory class, face flushy pink. *Havurah*
got you, foreign to your British ears, a liberal Jew
would know such groups you implied. I should talk
about this. Not just throw up these terms, skim over them,
assume others know. Should. Should. Should.

You know, people dress questions in different fashions.
This aggressive style, the one where you throw sticks

at me, agitates my southern soul. My adopted Yankee
persona only gets aggressive driving and direct
invitations. And she doesn't emerge at conferences.
Too anathema. If she did, she may have told you,
too bad so sad, stop whining just because you didn't
do your homework. Things and people exist outside
of our small vision, bless our hearts. Thank God, I
swallowed that response with the bran muffin. My shrug
meant here it comes, the story. Honey, the one I told
you consisted of terrible time constraints and research
procedures, how I let them label their own identity.
Havurot rose in the waves of the 70's consciousness
groups, many gay Jews felt welcome and centered themselves
there. Did you smile, walk away? Did we shake hands?
Later, when you greeted me with *Shabbat shalom*, handed
me your lottery ticket for luck at the research fundraiser,
I got it, the other story (but not the toys or videos).
We ascribe identities like address labels
because we need them. I held back about the street fair
in my new neighborhood, what locals call
The Westcott Nation. You assumed I was Jewish, right?
Well, so did the rabbi. I sat at his table with
the on-line *Yom Kippur* cards because he smiled;
I needed that to reconnect to this study.
He needed my name as I left, no cards purchased.
With white girl shame, I mumbled that not Jewish last
name, an out-group label. His eyebrow became a question
mark that dismissed me, though I fared better at the public
radio table. The cute woman there described
the stations women's programming, the lesbian
voices program the previous week. Do you get it?
I had on khaki cargo pants, tight T-shirt that read
I Will Not Kiss the Boys, and a *Girls Rule* hat
embossed with a rainbow flag. Maybe I'll
find the address and mail this letter to you. For sure,
next year, the lottery ticket is on me.

Dr. Faulkner Sandra

*Society for the Scientific Study of Sexuality

This epistle poem explores how my identities and enactment of identities as white,
bisexual, researcher, southern, teacher, and poet emerged, collided, and generally
became salient in formal conference and in informal, "on the street," presentations
of the research. Specifically, the poem addresses how multiple identities can conflict

and compete in the research process and the layered influences on the enactment of identities or communication style.

The tanka, a Japanese form, consists of 31 syllables and five lines (usually with a syllable count of 5-7-5-7-7, though in English some follow accented syllables of 2-3-2-3-3). Drury (2006) considers the tanka less formal than haiku, but the former still allows a poet make declarations, statements, and pay attention to imagery. The focus on mood, usually love, seasons, sadness, or the brevity of life, and the use of poetic devices like personification may make the tanka good for some research poems (Padgett, 1987).

This exercise requires an examination of how poetic forms can enhance data analysis:

- For the use of poetry as data analysis, use the four-step process that Furman et al. (2007) followed in their work on adolescent identity and development. In the first step, take a research poem(s) you have written, and in the second step, write another poem(s) in a form that explores themes from the first poem (or poems). You may try a letter poem, a pantoum, or a haiku. You will want to note your impressions of the first poem(s), reading and rereading to identify themes. Consider any characteristic words or phrases and see if this suggests a poetic form. The third step is to take the poem(s) in form and use a grounded theory approach to reflect on action words and meaning. In the fourth and final step, write responsive poems to the grounded theory analysis and original poems. This is an excellent exercise for a research team with different members writing poems in the various steps to encourage self-reflexivity and deep understanding.

Create Your Own Poetic Form

Another way to approach the use of writing exercises for constructing poems in your research is to create your own form. You can borrow ideas from any of the exercises described here, from books of writing exercises (e.g., Addonizio & Laux, 1997; Kooser, 2005; Thiel, 2001), and even create your own arbitrary (or not) rules. Creating rules that differ from a typical pattern or modus operandi in your own work could be helpful as a way to push your craft, avoid the usual, and flirt with originality (Longenbach, 2004). If you are using the poem as a means of data analysis, you may find some rules that will help you accomplish this (e.g., using form, using a persona, including key terms). It is easy to get stuck in a pattern in your writing. Consider lines and stanzas in your form. For example, what should the line length be in terms of syllables, stresses, words, and number of lines in the poem? Consider whether these lines should be enjambed, end-stopped, or some mixture. How many lines per stanza will you have? Will you use a rhyme scheme? Will your stanzas be structured with purpose (e.g., one scene/voice/idea/metaphor per stanza)?

I offer an exercise which I created when prompted in an editing workshop to make up my own form. The reason I chose to include a title from a song and use at least two borrowed lines was to clearly acknowledge influences on my writing, but I also made sure to include a verb in every line to avoid the didactic and keep the poem moving. The stanza and syllabic form decision was arbitrary.

- The title of the poem comes from a song.
- The poem should contain four stanzas.
- There should be three lines in each stanza.
- There should be one borrowed (stolen) line in two stanzas.
- Each line should have no more than 12 syllables.
- Two stanzas should have an end stop.
- There should be one image per stanza.
- There should be one metaphor in every other stanza.
- Use at least one verb in every line.

Textual and Visual Collage

Collage can be a good technique for Poetic Inquirers who are working with the visual arts, working in transdisciplinary research teams, and want to work in multiple-mediums. Forms of collage and hybrid work include cento, found poems, cut-up, erasure poetry, and video. Collage is also an excellent teaching tool in the methods classroom. For instance, some students in my qualitative research methods class and I presented our collaborative understanding of reflexivity using semester-long research journals, reflexivity models, collaborative poetry, and collage exercises (Faulkner et al., 2016). You may use a cut-up technique, which references manually or digitally cutting up text and rearranging it to create a new text (see Chapter 3 for examples). Poet-researchers can use online tools to help with digital cut-ups, for example using the Lazarus Corporation Text Mixing Desk (www. lazaruscorporation.co.uk/cutup). Another valuable online resource is the *Language is a Virus* site, which includes text generators, text manipulators, and writers' games to help cure writer's block and inspire creativity (www.languageisavirus.com/ creative-writing-techniques/william-s-burroughs-cut-ups.php#.XEdMrql7kkq). The process of doing collage can enhance reflective practice. "When creating cut-up or collage poems, the poet considers existing text reflexively or suspends their current deep understanding by repositioning and then reconsidering the text" (Lahman, Teman, & Richard, 2019, p. 212).

How To: 1. Choose an interview or interviews to re-present, research literature, research journal entries, and/or research themes to present in a collage poem/ project.

2. Gather materials to use such as: interview transcripts, photos, field notes, letters, email, texts, researcher journals, research memos, crayons, pencils, pens,

paint, double-sided tape, glue, research artifacts, yarn, magazines, cardboard, metals, fibers, recycled objects. If you want to go old-school and make a non-electronic collage, photocopy or make pdfs of important artifacts.

3. Choose a medium (e.g., electronic, installation art, cut and paste, fiber arts, craft boxes, video, painting, drawing, sculpture, mixed media).

4. Do a thematic analysis as described in the poetic analysis exercise above. Circle and cut out the highlighted themes and important ideas. Cut out any pictures that may be helpful. Think about how you could represent the theme(s) you wish to present.

5. Lay out all of the pieces. Rearrange. Commit to your collage by gluing/using double-sided tape. Use any other material that helps you present the story/theme/idea (e.g., magazine pictures, fiber, recycled objects). If you want to use Photoshop, collect material in the same way. You can arrange photos of the material you wish to use digitally and use the draw function.

6. Create an artist's statement to accompany the collage by answering these questions: What process did you use to create the collage? How does the collage re-present these themes? What did you learn about the research and yourself as a researcher by engaging in the collage making process?

- Variation 1: Video and Poetic Inquiry
  Follow the steps above and use iMovie or another program that will allow you to use audio and video files. Collect photos, video, and audio of your research. Use poems you have written about your research. Sheila Squillante's and my *Nasty Women Join the Hive* womanifesta (https://vimeo.com/230906797) and my *Woman, Running* video collage (www.youtube.com/watch?v=YIJrXhDdNV0) are examples of poetic collage using sound, video, photos, and poetry.
- Variation 2: Free-Form Collage Poem (adapted with permission of Sheila Squillante)

1. Find at least three different, non-poetry texts (the more removed from poetic language, the more surprising the result). Optional: a draft of your own work that isn't quite working.

2. Open each text at random, one after the next, and quickly scan to locate those words/phrases that jump out at you. Again, try not to think in terms of narrative, so much as texture and sonic pleasure.

3. Write these bits down on a piece of paper/type them into a document.

4. Once you have this source material, there are a number of ways to stitch/sculpt it:

   - work from top to bottom in order, removing words, connecting phrases.
   - work from bottom to top in order, etc.
   - surrender every third line, surrender every third word.
   - pick the phrasing that feels most like a beginning and begin there.

- pick the phrasing that feels most like an ending and begin there.
- which line makes you most uncomfortable emotionally? Syntactically? Start there.
- add articles, change tenses as needed.
- add nothing and create a poem *only* with the language on the page, unaltered.

You can make one poem, or many poems from the same raw material. You can create a series or a suite this way. You may be surprised by how your poem looks like you—that is, reflects your usual concerns and subjects— even though it is built on the language of others inside of a context not your own.

Exquisite Corpse and Working Collaboratively

Denise Duhamel and Maureen Seaton are two poets who have written collaborative poems, published in the collections, *Exquisite Politics* (1997), *Oyl* (2000), and *Little Novels* (2002). The title, *Exquisite Politics*, is a play on a surrealist game, Exquisite Corpse, where writers use images and words collectively but hide half of the writing they do until the end to see what can occur. The idea is to upturn our usual habits of thought (www.poets.org/poetsorg/text/play-exquisite-corpse). Playing Exquisite Corpse can help uncover group angst and reveal collective unconsciousness. Collage and the surrealist tradition are all about collaboration, which is why Poetic Inquirers may wish to play this game with their research teams.

> **Duhamel**: The most delightful part about our collaborating is the shared creative burden. Even when we think we are stumping one another, providing lines that seem almost impossible to finish, the other can usually think of something to follow right away. We are open to mess and mayhem. We have found what we believe to be a third voice, a voice that is neither Maureen's nor mine, but rather some poetic hybrid.
>
> *Duhamel, 2006, para. 6*

It is the possibility of finding a third vice that makes Exquisite Corpse appealing for Poetic Inquirers. We may find new insights into our research and different means of presenting our work because of the collaboration process. Duhamel and Seaton discussed their collaboration in an interview (2006), and give us some rules for successful collaboration:

1. Thou shalt trust thy collaborator's art with thy whole heart.
2. Thou shalt trust thy collaborator's judgment with thy whole mind.
3. Thou shalt trust thy collaborator's integrity with thy whole spirit.
4. Honor thy own voice.

5. Honor thy collaborator's spouse.
6. Thou shalt not be an egotistical asshole.
7. Thou shalt not covet all the glory.
8. Thou shalt love the same foods as your collaborator.
9. Thou shalt eat and tire at the same time.
10. Above all, honor the muse.

para. 11

Writing poems collaboratively can be a good way to do poetic analysis, and can be part of a reflective research practice. I offer a variation of the game Exquisite Corpse, a kind of collaborative writing that is good for difficult and sensitive topics. You may play this with a research team, use it in class as a teaching tool, or engage the audience in a game at a conference (I recommend this as it is great fun). Playing a version of this game is a way to re-story a research project, safely disclose, and reveal secrets (e.g., stigmatized identities, abuse) that need to be discussed. Though, I think the best reason to play is the fun factor.

To Play: 1. Choose a theme or themes to write about. These themes may come from your data analysis, interview transcripts, your research questions/research purpose, or a topic you wish to explore. For instance, Sheila Squillante and I used locker room talk, rape culture, misogyny, and feminist response as topics when we played an email version of the game to write about a Trump presidency.

2. You could begin by answering writing prompts to use in the game. These prompts should be related to the themes you identified in step one. For example, Sheila and I used the following prompts: What do you remember about talk related to women and girls in school (locker room talk)? What is a feminist response to political events? What do you remember about sexual assault and violence growing up, based on your personal experiences (rape culture)? What does being a feminist mean to you (misogyny)?

3. Next, write down some details to any of the prompts from step two. Choose the answers that you want to explore and that have emotional resonance with you. Answer the following questions: What impact did this have on your life?/What impact did this have on a participant's life?; What details do you remember about this?/What details did a participant talk about?; What did this feel like? Smell like? Sound like?

4. Choose a version of Exquisite Corpse to play:

   • Version One: Group Poem Construction

   Use a large piece of paper. Decide on the form of the poem beforehand. You could have players write words in a pattern (e.g., noun, verb, adjective, noun). You could have players write lines of poetry (e.g., a tercet for a villanelle).

Based on the writing prompts, choose the first line to a poem. When you finish writing your lines, fold the paper over before passing it to the next person.

Some variations to this game: Choose to look at the preceding lines or not. Decide to not use a predetermined form. Play via email or IM.

- Version Two: Three Poems and Responses

You could write three different poems: one about a single participant's story, a poem where the structure matches the experience you want to write about, and a poem about one theme that emerged.

After you write a poem, share the poem and have another person write a poem in response to your poem. You could write a response to the poem and so on. This could generate a series of poems.

Revising, Re-Visioning, Re-Imagining

Revision is important, if not vital, in a poetic project. Justice (2001) stated the first thing a poet should simply do is to cut out the bad parts. Of course, recognizing those parts is difficult when "writers are too much blinded by a love for their own creations" to have the will to accomplish this cutting (p. 249). Lynn Emmanuel (2001) takes a more brutal approach to revision by suggesting we get rid of manners and politeness and recognize that part of the difficulty rests in how we write to "promote a definition of the self in which we are highly invested" (p. 255).

> Writing presents to us the nullity of ourselves, the inaccuracies of our conceptions of selfhood. We are both nothing and everything—provisional, shifting, molten. Writing forces us to confront that fact. And we can't immune that fickle, promiscuous self with a model of writing and revision that resembles marriage: union, fidelity. As long as we try to be good, we cannot revise. Or this is what she, who has disappeared, thought at some earlier moment when we belonged to one another.
>
> *p. 256*

In yet another approach, Miller (2000) argued that revision is not all drudgery, and in fact, all writers engage in mental revision during the act of writing by deciding what words to use. She makes many suggestions for revising poems from throwing out the first stanza, using the first stanza as the last stanza, using few adjectives and adverbs but strong verbs, reading the poem out loud to see where the words do not work, taking two failed poems and interweaving the lines, to adding new material and replacing entire sections. For some, the most difficult part of revision is not being cruel to drafts or knowing what to cut and paste, but rather knowing when you have truly finished a poem.

> A "finished" poem should be greater than the sum of its words; it should express itself in a magical, individual way. It should, at the same time, speak clearly to the reader. All aspects of the finished poem should be intentional. The language should be elegant or efficient or potent—a little tighter than prose. If the language is diffuse, its lightness should accomplish part of what the poem communicates. The poem should say something you know, something that is important to you. It should be pleasing to you both in what it accomplishes, and how it does so.
>
> *Miller, 2000, p. 12*

Think of revision as part of your research process. In an interview with Jacqueline Alnes (2018), the long distance runner and writer, Jaclyn Gilbert, compares revision to habitual practice that lets you free up space think without reservation.

> I think revision is about learning to let go of all the closed off places in ourselves. It offers a repetition that's much like doing the same running loops over and over, to the point that you don't have to think about where you are going anymore, and your mind becomes more free to explore new thoughts and sensations, observations that have been there all along, waiting for you to pay attention.
>
> *para. 17*

Take any research poem that you have written and do the following three revisions, creating three new poems:

1. Reduce the poem's words by one third to one half of the original number.
2. Try a new voice in the poem (e.g., if you wrote in first person, use third person. Try a persona or a different persona. Add another speaker and/or narrator, subtract a speaker and/or narrator). You may decide to try step one and two in the same revision.
3. Revise the poem in step two, creating a third revision, by writing the poem in a different form (e.g., if you used long lines, try short lines. If you used irregular stanzas, try stanzas with the same number of lines. Change to couplets or tercets. Change the timing and location of the poem).

   - Ask yourself critical questions of the revisions: Is the choice of words clouding the narrative or lyric content? Are the lines successful? Did I get across what I intended? Is there music in the poem? If I wrote the poem as prose with no line breaks, would it still work? If not, then what needs to be adjusted (rhythm, language)? Should I put this poem aside for a few months? Have I used hackneyed expressions, images, or language? Extraneous language? Are my images and language fresh? Am I too attached to what is working in the poem?

- Another idea for a radical revision is to throw out what you have written and start a new poem entirely. Miller (2000) suggested writing a poem, turning the page and writing the same poem without looking at the previous version, and repeating this process until you can't think of anything you haven't used. This may take six attempts or more; the important thing is to do this in one sitting. Another version of radical revision is to find the essence of the poem in a line, image, or statement and throw out the rest of the poem. Now use that image, statement, or line to create the poem that wanted to live (Addonizio & Laux, 1997).

- Why not try a *Top Down, Bottom Up* revision as Parker (2018) suggests? This entails cutting as much as you can from the beginning and end of the poem. You may find the poem starts a few lines in and that the end you have is too dramatic in an effort to be profound. "Cut what you can get away with cutting; find the beginning that launches us and the ending that offers satisfaction without bluster or sentimentality" (p. 257).

- McGrath (2018) has us take a green and yellow highlighter to our poems: begin by looking at your poem as if it were "alien" to you, such as imagining it were a biology text. You want to be "cold-blooded" and objective as you revise your work. He talks of the process as *re-envisioning* our work. Highlight the passages in green that are "really *good*—a strong verb, a well-hewn line, a striking image or a sudden emotional leap" (p. 249). In the next pass, highlight passages in yellow that are essential to the poem, even if they are not "extraordinary in themselves." Consider the highlighted and un-highlighted passages and ask yourself what the uncolored lines are doing in your poem? You may need to "erase the poem down to its green core and rebuild from there" (p. 250).

- Mark Doty (2010) presents an exercise to help poets rid their writing of qualifiers, which writers may use when their nouns and verbs "aren't interesting enough":

…from a draft in progress, remove every adjective and adverb, and see what you've got left. Can you strengthen any of the nouns and verbs remaining, through greater specificity or precision? To illustrate my point, consider the difference between *tree* and *Sassafras*, between *tool* and *adze*. You can't say *sassafras* when you mean *tree*, but often there's a more exact term waiting to be employed. Now, which, if indeed any, of the qualifiers you've erased do you really miss, which ones are absolutely necessary?

p. 112

- You could try Diane Lockward's (2018) idea of an "infusion revision" by getting a journal or collection of poems by another author. Examine the work for "wonderful, distinctive language" and "circle five fabulous words" (p. 274). Take a poem you need to revise and find places to insert the words you circled.
- Nicole Cooley (2018) makes three suggestions for revising or *re-seeing* or *re-entering* a group of poems, which seems helpful for Poetic Inquirers using a series of poems in heir work. First, Cooley suggests thinking across the poems, "going shallow" and "interviewing" the poems by asking questions such as:

What color is this group of poems?

If this group of poems had a favorite food, what would it be?

If these poems could speak to me about their greatest problems, what would they say?

What should I do differently?

p. 266

Next, Cooley goes deep and reviews the poems for three or four themes. (Use your research skills and think thematic analysis.) She takes these themes and looks to the dictionary to find the definition and write poems based on the word's origin. These poems may or may not end up in the final collection, but the point of writing them is to do deep thinking about the themes and language in the work.

We are not fixing or editing our poems when we revise, especially when we revise a group of poems. Instead, we are taking risks of language and form and meaning. We are going places in our work we did not know we would go. We are challenging ourselves to write the best poems that we may not feel capable of writing, the poems we are meant to write.

p. 267

Below you will find an example of the three-step revision exercise above I tried in a class on ekphrastic poetry inspired by music. After completing the revisions, I found the last version to be better than the original and first and second revisions because the images were surreal, mirroring feelings about current politics and war. The lines seemed more musical and focused after taking away the extraneous details, and adding material about Detroit that complemented the goal of showing the cycle of war on multiple levels.

First Version

The Suicide Window
—after "World Wide Suicide" by Pearl Jam

a snowplow scrapes the church/house sidewalk
riddled with snow shovels, our angry boots
coagulate sand, politics, we slush along with booted feet,
branches rub the house with wind, wind tickles hard
under our chins until cramped fingers slide out—

we can't catch our breath   hey, hey
until heavy lifting gives way;

our stomachs sour with unease,
bobble heads burst on dashboards
from the drone of work trucks, bulky
with too many tires, controlled yell
to save the wind, the rumble beneath
the undulating hack of just enough,
we pare down the winter whip

beat our heads until we must stop

Revision 1 and 2

Outside the Suicide Window
—after "World Wide Suicide" by Pearl Jam

your angry boots coagulate sand
and spilled lattes, clutched
with mittened hands, maroon yarn
spun tight like your soldier's obituary,

a snowplow scrapes the riddled church;
your stomach sours with unease,
bobble heads burst on neighbor's dashboards
from the drone of work trucks,

the undulating hack of just enough,
beat your head until it stops

Revision 3

Suicide Window, Detroit

What if we rode a snowplow
like a corporate tank, scraped
the sidewalk outside a city church?
Citizens riddled with snow shovels, our angry
boots coagulate sand, the new urban detritus.
Beautiful branches erupt out of dead buildings,
and the drone of the suburban engine
whines into wild city corners
beside the rust belt graffiti—
Stop the Man, You Suck,
stick kids stuck inside a crumbled façade—
bubbled lines sprayed on the shells of lost jobs.
What if we spilled our lattes, clutched
with mittened hands, maroon yarn
spun tight like our city obituaries,
let our stomachs sour with unease.
Bobble heads burst on work truck dashboards,
listen to the rumble beneath
the undulating hack of just enough,
pare down the winter whip
beat our heads until we stop.

For Further Practice, Reading, and Reference

In sum, Poetic Inquirers can work out their poetry muscles though the use of poetic exercises. Found poetry and the use of formal constructions is a way to begin if one feels unsure of or frightened by the use of free verse. The goal is to make poetry a habit through exercise that is playful and useful, stretchy and snappy. This includes revising our work. Revision is an important part of the Poetic Inquiry process; it is through revision that we may fully realize our Poetic Inquiry goals and make our work what we want and need it to be.

> The real work of the poet is revision, the test for which it is wise to adopt more workmanlike persona. Revision is the salt mine to which, pick in hand, we must all descend in time, the day job to keep a roof over our metaphorical heads. For this work—reshaping and unclogging and fine-tuning a poem—it is better to act like an engineer, or a plumber, or even an accountant, then a sleepy eye dreamer wandering through the garden waiting for poems to pop out of the roses.
>
> *McGrath, 2018, p. 249*

When you think and dream of poems regularly, exercise the poetry muscle, your subconscious becomes agile and ready for the habitual exploration of ideas (Miller, 2000). You strengthen your poetry muscles, so that you can make your practice regular and mindful as Jaclyn Gilbert articulates:

> My best writing comes when I let go, when I let my mind wander long enough to feel fully present in the writing process. My best races have tended to work similarly. If I can let go and trust my body to do the work I've trained it to do, I open up my mind to really listen to it, moment by moment, and I can tap into a confidence that will let me push boundaries without hurting myself. It's when I get scared, unsure of whether I can survive the pain or reach a deadline, that my body tightens up. I lose my breath and the courage to really explore what's possible inside the work. And I think the reader can feel that too, my lack of faith in what I'm saying.
>
> *Alnes, 2018, para. 16*

I close by offering some books on poetic practice and critique that you can use to develop and stretch your own aesthetics, to join the conversation, and to further your Poetic Inquiry. Happy reading, writing, and poetry making.

Further Reading

Addonizio, K., & Laux, D. (1997). *The Poet's Companion: A Guide to the Pleasures of Writing Poetry*. New York: W.W. Norton & Company.

Addonizio, K. (2009). *Ordinary Genius: A Guide for the Poet Within*. New York: W.W. Norton & Company.

Behn, R., & Twichell, C. (Eds.) (2001). *The Practice of Poetry: Writing Exercises from Poets Who Teach*. New York: Quill/Harperresource.

Buckley, C. B., & Merrill, C. (Eds.) (1995). *What Will Suffice: Contemporary American Poets on the Art of Poetry*. Salt Lake City, UT: Gibbs Smith.

Butler-Kisber, L., Guiney Yallop, J. J., Stewart, M., & Wiebe, S. (Eds.) (2017). *Poetic Inquiries of Reflection and Renewal*. Nova Scotia: MacIntyre Purcell.

Doty, M. (2010). *The Art of Description: World into Word*. Minneapolis, MN: Graywolf Press.

Drury, J. (2006). *The Poetry Dictionary* (2nd ed.). Cincinnati, OH: Writer's Digest Books.

Duhamel, D., & Seaton, M. (1997). *Exquisite Politics*. Chicago, IL: Tia Chucha Press.

Faulkner, S. L., & Cloud, A. (Eds.) (2019). *Poetic Inquiry as Social Justice and Political Response*. Wilmington, DE: Vernon Press.

Finch, A. (2005). *The Body of Poetry: Essays on Women, Form, and the Poetic Self*. Ann Arbor, MI: University of Michigan Press.

Galvin, K., & Prendergast, M. (Eds.) (2016). *Poetic Inquiry II: Seeing, Caring, Understanding: Using Poetry as and for Inquiry*. Rotterdam: Sense/Brill.

Hirshfield, J. (1997). *Nine Gates: Entering the Mind of Poetry*. New York: HarperCollins.

Hoagland, T. (2006). *Real Sofistikashun: Essays on Poetry and Craft*. Saint Paul, MN: Graywolf Press.

Hugo, R. (1992). *The Triggering Town: Lectures and Essays on Poetry and Writing.* New York: W. W. Norton & Company.

Kasdorf, J. S., & Rubin, S. (2018), *Shale Play: Poems and Photographs from the Fracking Fields.* University Park, PA: The Pennsylvania State University Press.

Kooser, T. (2005). *The Poetry Home Repair Manual: Practical Advice for Beginning Poets.* Lincoln, NE: University of Nebraska Press.

Longenbach, J. (2004). *The Resistance to Poetry.* Chicago, IL: University of Chicago Press.

Longenbach, J. (2008). *The Art of the Poetic Line.* Saint Paul, MN: Graywolf Press.

Oliver, M. (1998). *Rules for the Dance: A Handbook for Writing and Reading Metrical Verse.* New York: Houghton Mifflin.

Pack, R., & Parini, J. (Eds.) (1995). *Introspections: American Poets on One of Their Own Poems.* Hanover, NH: Middlebury College.

Padgett, R. (1987). *The Teachers and Writers Handbook of Poetic Forms.* New York: Teachers & Writers Collaborative.

Parini, J. (2008). *Why Poetry Matters.* New Haven, CT: Yale University Press.

Prendergast, M., Leggo, C., & Sameshima, P. (Eds.) (2009). *Poetic Inquiry: Vibrant Voices in the Social Sciences.* Rotterdam: Sense/Brill Publishers.

Raab, L. (2016). *Why Don't We Say What We Mean: Essays Mostly about Poetry.* North Adams, MA: Tupelo.

Revell, D. (2007). *The Art of Attention: A Poet's Eye.* Minneapolis, MN: Graywolf Press.

Rosko, E., & Vander Zee, A. (Eds.) (2011). *A Broken Thing: Poets on the Line.* Iowa City: University of Iowa Press.

Sameshima, P., Fidyk, A., James, K., & C. Leggo (Eds.) (2017). *Poetic Inquiry III: Enchantments of Place.* Wilmington, DE: Vernon Press.

See, C. (2002). *Making a Literary Life: Advice for Writers and Other Dreamers.* New York: Ballantine Books.

Simic, C. (1990). *Wonderful Words, Silent Truth: Essays on Poetry and a Memoir.* Ann Arbor, MI: University of Michigan Press.

Simic, C. (1994). *The Unemployed Fortune-teller.* Ann Arbor, MI: University of Michigan Press.

Strand, M., & Boland, E. (2000). *The Making of a Poem: A Norton Anthology of Poetic Forms.* New York: W.W. Norton & Company.

Thiel, D. (2001). *Writing Your Rhythm: Using Nature, Culture, Form and Myth.* Ashland, OR: Story Line Press.

Thomas, S., Cole, A., & Stewart S. (Eds.) (2012). *The Art of Poetic Inquiry.* Nova Scotia: Backalongbooks.

Townsend, A., & Baker, D. (2007). *Radiant Lyre: Essays on Lyric Poetry.* Saint Paul, MN: Graywolf Press.

Voight, E. B. (2009). *The Art of Syntax: Rhythm of Thought, Rhythm of Song.* Minneapolis, MN: Graywolf Press.

Wiegers, M. (Ed.) (2003). *This Art: Poems about Poetry.* Port Townsend, WA: Copper Canyon Press.

Young, D. (2010). *The Art of Recklessness: Poetry as Assertive Force and Contradiction.* Minneapolis, MN: Graywolf Press.

REFERENCES

Addonizio, K. (2009). *Ordinary Genius: A Guide for the Poet Within.* New York: W.W. Norton & Company.

Addonizio, K., & Laux, D. (1997). *The Poet's Companion: A Guide to the Pleasures of Writing Poetry.* New York: W.W. Norton & Company.

Aitken, K. (2012). Why visual art? In S. Thomas, A. Cole, & S. Stewart (Eds.), *The Art of Poetic Inquiry* (pp. 66–72). Nova Scotia: Backalongbooks.

Alnes, J. (2018). The need for distance: Jaclyn Gilbert on writing and running. *Longreads*, December, 2018. Available at: https://longreads.com/2018/12/03/the-need-for-distance-jaclyn-gilbert-on-writing-and-running/

Ahmed, S. (2017). *Living a Feminist Life.* Durham, NC: Duke University.

Alexander, P. (1991). *Commonwealth of Wings.* Hanover, NH: Wesleyan University Press.

Anderson, M. (2001). Important elements: Writing groups of related poems. In R. Behn & C. Twichell (Eds.), *The Practice of Poetry: Writing Exercises from Poets Who Teach* (pp. 160–163). New York: Quill/Harperresource.

Andrews, T. (1995). Ars Poetica. In C. B. Buckley & C. Merrill (Eds.), *What Will Suffice: Contemporary American Poets on the Art of Poetry* (p. 2). Salt Lake City, UT: Gibbs Smith.

Anzaldúa, G. (1981). *This Bridge Called My Back: Writings by Radical Women of Color.* Watertown, MA: Persephone Press.

Anzaldúa, G. (2013). The new mestiza nation: A multicultural movement. In Carole R. McCann & Seung-Kyung Kim (Eds.), *Feminist Theory Reader, Local and Global Perspectives* (3rd ed.) (pp. 277–284). New York: Routledge.

Archambeau, R. (2008). A guildhall summons: Poetry, politics, and leanings-left. *Poetry*, 193, 169–176.

Alcoff, L. M. (2003). Introduction. In L. M. Alcoff (Ed.), *Singing in the Fire: Stories of Women in Philosophy* (pp. 1–13). Lanham, MD: Rowman & Littlefield.

Badley, G. F. (2019). Post-academic writing: Human writing for human readers. *Qualitative Inquiry*, 25(2), 180–191. doi:10.1177/1077800417736334

Baxter, L. (2011). *Voicing Relationships: A Dialogic Perspective.* Thousand Oaks, CA: Sage.

Becker, R. (1995). Dreaming at the Rexall drug. In C. B. Buckley & C. Merrill (Eds.), *What Will Suffice: Contemporary American Poets on the Art of Poetry* (pp. 4–5). Salt Lake City, UT: Gibbs Smith.

Becker, R. (2000). *The Horse Fair*. Pittsburgh, PA: University of Pittsburgh.

Behar, R. (1996). *The Vulnerable Observer: Anthropology that Breaks Your Heart*. Boston, MA: Beacon Press.

Behar, R. (2008). Between poetry and anthropology: Searching for languages of home. In M. Cahnmann-Taylor & R. Siegesmund (Eds.), *Arts-based Research in Education: Foundations for Practice* (pp. 55–71). New York: Routledge.

Berger, L. (2001). Inside out: Narrative autoethnography as a path toward rapport. *Qualitative Inquiry*, 7, 504–518.

Bhattacharya, K. (2008). Voices lost and found: Using found poetry in qualitative research. In M. Cahnmann-Taylor & R. Siegesmund (Eds.), *Arts-based Research in Education: Foundations for Practice* (pp. 83–88). New York: Routledge.

Biley, F. (2016). Waking up following breast surgery: An insight from the Beats, Burroughs and the cut-up technique. In K. Galvin & M. Prendergast (Eds.), *Poetic Inquiry II: Seeing, Caring, Understanding: Using Poetry as and for Inquiry* (pp. 205–210). Rotterdam: Sense.

Bingham, R. L. (2004). Giant crickets attacking America: An interview with Tim Seibles. *New Letters: A Magazine of Writing and Art*, 70(3&4), 213–225.

Bischoff, T. (2001). Interview with Frank X. Walker. Available at: www.ket.org/bookclub/books/2001_apr/interview.htm

Bjorneby, K. (2002). Persephone's crown. *The Threepenny Review*, 23(1), 89.

Bloom J. (2003). *Gravity Fails: The Comic Jewish Shaping of Modern America*. Westport, CT: Praeger.

Bochner, A. (2000). Criteria against ourselves. *Qualitative Inquiry*, 6, 278–291.

Boylorn, R. M. (2014). From here to there: How to use auto/ethnography to bridge difference. *International Review of Qualitative Research*, 7(3), 312–326. doi:10.1525/irqr.2014.7.3.312

Brady, I. (2000). Anthropological poetics. In N. K. Denzin & Y. S. Lincoln (Eds.), *Handbook of Qualitative Research* (2nd ed., pp. 949–979). Thousand Oaks, CA: Sage.

Brady, I. (2004). In defense of the sensual: Meaning construction in ethnography and poetics. *Qualitative Inquiry*, 10, 622–644.

Brady, I. (2005). Poetics for a planet: Discourse on some problems of being-in-place. In N. K. Denzin & Y. S. Lincoln (Eds.), *Handbook of Qualitative Research* (3rd ed., pp. 979–1026). Thousand Oaks, CA: Sage.

Buch, E. D., & Staller, K. M. (2014). What is feminist ethnography? In S. N. Hesse-Biber (Ed.), *Feminist Research Practice: A* Prime (107–144). Thousand Oaks, CA: Sage.

Buckley, C. B., & Merrill, C. (Eds.). (1995). *What Will Suffice: Contemporary American Poets on the Art of Poetry*. Salt Lake City, UT: Gibbs Smith.

Bugeja, M. J. (1994). *The Art and Craft of Poetry*. Cincinnati, OH: Writer's Digest Books.

Burford, J. (2018). Sketching possibilities: Poetry and politically-engaged academic practice. *Art/Research International: A Transdisciplinary Journal*, 3(1), 229–246.

Butler-Kisber, L. (2002). Artful portrayals in qualitative inquiry: The road to found poetry and beyond. *The Alberta Journal of Educational Research*, XLVIII(3), 229–239.

Butler-Kisber, L. (2012). Poetic inquiry. In S. Thomas, A. Cole & S. Stewart (Eds.), *The Art of Poetic Inquiry* (pp. 142–176). Nova Scotia: Backalongbooks.

Cahnmann, M. (2003). The craft, practice, and possibility of poetry in educational research. *Education Researcher*, 32(3), 29–36.

Cahnmann, M. (2005). *Reverse the Charges.* Athens, GA: SL Mirth Edition.

Calafell, B. M. (2004). Disrupting the dichotomy: 'Yo Soy Chicana/o?' in the New Latina/o south. *The Communication Review,* 7, 175–204.

Calafell, B. M. (2014). The future of feminist scholarship: Beyond the politics of inclusion. *Women's Studies in Communication,* 37, 266–270. doi:10.1080/07491409.2014.955436

Carr, J. M. (2003). Poetic expressions of vigilance. *Qualitative Health Research,* 13, 1324–1331. doi:10.1177/1049732303254018

Carruth, H. (1992). *Collected Shorter Poems, 1946–1991.* Port Townsend, WA: Copper Canyon Press.

Chang, H. (2008). *Autoethnography as Method.* Walnut Creek, CA: Left Coast Press, Inc.

Chang, H., Ngunjiri, F. W., & Hernandez, K-A. C. (2013). *Collaborative Autoethnography.* Walnut Creek, CA: Left Coast Press, Inc.

Chang, J. (2018). "Each time the light changed": A Micro(inter)view with Jennifer Chang, curated by Lisa Olstein. *Tupelo Quart*erly, June 14, 2018. Available at: www.tupeloquarterly.com/each-time-the-light-changed-a-microinterview-with-jennifer-chang-curated-by-lisa-olstein/

Chilton, G., & Leavy, P. (2014). Arts-based research practice: Merging social research and the creative arts. In P. Leavy (Ed.), *The Oxford Handbook of Qualitative Research* (pp. 403–422). New York: Oxford University.

Clement, C., & Prendergast, M. (2012). *Poetic Inquiry: An Annotated Bibliography: Update, 2007–2012* (595 page bibliography). Victoria, British Columbia, Canada: Department of Curriculum & Instruction, University of Victoria.

Clough, P. T. (2000). Comments on setting criteria for experimental writing. *Qualitative Inquiry,* 6, 278–291.

Collins, M. (2006). *Blue Front: A Poem.* Saint Paul, MN: Graywolf Press.

Collins, M. (2007, March). History into poetry, poetry into history. Panel presentation at the annual meeting of the Associated Writing Programs, Atlanta, GA.

Collins, P. H. (2000). *Black Feminist Thought: Knowledge, Consciousness, and the Politics of Empowerment.* New York: Routledge.

Cooley, N. (2001). Three poems introduction. *Common-Place* [online journal], 1(3), Available at: www.common-place.org/vol-01/no-03/cooley/

Cooley, N. (2004). *The Afflicted Girls: Poems.* Baton Rouge, LA: Louisiana State University.

Cooley, N. (2018). Craft tip #27: The shallow and the deep: How to revise a group of poems. In D. Lockward (Ed.), *The Practicing Poet: Writing beyond the Basics* (pp. 265–267). West Caldwell, NJ: Terrapin.

Craigo, K. (January 7, 2019). When the poem writes back. Available at: https://betterviewofthemoon.blogspot.com/2019/01/when-poem-writes-back.html?fbclid=IwAR1EJ-2fulGKdgyFbI7ojOl50p08jxV0oCgKot_vAUvwC48j53FCmfM88KI

Craigo, K. (March 23, 2016). Bias and the literary review. Available at: http://betterviewofthemoon.blogspot.com/2016/03/bias-and-literary-review.html.

Cummins, J. (1986). *The Whole Truth: A Poem.* San Francisco: North Point Press.

Dark. K. (2009). Examining praise from the audience: What does it mean to be a successful poet-researcher? In M. Prendergast, C. Leggo, & P. Sameshima (Eds.), *Poetic Inquiry: Vibrant Voices in the Social Sciences* (pp. 171–185). Rotterdam: Sense/Brill Publishers.

Davis, A. M. (2007). S.I.P. (School Induced Psychosis): Poem for my daughter. *Qualitative Inquiry,* 13(7), 919–924.

Denzin, N. K. (1997). *Interpretive Ethnography: Ethnographic Practices for the 21st Century*. Thousand Oaks, CA: Sage.

Denzin, N. K. (2005). *Performance Ethnography: Critical Pedagogy and the Politics of Culture*. Thousand Oaks, CA: Sage.

Denzin, N. K. (2014). *Interpretive Autoethnography* (2nd ed.). Thousand Oaks, CA: Sage.

Doty, M. (2010). *The Art of Description: World into Word*. Minneapolis, MN: Graywolf Press.

Dove, R. (2012). Video: Breaking the Line, Breaking the Narrative. Available at: www.poets.org/poetsorg/text/video-breaking-line-breaking-narrative

Dove, R. (2018). *Q and A on Poetry*. Bowling Green State University, September, 20

Drury, J. (2006). *The Poetry Dictionary* (2nd ed.). Cincinnati, OH: Writer's Digest Books.

Duck, S. (2011). *Rethinking Relationships*. Thousand Oaks, CA: Sage.

Duhamel, D. (2006). Poetry and Collaboration: Denise Duhamel & Maureen Seaton. poets.org, December 21, 2006. Available at: www.poets.org/poetsorg/text/poetry-and-collaboration-denise-duhamel-maureen-seaton

Duhamel, D., & Seaton, M. (1997). *Exquisite Politics*. Chicago, IL: Tia Chucha Press.

Duhamel, D., & Seaton, M. (2000). *Oyl*. Long Beach, CA: Pearl Editions.

Duhamel, D., & Seaton, M. (2002). *Little Novels*. Long Beach, CA: Pearl Editions.

Eady, C. (2001). *Brutal Imagination*. New York: G. P. Putnam's Sons.

Eisner, E. (2005). *Reimagining Schools: The Selected Works of Elliot W. Eisner*. New York: Routledge.

Ellingson, L. (2017). *Embodiment in Qualitative Research*. New York: Routledge.

Ellis, C. (2000). Creating criteria: An ethnographic short story. *Qualitative Inquiry*, 6, 273–277.

Emmanuel, L. (2001). In praise of malice: Thoughts on revision. In R. Behn & C. Twichell (Eds.), *The Practice of Poetry: Writing Exercises from Poets Who Teach* (pp. 251–256). New York: Quill/Harperresource.

Fairchild, B. H. (2003, June). *The motions of being: On the intersections of lyric and narrative (a work in progress)*. Paper presented at the West Chester University Poetry Conference on Form and Narrative, West Chester, PA.

Fairchild, B. H. (2007). A way of being: Observations on the ends and means of poetry. *New Letters*, 74(1), 53–69.

Faulkner, S. L. (2018a). Crank up the feminism. *Rise Up Review!* Summer, 2018. Available at: www.riseupreview.com/Sandra-Faulkner.html

Faulkner, S. L. (2018b). Queering sexuality education in family and school. In A. Harris, S. Holman Jones, S. L. Faulkner, & E. Brook, *Queering Families, Schooling Publics: Keywords* (pp. 25–41). New York: Routledge.

Faulkner, S. L. (2018c). *Real Women Run: Running as Feminist Embodiment*. New York: Routledge.

Faulkner, S. L. (2018d). Shaming as a form of social activism: Autoethnographic stories. *Qualitative Inquiry*. doi:10.1177/1077800418806608

Faulkner, S. L. (2018e). Crank up the feminism: Poetic inquiry as feminist methodology. *Humanities*, 7(3), 85. doi:10.3390/h7030085

Faulkner, S. L. (2017a). Poetic inquiry: Poetry as/in/for social research. In P. Leavy (Ed.), *The Handbook of Arts-Based Research* (pp. 208–230). New York: Guilford Press.

Faulkner, S. L. (2017b) Faulkner writes a middle-aged *Ars Poetica*. In L. Butler-Kisber, J. J. Guinney Yallop, M. Stewart, & S. Wiebe (Eds.), *Poetic Inquiries of Reflection and Renewal* (pp. 147–152). Nova Scotia: MacIntyre Purcell Publishing Inc.

Faulkner, S.L. (2017c). Mother-poems: Using the confessional as critique in autoethnographic poetry. In S. Holman Jones & M. Pruyn (Eds.), *Creative Selves/Creative Cultures: Critical Autoethnography, Performance, and Pedagogy*. Cham, Switzerland: Palgrave-MacMillan.

Faulkner, S. L. (2017d). MotherWork collage (a queer scrapbook). *QED: A Journal in GLBTQ Worldmaking*, 4(1), 166–179.

Faulkner, S. L. (2017e). Poetry is politics: A poetry manifesto. *International Review of Qualitative Research*, 10(1), 89–96. doi:10.1525/irqr.2017.10.1.89

Faulkner, S. L. (2016a). TEN: The promise of arts-based, ethnographic, and narrative research in critical family communication research and praxis. *Journal of Family Communication*, 16(1), 9–15. doi:10.1080/15267431.2015.1111218

Faulkner, S. L. (2016b). Postkarten aus Deutschland: A chapbook of ethnographic poetry. *Liminalities*, 12(1). Available at: http://liminalities.net/12-1/postkarten.html

Faulkner, S. L. (2015). *Knit Four, Make One: Poems*. Somerville, MA: Kattywompus Press.

Faulkner, S. L. (May, 2015). "Critical qualitative rigor: Found poems as *ars criteria*" on Rigor in qualitative methods. Panel presentation at the 11th International Congress of Qualitative Inquiry, University of Illinois at Urbana-Champaign.

Faulkner, S. L. (2014a). *Family Stories, Poetry, and Women's Work: Knit Four, Frog One (Poems)*. Rotterdam: Sense/Brill Publishers.

Faulkner, S. L. (2014b). Bad mom(my) litany: Spanking cultural myths of middle-class motherhood. *Cultural Studies ↔ Critical Methodologies*, 14(2), 138–146. doi:10.1177/1532708613512270

Faulkner, S. L. (2012a). That baby will cost you: An intended ambivalent pregnancy. *Qualitative Inquiry*, 18(4), 333–340.

Faulkner, S. L. (2012b). *Hello Kitty Goes to College: Poems* (chapbook). Chicago, IL: dancing girl press.

Faulkner, S. L. (2012c). Frogging it: A poetic analysis of relationship dissolution. *Qualitative Research in Education*, 1(2), 202–227. doi:10.4471/qre.2012.10

Faulkner, S. L. (2009). *Poetry as Method: Reporting Research through Verse*. New York: Routledge.

Faulkner, S. L. (2007). Concern with craft: Using *ars poetica* as criteria for reading research poetry. *Qualitative Inquiry*, 13(2), 218–234.

Faulkner, S. L. (2006). Reconstruction: LGBTQ and Jewish. *International and Intercultural Communication Annual*, 29, 95–120.

Faulkner, S. L. (2005). Method: 6 poems. *Qualitative Inquiry*, 11(6), 941–949.

Faulkner, S. L. (nd). Real women run: Running as feminist embodiment. Available at: http://innovativeethnographies.net/realwomenrun

Faulkner, S. L., & Squillante, S. (2018) Nasty women join the hive: A womanifesto invitation for white feminists. *Women & Language Online*, 40(2). Available at: www.womenandlanguage.org/40-2

Faulkner, S. L., Guiney Yallop, J., Wiebe, S., & Honein, N. (2017). Playing exquisite corpse: Villanelles on family. In P. Sameshima, A. Fidyk, K. James, & C. Leggo (Eds.), *Poetic Inquiry III: Enchantments of Place* (pp. 87–95). Wilmington, DE: Vernon Press.

Faulkner, S. L., Kaunert, C., Kluch, Y., Koc, E. S., & Trotter S. (2016). Using arts-based research exercises to foster understanding of reflexivity in qualitative research. *LEARNing Landscapes*, 9(2), 197–212. Available at: http://learninglandscapes.ca/images/documents/ll-no18/llspring2016_final_lr.pdf

Faulkner, S. L., & Nicole, C. (2016). Embodied poetics in mother poetry: Dialectics and discourses of mothering. In K. Galvin & M. Prendergast (Eds.), *Poetic Inquiry II: Seeing, Caring, Understanding: Using Poetry as and for Inquiry* (pp. 81–98). Rotterdam: Sense.

Faulkner, S. L., & Ruby, P. D. (2015). Feminist identity in romantic relationships: A relational dialectics analysis of email discourse as collaborative found poetry. *Women's Studies in Communication*, 38(2), 206–226. doi:10.1080/07491409.2015.1025460

Faulkner, S. L., & Hecht, M. L. (2011). The negotiation of closetable Identities: A Narrative Analysis of LGBTQ Jewish Identity. *Journal of Social and Personal Relationships*, 28(6), 829–847. doi:10.1177/0265407510391338

Faulkner, S. L., Calafell, B. M., & Grimes, D. S. (2009). Hello Kitty goes to college: Poems about harassment in the academy. In M. Prendergast, C. Leggo, & P. Sameshima (Eds.), *Poetic Inquiry: Vibrant Voices in the Social Sciences* (pp. 187–208). Rotterdam: Sense/Brill Publishers.

Ferris, J. (2004). The enjambed body: A step toward a crippled poetics. *The Georgia Review*, 58(2), 219-233.

Finch, A. (2005). *The Body of Poetry: Essays on Women, Form, and the Poetic Self.* Ann Arbor, MI: University of Michigan Press.

Finch, A. (2007). A METER DOCTOR REPORTS FROM THE FIELD: Towards a metrical diversity cure (or, why free verse isn't free). *Educational Insights: Studio* [online journal], 1(1). Available at: http://ccfi.educ.ubc.ca/publication/insights/studio/c01n01/studio5a1.html

Finley, S. (2008). Arts-based research. In G. J. Knowles & A. L. Cole (Eds.), *Handbook of the Arts in Qualitative Research: Perspectives, Methodologies, Examples, and Issues* (pp. 71–81). Thousand Oaks, CA: Sage.

Fisher, T. (2009). Outside the republic: A visionary political poetics. *Textual Practice*, 23, 975–986. doi:10.1080/09502360903361600

Fitzpatrick, E., & Fitzpatrick, K. (2014). Disturbing the divide: Poetry as improvisation to disorder power relationships in research supervision. *Qualitative Inquiry*, 12(1), 50–58. doi:10.1117/1077800414542692

Fitzpatrick, E., Worrell, F. C., Alansari, M., & Li, A. Y. (2018). Let us dance. *Qualitative Inquiry*, 23(7), 495–501. doi:10.1177/1077800417718286

Fitzpatrick, E., & Alansari, M. (2018). Creating a warmth against the chill: Poetry for the doctoral body. *Art/Research International: A Transdisciplinary Journal*, 3(1), 208–228.

Frost, R. (1995). The figure a poem makes. In R. Poirier & M. Richardson (Eds.), *Robert Frost: Collected Poems, Prose, and Plays* (pp. 776–780). New York: The Library of America.

Furman, R. (2003). Exploring step-fatherhood through poetry. *Journal of Poetry Therapy*, 16(2), 91–96.

Furman, R. (2006a). Poetic forms and structures in qualitative health research. *Qualitative Health Research*, 16, 560–566.

Furman, R. (2006b). Poetry as research: Advancing scholarship and the development of poetry therapy as a profession. *The Journal of Poetry Therapy*, 19(3), 133–145.

Furman, R., Lietz, C., & Langer, C. L. (2006). The research poem in international social work: Innovations in qualitative methodology. *International Journal of Qualitative Methods*, 5(2). Available at: www.ualberta.ca/~iiqm/backissues/5_3/PDF/furman.pdf

Furman, R., Langer, C. L., Davis, C. S., Gallardo, H. P., & Kulkarni, S. (2007). Expressive, research and reflective poetry as qualitative inquiry: A study of adolescent identity. *Qualitative Research*, 7(3), 301–315.

Galvin, K. T., & Prendergast, M. (2016). Introduction. In K. T. Galvin & M. Prendergast (Eds.), *Poetic Inquiry II – Seeing, Caring, Understanding* (pp. xi-xvii). Rotterdam: Sense/Brill.

Galvin, J. (2005). Art class. In C. B. Buckley & C. Merrill (Eds.), *What Will Suffice: Contemporary American Poets on the Art of Poetry* (p. 36). Salt Lake City, UT: Gibbs Smith.

Garratt, D., & Hodkinson, P. (1998). Can there be criteria for selecting research criteria?—A hermeneutical analysis of an inescapable dilemma. *Qualitative Inquiry*, 4, 515–539.

Gee, J. (1985). The narrativization of experience in the oral style. *Journal of Education*, 167(1), 9–35.

Glaser, B. G. (1978). *Theoretical Sensitivity: Advances in the Methodology of Grounded Theory*. Mill Valley, CA: Sociology Press.

Glesne, C. (1997). That rare feeling: re-presenting research through poetic transcription. *Qualitative Inquiry*, 3, 202–222.

González, M. C. (2002). Painting the white face red: Intercultural contact through poetic ethnography. In J. N. Martin, T. K. Nakayama, & L. A. Flores (Eds.), *Readings in Intercultural Communication: Experiences and Contexts* (2nd ed.). Boston, MA: McGraw-Hill.

Goodall, H. L. (2000). *Writing the New Ethnography*. Walnut Creek, CA: Alta Mira.

Gordon, N. E. (2007). Considering chapbooks: A brief history of the little book. *Jacket*, 34. Available at: http://jacketmagazine.com/34/gordon-chapbooks.shtml

Gradle, S. (2017). Art at the end of time. In L. Butler-Kisber, J. J. Guiney Yallop, M. Stewart, & S. Wiebe (Eds.), *Poetic Inquires of Reflection and Renewal* (pp. 234–243). Nova Scotia: MacIntyre Purcell.

Grasso, S. (2018). Art student delivers perfect response to teacher's request to 'dial back the feminism'. *The Daily Dot*, February 8, 2018. Available at: www.dailydot.com/irl/dial-down-the-feminism/

Gingrich-Philbrook, C. (2005). Autoethnography's family values: Easy access to compulsory experiences. *Text and Performance Quarterly*, 25(4), 297–314.

Guiney Yallop, J. J., Wiebe, S., & Faulkner, S. L. (2014). Poetic inquiry in/for/as (editorial for special issue on *the practices of poetic inquiry*). *in education*, 20(2), 1–11. Available at: http://ineducation.ca/ineducation/issue/view/21

Gulla, A. (2018). Ekphrastic conversations: Writing poems as dialogues with works of art. *Canadian Review of Art Education*, 45(1), 23–31.

Hahn, K. (2009). Chapbook renaissance: The little book in the age of digital and DIY. *Poets & Writers*, September/October, 63–65.

Halberstam, J. (1998). *Female Masculinity*. Durham, NC: Duke University Press.

Hartnett, S. J. (2003). *Incarceration Nation: Investigative Prison Poems of Hope and Terror*. Walnut Creek, CA: AltaMira.

Hartnett, S. J., & Engels, J. D. (2005). "Aria in time of war": Investigative poetry and the politics of witnessing. In N. K. Denzin & Y. S. Lincoln (Eds.), *Handbook of Qualitative Research* (3rd ed., pp. 1043–1067). Thousand Oaks, CA: Sage.

Hirshfield, J. (1997). *Nine Gates: Entering the Mind of Poetry*. New York: HarperCollins.

Hoagland, T. (2006). *Real Sofistikashun: Essays on Poetry and Craft*. Saint Paul, MN: Graywolf Press.

Hudgins, A. (1988). *After the Lost War: A Narrative*. Boston, MA: Houghton Mifflin.

Hudgins, A. (2003). *Ecstatic in the Poison*. New York: Sewanee/Overlook Hardcover.

Hudgins, A. (2007, March). History into poetry, poetry into history. Panel presentation at the annual meeting of the Associated Writing Programs, Atlanta, GA.

Hugo, R. (1977). *31 Letters and 13 Dreams: Poems*. New York: Norton.

Hugo, R. (1992). *The Triggering Town: Lectures and Essays on Poetry and Writing*. New York: W. W. Norton & Company.

Hurren, W. (2009). The convenient portability of words: Aesthetic possibilities of words on paper/postcards/maps/etc. In M. Prendergast, C. Leggo, & P. Sameshima (Eds.),

Poetic Inquiry: Vibrant Voices in the Social Sciences (pp. 23–27). Rotterdam: Sense/ Brill.

James, K. (2017). What lovely words may also mean. In P. Sameshima, A. Fidyk, K. James, & C. Leggo (Eds.), *Poetic Inquiry: Enchantment of Place* (pp. 23–27). Wilmington, DE: Vernon Press.

Janas, M. (1991). Why poetry and prose matter: A conversation with Pamela Alexander and Martha Collins. Available at: www.oberlin.edu/wwwcomm/ats/atscurrent/ats0399/ atsmar99_poetry.html

Janesick, V. (2003). *Stretching Exercises for Qualitative Researchers* (2nd ed.). Thousand Oaks, CA: Sage.

Jarman, M. (1995). What only poetry can do. In C. B. Buckley & C. Merrill (Eds.), *What Will Suffice: Contemporary American Poets on the Art of Poetry* (pp. 72–73). Salt Lake City, UT: Gibbs Smith.

Johnson, T. H., & Ward, T. V. W. (1958). *Letter to Thomas Wentworth Higginson (1870), letter #342a. The Letters of Emily Dickinson* (1958). Cambridge, MA: Belknap Press of Harvard University Press.

Jones, S. H., Adams, T. E., & Ellis, C. (2013). Coming to know autoethnography as more than method. In S. H. Jones, T. E. Adams, & C. Ellis (Eds.), *Handbook of Autoethnography* (pp. 17–48). Walnut Creek, CA: Left Coast Press, Inc.

Justice, D. (2001). Of revision. In R. Behn & C. Twichell (Eds.), *The Practice of Poetry: Writing Exercises from Poets Who Teach* (pp. 249–250). New York: Quill/ Harperresource.

Kidd, J. (2016). White skin, brown body. In K. T. Galvin & M. Prendergast (Eds.), *Poetic Inquiry II-Seeing, Caring, Understanding* (pp. 135–140). Rotterdam: Sense/Brill.

Krizek, R. L. (2003). Ethnography as the excavation of personal narrative. In R. P. Clair (Ed.), *Expressions of Ethnography: Novel Approaches to Qualitative Methods* (pp. 141–151). Albany, NY: SUNY.

Kooser, T. (2005). *The Poetry Home Repair Manual: Practical Advice for Beginning Poets.* Lincoln, NE: University of Nebraska Press.

Kusserow, A. (2008). Ethnographic poetry. In M. Cahnmann-Taylor & R. Siegesmund (Eds.), *Arts-based Research in Education: Foundations for Practice* (pp. 72–78). New York: Routledge.

Lafrenière, D., & Cox, S. M. (2012). "If you can call it a poem": Toward a framework for the assessment of arts-based works. *Qualitative Research*, 13, 318–336. doi:10.1177/ 1468794112446104

LaFollette, K. (2018). "The opposite of the skeleton inside me": Women's poetry as feminist activism. *Art/Research International: A Transdisciplinary Journal*, 3(1), 178–189. doi:10.18432/ari28922

Lahman, M. K., Teman, E. D., & Richard, V. M. (2019). IRB as poetry. *Qualitative Inquiry*, 25(2) 200–214. doi:10.1177/10778

Lahman, M. K., Richard, V. M., & Teman, E. D. (2019). ish: How to write poemish (research) poetry. *Qualitative Inquiry*, 25(2), 215–227. doi:10.1177/1077800417750182

Lahman, M. K., & Richard, V. M. (2014). Appropriated poetry: Archival poetry in research. *Qualitative Inquiry*, 20(3) 344–355. doi:10.1177/1077800413489272

Lahman, M. K., Rodriquez, K. L., Richard, V. M., Geist, M. R., Schendel, R. K., & Graglia, P. E. (2011). (Re)forming research poetry. *Qualitative Inquiry*, 17(9), 887–896. doi:10.1177/1077800411423219

Langer, C. L., & Furman, R. (2004, March). Exploring identity and assimilation: Research and interpretive poems [19 paragraphs]. Forum Qualitative Sozialforschung/Forum: *Qualitative*

Social Research [online journal], 5(2), Arts. 5. Available at: www.qualitativeresearch.net/fqs-texte/2-04/2-04langerfurman-e.htm

Leavy, P. (2009). *Method Meets Art: Arts-based Research Practice.* New York: Guilford.

Leavy, P. (2015). *Method Meets Art: Arts-based Research Practice* (2nd ed). New York: Guilford.

Leggo, C. (2005). The heart of pedagogy: On poetic knowing and living. *Teachers and Teaching: Theory and Practice*, 11(5), 439–455.

Leggo, C. (2008a). The ecology of personal and professional experience: A poet's view. In M. Cahnmann-Taylor & R. Siegesmund (Eds.), *Arts-based Research in Education: Foundations for Practice* (pp. 87–97). New York: Routledge.

Leggo, C. (2008b). Astonishing silence: Knowing in poetry. In G. J. Knowles & A. L. Cole (Eds.), *Handbook of the Arts in Qualitative Research: Perspectives, Methodologies, Examples, and Issues* (pp. 165–174). Thousand Oaks, CA: Sage.

Leggo, C. (2012). Where the wild words are: Provoking pedagogic imagination. In S. Thomas, A. Cole & S. Stewart (Eds.), *The Art of Poetic Inquiry* (pp. 378–394). Nova Scotia: Backalongbooks.

Lieblich, A., Tuval-Mashiach, R., & Zilber, T. (1998). *Narrative Research: Reading, Analysis, and Interpretation.* Thousand Oaks, CA: Sage.

Liu, L. (2019). A conversation with Nomi Stone. *NEOCOLLOGUY*, January, 5, 2019. Available at: www.neocolloquy.com/home/nomi-stone

Lockward, D. (2018). Bonus prompt: The revision infusion poem. In D. Lockward (Ed.), *The Practicing Poet: Writing beyond the Basics* (p. 274). West Caldwell, NJ: Terrapin.

Longenbach, J. (2004). *The Resistance to Poetry.* Chicago, IL: University of Chicago Press.

Longenbach, J. (2008). *The Art of the Poetic Line.* Saint Paul, MN: Graywolf Press.

Madison, D. S. (1991). "That was my occupation": Oral narrative, performance, and black feminist thought. *Text and Performance Quarterly*, 13, 213–232.

Madison, D. S. (1994). Story, history, and performance: Interpreting oral history through Black performance traditions. *Black Sacred Music: A Journal of Theomusicology*, 8, 43–63.

Madison, D. S. (2004). Performance, personal narratives, and the politics of possibility. In Y. S. Lincoln & N. K. Denzin (Eds.), *Turning Points in Qualitative Research: Tying Knots in a Handkerchief* (pp. 469–486). Walnut Creek, CA: AltaMira.

Madison, D. S. (2005). *Critical Ethnography: Method, Ethics, and Performance.* Thousand Oaks, CA: Sage.

Manning, J. (2014). A constitutive approach to interpersonal communication. *Communication Studies*, 65, 432–440. doi:10.1080/10510974.2014.927294

Manning, J., & Kunkel, A. (2015). Qualitative approaches to dyadic data analyses in family communication research: An invited essay. *Journal of Family Communication*, 15, 185–192. doi:10.1080/15267431.2015.1043434

Margolis, G. (1997). Perhaps before we both must leave. In R. Pack & J. Parini (Eds.), *Introspections: American Poets on One of Their Own Poems* (pp. 150–152). Hanover, NH: Middlebury College.

Maynard, K. & Cahnmann-Taylor, M. (2007, October). Anthropology at the edge of words: Where poetry and ethnography meet. Paper presentation at the 1st International Symposium on Poetic Inquiry, Vancouver, BC.

McAdams, D. P. (1993). *The Stories We Live By: Personal Myths and the Making of the Self.* New York: William Morrow.

McCarriston, L. (1991). *Eva-Mary.* Evanston, IL: TriQuarterly Books.

McCaughey, M. (1997). *Real Knockouts: The Physical Feminism of Women's Self-defence.* New York: New York City Press.

McGrath, C. (2018). Craft tip #25: Life in the salt mines: A revision strategy. In D. Lockward (Ed.), *The Practicing Poet: Writing beyond the Basics* (pp. 249–254). West Caldwell, NJ: Terrapin.

McHugh, H. (1995). What he thought. In C. B. Buckley & C. Merrill (Eds.), *What Will Suffice: Contemporary American Poets on the Art of Poetry* (pp. 97–98). Salt Lake City, UT: Gibbs Smith.

Memmer, P. (2008). *Threat of Pleasure.* Cincinnati, OH: Word Press.

Miller, P. (2000). Revising poetry. *The Writer,* 113(4), 12.

Miller, W. (2005). Chapbooks: Democratic ephemera. *American Book Review,* March–April, 1–6.

Moraga, C., & Anzaldúa, G. (Eds.). (1981). *This Bridge Called My Back: Writings by Radical Women of Color.* New York: Kitchen Table.

Morse, J. M., Coulehan, J., Thorne, S., Bottorff, J. L., Cheek, J. & Kuzel, A. J. (2009). Data expressions or expressing data. *Qualitative Health Research,* 19(8), 1035–1036. doi:10.1177/1049732309338719

Moustakas, C. (1994). *Phenomenological Research Methods.* Thousand Oaks, CA: Sage.

Neilsen, L. (2008). Lyric inquiry. In J. G. Knowles & A. L. Cole (Eds.), *Handbook of the Arts in Qualitative Research: Perspectives, Methodologies, Examples, and Issues* (pp. 93–102). Thousand Oaks, CA: Sage.

Nelson, M. (2001). *Carver: A Life in Poems.* Asheville, NC: Front Street.

Nelson, M. (2007, March). History into poetry, poetry into history. Panel presentation at the annual meeting of the Associated Writing Programs, Atlanta, GA.

Ohito, E. O., & Nyachae, T. M. (2018). Poetically poking at language and power: Using black feminist poetry to conduct rigorous feminist critical discourse analysis. *Qualitative Inquiry,* 1–12. doi:10.1177/1077800418786303

Olesen, V. (2005). Early millennial feminist qualitative research. In N. K. Denzin & Y. S. Lincoln (Eds.), *The Sage Handbook of Qualitative Research* (3rd ed., pp. 235–278). Thousand Oaks, CA: Sage.

Oliver, M. (1998). *Rules for the Dance: A Handbook for Writing and Reading Metrical Verse.* New York: Houghton Mifflin.

Oughton, J. (2012). Poetry: Way to know, art. In S. Thomas, A. Cole, & S. Stewart (Eds.), *The Art of Poetic Inquiry* (pp. 73–85). Nova Scotia: Backalongbooks.

Owen, W. F. (1984). Interpretive themes in relational communication. *Quarterly Journal of Speech,* 70, 274–287.

Orr, D. (2008). The politics of poetry. *Poetry,* 192(4), 409–418.

Padgett, R. (Ed.) (1987). *The Teachers and Writers Handbook of Poetic Forms.* New York: Teachers & Writers Collaborative.

Parini, J. (2008). *Why Poetry Matters.* New Haven, CT: Yale University Press.

Parker, A. M. (2018). Craft tip #26: Top, down, bottom, up. In D. Lockward (Ed.), *The Practicing Poet: Writing beyond the Basics* (pp. 257–258). West Caldwell, NJ: Terrapin.

Patton, M. (2001). *Qualitative Research and Evaluation Methods* (4th ed.). Thousand Oaks, CA: Sage.

Pelias, R. J. (2004). *A Methodology of the Heart: Evoking Academic & Daily Life.* Walnut Creek, CA: Altamira.

Pelias, R. J. (2005). Performative writing as scholarship: An apology, an argument, and anecdote. *Cultural Studies ↔ Critical Methodologies,* 5(4), 415–424.

Pelias, R. J. (2007). Jarheads, girly men, and the pleasures of violence. *Qualitative Inquiry,* 13(7), 945–959.

Penwarden, S. (2017). Poetry as therapy/research: Hearing the poetic in ordinary talk. In L. Butler-Kisber, J. J. Guiney Yallop, M. Stewart, & S. Wiebe (Eds.), *Poetic Inquires of Reflection and Renewal* (pp. 224–233). Nova Scotia: MacIntyre Purcell.

Percer, L. H. (2002, June). Going beyond the demonstrable range in educational scholarship: Exploring the intersections of poetry and research. *The Qualitative Report*, 7(2). Available at: www.nova.edu/ssss/QR/QR7-2/hayespercer.html

Perloff, M. (1998). Collage and poetry. In M. Kelly (Ed.), *Encyclopedia of Aesthetics*, 1, 384–387. New York: Oxford University Press. Available at: http://marjorieperloff.com/essays/collage-poetry/

Poetry Foundation. (2012). Adrienne Rich: 1929–2012. Available at: www.poetryfoundation.org/poets/adrienne-rich

Poetry Foundation. (n.d.). Collage. Available at: www.poetryfoundation.org/learn/glossary-terms/collage

Piirto, J. (2002). The quality and qualifications: Writing inferior poems as qualitative research. *International Journal of Qualitative Studies in Education*, 15(4), 431–445.

Poindexter, C. (2002). Research as poetry: A couple experiences HIV. *Qualitative Inquiry*, 8, 707–714.

Prendergast, M. (2006). Found poetry as literature review: Research poems on audience and performance. *Qualitative Inquiry*, 12, 369–388.

Prendergast, M. (2009). "*Poem* is what?": Poetic inquiry in qualitative social science research. In M. Prendergast, C. Leggo, & P. Sameshima (Eds.), *Poetic Inquiry: Vibrant Voices in the Social Sciences*. Rotterdam: Sense Publishers.

Prendergast, M. (2012). Poetic inquiry and the social poet. In S. Thomas, A. Cole & S. Stewart (Eds.), *The Art of Poetic Inquiry* (pp. 488–502). Nova Scotia: Backalongbooks.

Prendergast, M. (2015). Poetic inquiry, 2007–2012: A surrender and catch found poem. *Qualitative Inquiry*, 21(8) 678–685. doi:10.1177/1077800414563806

Raab, L. (2016). *Why Don't We Say What We Mean: Essays Mostly about Poetry*. North Adams, MA: Tupelo.

Reale, M. (2015a). "We never thought it would be like this": Refugees' experiences in Sicily. *The Qualitative Report*, 20(1), Article 6, 107–114. Available at: www.nova.edu/ssss/QRQR20/1/reale6.pdf

Reale, M. (2015b). Can I call this place home? Poetic representation of a border crossing by sea. *Cultural Studies ↔ Critical Methodologies*, 15(1), 30–31. doi:10.1177/1532708613516432

Reale, M. (2015c). *How do you think I feel?*: Poetic representation of African and Syrian refugees in a Sicilian refugee camp in wake of the Lampedusan tragedy. *Cultural Studies ↔ Critical Methodologies*, 15(3), 167–168. doi:10.1177//1532708614562882

Reale, M. (2015d). Living one day is easy, living a life is hard: A Sudanese refugee in Sicily. *Cultural Studies ↔ Critical Methodologies*, 15(6), 490–491. doi:10.177//1532708615614023

Reed, T.V. (2013). The poetic is political: Feminist poetry and the poetics of women's rights. In Carole R. McCann and Seung-Kyung Kim (Eds.)., *Feminist Theory Reader, Local and Global Perspectives* (3rd ed.), pp. 85–97. New York: Routledge.

Reilly, R. C., Lee, V., Laux, K., & Robitaille, A. (2018). Using found poetry to illuminate the existential and posttraumatic growth of women with breast cancer engaging in art therapy. *Qualitative Research in Psychology*. doi:10.1080/14780887.2018.1429863

Revell, D. (2007). *The Art of Attention: A Poet's Eye*. Minneapolis, MN: Graywolf Press.

Richardson, L. (1997a). Skirting a pleated text: de-disciplining an academic life. *Qualitative Inquiry*, 3, 295–304.

Richardson, L. (1997b). *Fields of Play: Constructing an Academic Life*. New Brunswick, NJ: Rutgers University.

Richardson, L. (2000). Evaluating ethnography. *Qualitative Inquiry*, 6, 253–255.

Richardson, L. (2002). Poetic representations of interviews. In J. F. Gubrium & J. A. Holstein (Eds.), *Handbook of Interview Research: Context and Method* (pp. 877–891). Thousand Oaks, CA: Sage.

Richardson, M. (1998). Poetics in the field and on the page. *Qualitative Inquiry*, 4, 451–462.

Richardson, P. (2017). The mermaid & the minotaur: The imagined inner life of women intellectuals in love. In L. Butler-Kisber, J. J. Guiney Yallop, M. Stewart, & S. Wiebe (Eds.), *Poetic Inquires of Reflection and Renewal* (pp. 121–136). Nova Scotia: MacIntyre Purcell.

Richardson, P., & Walsh, S. (2018). Endless open heart: Collaborative poetry and image as contemplative and restorative practice. *Canadian Review of Art Education*, 45(1), 153–164.

Riessman, C. K. (1993). *Narrative Analysis*. Newbury Park, CA: Sage.

Rose, D. (1990). *Living the Ethnographic Life*. Thousand Oaks, CA: Sage.

Rothman, D. J. (2007, March). Narrative poetry: Past, present and future. Panel presentation at the annual meeting of the Associated Writing Programs, Atlanta, GA.

Saarnivaara, M. (2003). Art as inquiry: The autopsy of an [art] experience. *Qualitative Inquiry*, 9(4), 580–602.

Sahlstein, E. (2014). Reflecting on the study: Excerpts from an interview with Erin Sahlstein. In J. Manning & A. Kunkel (Eds.), *Researching Interpersonal Relationships: Qualitative Methods, Studies, and Analysis* (pp. 110–115). Los Angeles, CA: Sage.

Sameshima, P., Vandermause, R., & Santucci, C. (2012). Motherhood and meth: Ekphrastic intervention. In S. Thomas, A. Cole & S. Stewart (Eds.), *The Art of Poetic Inquiry* (pp. 187–202). Nova Scotia: Backalongbooks.

Shidmer, N. (2014). Poetic inquiry and its lyrical potentials for research. *in education*, 20(2), 12–20. Available at: https://ineducation.ca/ineducation/article/view/180

See, C. (2002). *Making a Literary Life: Advice for Writers and Other Dreamers*. New York: Ballantine Books.

Siegesmund, R., & Cahnmann-Taylor, M. (2008). The tensions of arts-based research in education reconsidered: The promise of practice. In M. Cahnmann-Taylor & R. Siegesmund (Eds.), *Arts-based Research in Education: Foundations for Practice* (pp. 231–246). New York: Routledge.

Simic, C. (1990). *Wonderful Words, Silent Truth: Essays on Poetry and a Memoir*. Ann Arbor, MI: The University of Michigan Press.

Simic, C. (1994). *The Unemployed Fortune-teller*. Ann Arbor, MI: University of Michigan Press.

Smith, W. J. (2000). *The Cherokee Lottery: A Sequence of Poems*. Willimantic, CT: Curbstone Press.

Soniat, K. (1997). On reading histories: "The captain's advice to those headed for the trees: 1609." In R. Pack & J. Parini (Eds.), *Introspections: American Poets on One of Their Own Poems* (pp. 259–262). Hanover, NH: Middlebury College.

Snowber, C. (2016). *Embodied Inquiry: Writing, Living and Being Through the Body*. Rotterdam: Brill/Sense.

Strand, M., & Boland, E. (2000). *The Making of a Poem: A Norton Anthology of Poetic Forms*. New York: W. W. Norton & Company.

Stewart, R. (2004). The end of boredom: An interview with Billy Collins. *New Letters: A Magazine of Writing and Art*, 70(2), 143–159.

Strine, M. S. (1989). The politics of asking women's questions: Voice and value in the poetry of Adrienne Rich. *Text and Performance Quarterly*, 1, 24–41. doi:10.1080/10462938909365910

Sullivan, A. M. (2009). On poetic occasion in inquiry: Concreteness, voice, ambiguity, tension, and associative logic. In M. Prendergast, C. Leggo, & P. Sameshima (Eds.), *Poetic Inquiry: Vibrant Voices in the Social Sciences* (pp. 111–126). Rotterdam: Sense/Brill.

Suter, E. A. (2018). The promise of contrapuntal and intersectional methods for advancing critical interpersonal and family communication. *Communication Monographs*, 85, 123–139. doi.org/10.1080/03637751.2017.1375131

Tedlock, D. (1983). *The Spoken Word and the Work of Interpretation*. Philadelphia, PA: University of Pennsylvania.

Thiel, D. (2001). *Writing Your Rhythm: Using Nature, Culture, Form and Myth*. Ashland, OR: Story Line Press.

Thomas, T. (n.d.) The Skinny poetry form. *The Skinny Poetry Journal*. Available at: https://theskinnypoetryjournal.wordpress.com/about/

Tillinghast, R. (2001). Household economy, ruthlessness, romance, and the art of hospitality. In R. Behn & C. Twichell (Eds.), *The Practice of Poetry: Writing Exercises from Poets Who Teach* (pp. 245–248). New York: Quill/Harperresource.

Todres, L., & Galvin, K. T. (2008). Embodied interpretation: a novel way of evocatively re-presenting meanings in phenomenological research. *Qualitative Research*, 8(5), 568–583. doi:10.1177/1 468794108094866

Townsend, A., & Baker, D. (2007). *Radiant Lyre: Essays on Lyric Poetry*. Saint Paul, MN: Graywolf Press.

Vander Zee, A. (2011). New minds. New lines. E. Rosko & A. Vander Zee (Eds.), *A Broken Thing: Poets on the Line* (pp. 5–24). Iowa City, IA: University of Iowa Press.

Velija, P., Mierzwinski, M., & Fortune, L. (2013). "It made me feel powerful": Women's gendered embodiment and physical empowerment in the martial arts. *Leisure Studies*, 32(5), 524–541. doi:10.1080/02614367.2012.696128

Vincent, A. (2018). Is there a definition? Ruminating on Poetic Inquiry, strawberries, and the continued growth of the field. *Art/Research International: A Transdisciplinary Journal*, 3(2), 48–76. doi: 10.18432/ari29356

Voight, E. B. (2009). *The Art of Syntax: Rhythm of Thought, Rhythm of Song*. Minneapolis, MN: Graywolf Press.

Walker, F. X (2007, March). History into poetry, poetry into history. Panel presentation at the annual meeting of the Associated Writing Programs, Atlanta, GA.

Walker, F. X (2008). *When Winter Come: The Ascension of York*. Lexington, KY: University Press of Kentucky.

Walsh, S. (2006). An Irigarayan framework and resymbolization in an arts-informed research process. *Qualitative Inquiry*, 12(5), 976–993.

Ward, E. (2011). "Bringing the message forward": Using poetic re-presentation to solve research dilemmas. *Qualitative Inquiry*, 17(4) 355–363. doi:10.1177/1077800411401198

Walsh, S. (2012). Contemplation, artful writing: Research with internationally educated female teachers. *Qualitative Inquiry*, 18(3), 273–285. doi: 10.1177/1077800411431553

Weems, M. (2010). Till the well runs. *Qualitative Inquiry*, 16(9), 742–746. doi:10.1177/1077800410374441

Wiegers, M. (Ed.) (2003). *This Art: Poems about Poetry*. Port Townsend, WA: Copper Canyon Press.

Welsch, G. (2006). *Dirt and All Its Dense Labor*. Cincinnati, OH: WordTech Editions.

Witkin, S. L. (2007). Relational poetry: Expressing interweaving realities. *Qualitative Social Work*, 6(4), 477–481.

Young, D. (2010). *The Art of Recklessness: Poetry as Assertive Force and Contradiction.* Minneapolis, MN: Graywolf Press.

Xiao, J. (2017, April 9). The white feminism of the women's march is still on my mind. *Everyday Feminism.* Available at: http://everydayfeminism.com/2017/04/white-feminism-womens-march/

INDEX

Lockwood, D. 181
Longenbach, J. 12, 15, 24, 133, 139, 145–146, 148, 160, 173

Madison, D. S. 40, 51, 63–65, 74, 139, 143
Manning, J. 26, 37
Margolis, G. 134
McAdams, D. P. 70
McCarriston, L. 109–110
McCaughey, M. 24
McGrath, C. 180, 183
McHugh, H. 134
Memmer, P. 115, 136
metaphor 11, 40–41, 98, 111, 115–116, 120, 126–127, 133, 139, 143–144, 146, 155, 158, 162, 164, 173–174, 183
meter 11–12, 15, 51, 120, 135, 144, 168
Miller, P. 178–180, 184
Miller, W. 80
mindfulness 154, 184
Moraga, C. 19
Morse, J. M. 154
motherhood/mothering 2–4, 8, 10, 88, 94–95, 118, 165; middle-class 7, 8, 10, 94, 97
Moustakas, C. 104–105, 127, 129

narrative: analysis 74; construction of 47, 118; historical 50; participant 52, 65, 74–75, 138, 169; in poetry, 74, 118, 169–175, 179; research 4, 7, 10, 13, 70, 73, 138, 163–164; of the self 77, 140; structure 79; theory 2, 70; truth 27, 75, 101, 142, 144, 146–147; *see also* poetic forms
Neilsen, L. 15, 155, 157
Nelson, M. 48–49

Ohito, E. O. 51, 62–63, 156
Olesen, V. 25, 90
Oliver, M. 131
Orr, D. 30–31
Oughton, J. 158–159
Owen, W. F. 67

Padgett, R. 54, 75, 78–79, 159, 160, 169–170, 173
Parini, J. 11, 15, 28, 30, 43, 124, 142, 144–146
Parker, A. M. 180
participant observation 48, 155
participants 58–59, 63–65, 70–71, 74–75, 78–79, 96, 104–105, 129–130, 146, 151, 156–158, 163–164, 167, 170, 177–178

Patton, M. 52, 163
pedagogy 2–3, 7, 16, 18, 29, 37, 80, 100, 102, 147, 151, 174, 177
Pelias, R. J. 17, 40, 77–78
Penwarden, S. 164
Percer, L. H. 40, 130–131, 143
Perloff, M. 92–93
phenomenology 100, 104, 127, 129, 158
Piirto, J. 102, 129, 131, 143–144
poetry: as data analysis 31, 39, 44–45, 51, 61–62, 89, 92, 151, 155–156, 159, 169, 173, 177; defining 11; in fieldwork 5, 21–22, 24, 27, 61, 80, 95, 158–159; the line of 11–12, 15, 18, 20, 22, 24, 44, 46, 49, 51, 57, 62, 64–65, 75, 77, 86, 88–92, 107, 112, 117–118, 121–122, 124–126, 128, 133, 137–141, 144–147, 153, 155, 159–160, 163, 166–169, 173–174, 176–178; as method 1, 5–6, 11, 13, 38–99, 131, 140, 148; as political response 11, 19–20, 29–32, 98, 103, 145, 177; power of 11, 15, 28–29, 30–31, 39, 41, 69, 80, 89, 92, 111, 135, 141, 146, 149, 155, 161; as representation 1, 11, 17, 19, 21, 24, 27, 39, 50, 59, 63, 74–75, 79, 87, 98–99, 104, 109, 129, 131, 139, 143, 146, 151, 154, 157, 169–170; as resistance 24–25, 37, 45–47, 73, 124, 145; use of research in 1–2, 6, 12, 14, 22, 25, 31, 41, 51–63; as social justice 11, 28–30; as universal 10, 14–15, 32, 70, 113–114, 117, 128; uses of 14; as way of knowing 14–15
poetic analysis 22, 24, 51–52, 61, 89, 94–95, 165–166, 175, 177
poetic craft 13, 43, 51–52, 99, 100–104, 118, 124, 128, 130–135, 138, 142–144, 146–150, 152–154, 168, 173
poetic criteria: artistic concentration 101, 131, 142–144, 146–147, 149; authenticity 40, 46–47, 50, 54, 106, 109–111, 143–144, 149; as conditional 75, 101, 133, 142, 144, 146–147, 149; deep suspicion 105–109; discovery/surprise 30, 101, 106–108, 118, 133, 136, 139, 142–145, 147, 158; embodied experience 101, 133, 144–145, 147; fragmentation/flux/ineffable 117–119; flexing the poetry muscle 119–123, 152–154, 157, 183–184; good and effective 105–129; good enough poetry 100–101, 120, 150–152, 155; imagined reality 106, 123–125; mystery 125–127; as narrative connectedness 109–114;

psychological and emotional effect 111–114; pushing the boundaries 114–117; question of 100–103; as transformation 101, 142–144, 147, 150, 158; vigor 102, 143, 150; visual of 144; *see also* narrative: truth

poetic forms: archival 43, 45–46, 48, 50, 63, 70, 103, 139; autoethnographic 12, 58, 94–95; cento 18, 93, 174; chapbooks 21, 32, 79–81, 89; cluster 79, 86–89; confessional 8, 118, 124; dialogue poem 8, 71–73, 88, 164–165; dramatic monologue 157; dream 57–58; ekphrastic 3, 158–159; epistle 5, 57–58, 131, 158, 170–173; erasure 93–94, 174; ethnographic 12, 20–21, 81; ethnopoetics 21, 77; exquisite corpse 91, 98, 176–177; free verse 8, 62–63, 88, 90, 123, 135–136, 152, 160, 183; and function 1, 4, 15, 93, 101, 128, 138, 144, 169–173; haiku 22–24, 168, 173; hybrid 45, 92–95, 174–176; Institutional Review Board (IRB) 5, 57–59; interpretive 12–13, 77, 90; investigative poem 28–30; list 54, 62–63; long poem 43, 79–89, 168–169; lyric 10–11, 15, 38, 42, 45, 51, 74, 78–79, 90, 99, 131, 168; mother-poems 7, 10, 95; narrative 7, 13, 22, 24, 45, 70–71, 75, 78–79, 90, 118; pantoum 61, 75, 121, 169, 172–173; performance 12, 30, 39, 63, 65, 77, 89–90; persona 47, 131, 138, 149, 157–158, 173, 179, 183; response 3, 30–31, 40, 61–62, 91–92, 98, 158–159, 177–178; series 66, 81, 78–91, 94, 99, 113–114, 121, 124, 138, 147, 165, 168–169, 176, 178, 181; short poem 52, 80, 125, 167–168; sonnet 8, 32, 46, 86, 88, 117, 160, 168–169; surrender and catch poem 161–162, 164; tanka 61, 90, 92, 168, 173; textual, aural, and visual collage 8, 10, 31, 38, 45, 58, 79–88, 92–95, 99, 118, 166, 174–176; triptych 166–167; villanelle 90–92, 177

poetic image/imagery 11–12, 41, 44, 49, 79–81, 90–91, 93–95, 98, 106–107, 109, 111, 113, 123–124, 126, 133, 137, 145–146, 153, 156, 159, 162, 164, 168, 173–174, 176, 180–181

poetic inquirers: challenges for 102, 153–157, 161, 170; definition 11, 28; goals of 14, 31, 38, 51, 99; techniques for 45, 70, 80, 87, 93, 95, 170, 174, 176, 181, 183

poetic inquiry goals 2, 16, 18, 25, 32, 38–43, 45, 47–48, 59, 98–100, 102, 104, 128, 132, 138, 142–143, 149, 153–156, 168, 183

poetic labels 12–13, 39

poetic language 1, 11–12, 14–15, 17, 20–22, 24, 30–31, 40, 43, 47, 50–51, 63, 65, 70, 73–74, 78–79, 93, 110–111, 113, 118, 122–126, 128–130, 134, 140, 143–146, 149, 156, 159–160, 164, 168, 170, 175–176, 179–181

poetic occasion 43–45, 48, 69, 133, 155, 159

poetic practice 2, 4, 6, 18, 22, 42, 91, 103, 106, 118, 135, 151–154, 184

poetic process 1–2, 15, 17, 22, 24, 30–31, 37–39, 42–44, 46, 51–64, 67, 75, 80, 89–93, 102–104, 107, 109–110, 112, 117, 120–121, 125, 127, 129, 132, 142, 150, 153–156, 158–159, 161, 164–165, 168, 170, 173–176, 179–180, 183–184

poetic structure 11–12, 78, 88, 113, 126, 150, 173

poetic syntax 11–12, 42, 74, 124, 133, 140, 145, 160

poetic voice 9, 19–20, 30–31, 39, 41, 43, 45–51, 57, 59, 62–64, 77, 88, 90, 106–107, 109–110, 113, 124–125, 129, 133, 136–137, 139, 144, 146, 155–157, 163, 173, 176, 179

poet-researchers 41–42, 45, 89–90, 99, 102–104, 129–130, 133, 142, 150–152, 154, 156, 164, 168, 174

poetic transcription 12–13, 22, 24–27, 31, 51, 61, 63–70, 90, 104, 151, 159–165

poets and qualitative researchers 41–43, 50–51, 89, 98, 103, 108, 153, 156

Poindexter, C. 40, 65

political action 29–32, 38–40, 62, 80, 90, 99, 104, 143, 161, 177

power differences 15, 21, 77, 81, 157

Prendergast, M. 6, 13–14, 17, 28, 39, 41, 63, 71, 102–103, 158, 161–163

qualitative research 1–4, 6, 10, 12, 13–18, 31, 37–41, 44–45, 51–52, 62, 70, 79, 99–103, 135, 143–144, 146–150, 152–156, 174

queer: theory 2; methodology 10, 93–95

race 13, 17, 19, 90

racism 19–20, 32, 98

reactions to poetic inquiry 10–11, 32–33, 35, 47, 92, 111